MARK

Other Focus on the Bible Commentaries

Old Testament

New Testament

MARK

Geoffrey Grogan

CHRISTIAN FOCUS

Rev Geoffrey Grogan is Principal Emeritus of Glasgow Bible College (now the International Bible College). His theological studies were undertaken there and at the London Bible College. He served the College as a full-time lecturer for fourteen years before going south in 1965 to teach at LBC. In 1969 he returned to Glasgow as principal. He has served on four missionary councils, on the Strathclyde Education Committee and the Management Committee for the Cambridge University Diploma in Religious Studies. He has written various books, *Christ of the Bible & the Church's Faith* (ISBN 1 85792 6625), *Prayer, Praise & Prophecy* (ISBN 1 85792 6420) and a commentary on *2 Corinthians* (ISBN 1 85792 2204).

ISBN 1 85792 905 5

© Geoffrey W. Grogan 1995

First published in 1995
Revised and enlarged edition published in 2003,
by
Christian Focus Publications, Geanies House,
Fearn, Ross-shire, IV20 1TW, Scotland.

www.christianfocus.com

Cover design by Alister MacInnes

Printed and bound by
Mackays of Chatham

Contents

Introduction

1. How they brought the good news from Jerusalem to Rome

'Jerusalem!' What feelings are aroused by that name!

It is so today, for it is a holy city to the Christian, the Jew and the Moslem. This was also true in Bible times. It stirred the emotions of the Jews. It was the capital of their country. More than this, it was the place where God's holy temple was.

To be away and unable to visit it was agony for the godly Jew. 'As the deer pants for streams of water, so my soul pants for you, O God. My soul thirsts for God, for the living God. When can I go and meet with God?' (Ps. 42:1,2). What eager and frustrated longing is concentrated into that word, 'When...?' Meet with God – where? Why, in Jerusalem and at the temple, of course!

Then there were the longer-term exiles, the folk who did not even live in the Holy Land, but who were born of Jewish parents in places like Antioch and Alexandria, like Corinth or Carthage. Many of them saved up for years to make the journey, sometimes in the midst of danger, to be at Jerusalem at the time of one of the religious feasts. Most of all there were the folk in enforced exile in Babylon, six hundred years or so before Christ. One of them wrote, 'If I forget you, O Jerusalem, may my right hand forget its skill' (Ps 137:5).

As we read the Bible it seems to present so many people wanting to get to Jerusalem. Isaiah says, 'The mountain of the Lord's temple will be established as chief among the mountains; it will be raised above the hills, and all nations will stream to it' (Isa. 2:2). The New Testament says, even of Abraham the nomad, that 'he was looking forward to the city with foundations, whose architect and builder is God' (Heb. 11:10).

Yet there is one Bible book where the movement is all the other way. In the Acts of the Apostles, Jerusalem is a place of emigration not of immigration, not of destination but of exodus. Why?

The secret is to be found in the Gospel of Luke. There is no lack of emphasis there on Jerusalem as a place of destination, in fact of destiny. More than thirty times the name comes, nearly as many as in the other three Gospels put together, and so often with a sense that something of immense importance is going to happen there. You will see this very clearly if you read Luke 2:38; 9:31, 51; 13:33-35; 18:31; 19:11; 21:20-24 and 23:28.

This is why the movement in Acts is outward and not inward. At Jerusalem, the most important events since the foundation of the world – the death and resurrection of Jesus – had taken place, and it was urgent that everybody should know about them. Luke in fact prepares his readers for this at the end of his Gospel, where Jesus says to his disciples about himself as the Christ, 'repentance and forgiveness of sins will be preached in his name to all nations, beginning at Jerusalem' (Luke 24:47). This then set the theme for his second book.

If you stand at the door of a great newspaper's printing works at the right time of day, you will see streams of vans going out in many directions, moving with all speed to every point of the compass. Why? To bring the latest news to as many people as can be reached. And what is this news? Why, so often it is about war or famine, about adultery or murder. Martyn Lewis, the BBC news-reader, went on record as declaring his concern that so often what is published and broadcast is bad news, when there is so much good news available.

Here in Jerusalem were men and women with the best news ever to be published. It was not only an urgent matter to get it out; it was their greatest joy. Out they went – but at first they only felt free to take this message to people who shared their religion.

Jesus was the expected Messiah of the Jewish people. They might not accept him, but at least the Christians knew it was right to tell them about him and to seek to win them to faith in him. There was no problem either with proselytes, for these were non-Jews who were attracted to the Jewish faith and had gone so far as to become officially Jewish in their religion. But other Gentiles were another matter. The first Christians had all been taught the Old Testament in the synagogues in their earlier days, and the teaching was in the hands of men who were afraid that contact with Gentiles would pollute good Jews. This kind of teaching can go very deep and it cannot have been easy to contemplate acting in a manner contrary to it.

A series of events shook these first Christians out of their exclusively Jewish nest. First of all, Jesus told them that the good news about him was meant for the whole world (Matt. 28:19; Mark 16:15; Luke 24:47; Acts 1:8). Then the gospel began to spread among the Samaritans (Acts 8:5-25), the 'mongrel' race who lived between Judaea and Galilee. Finally the Lord gave Peter not only a vision to reassure him, but also immediately after it an opportunity of proclaiming Christ to a group of Gentile enquirers (Acts 10). How then did the gospel get from the capital of Israel to the capital of the Empire? The Acts of the Apostles does not tell us explicitly, but it is easy enough to read between the lines.

Luke tells us that there were Jews and proselytes from Rome present at Jerusalem on the Day of Pentecost when the gospel was preached there (Acts 2:10,11). We can be pretty sure that some of them would have been among the 3,000 people who were converted that day (Acts 2:41). Can there be any real doubt that, on their return to Rome, they would establish at least one local Christian church there?

Then, of course, their numbers would swell. This growth would be in part through their own witness to Christ, but there was another important factor. Evangelistic missions were being conducted by Paul and others in the eastern parts of the Empire. At that time it was almost literally true that 'all roads lead to Rome', and there can be little doubt that some of these folk would find their way to that city and, tapping the local 'grapevine', would discover and join the local Christians or else perhaps start another Christian church elsewhere in the city.

2. The story of Jesus in written form

Was Mark's book the first Gospel to be written? Most scholars think so, although there are some who reckon Matthew earlier. The question is interesting, but it is not of crucial importance. We will assume the priority of Mark.

Here is the start of a somewhat but not entirely new type of literature. A book recently published under the editorship of Richard Bauckham (*The Gospels for all Christians: Rethinking the Gospel Audiences,* T. and T. Clark, 1998), argues that although the Gospels are not much like modern biographies, because of their almost exclusive concentration on the ministry and death of Jesus, they are similar in many respects to the various biographies produced in the Graeco-Roman world in the few centuries which preceded and followed the ministry of our Lord. Bauckham and his colleagues argue their case persuasively, and there can be little doubt that the Gospels would have been recognised by their early readers as biographies of Jesus. There was however one important difference. Other biographies were not a preaching of good news. After all, the men who were the subjects of them were dead. There was no good news in that. But Mark and the other three Gospel writers were telling the story of Somebody who had conquered death. Their books then were truly Gospels, the proclamation of good news, and so theirs was, in this important respect, a new literary venture.

There is in fact no book that presents us with so many significant beginnings as does the Bible.

Did Abraham realise that he was to be the father of the race that was to be the people of God and the father of the whole family of the faithful? Did Jacob know that the new name God gave him ('Israel') would be the most frequent name found in Scripture and that the nation that sprang from him would be the cradle in which God's Son was born? Did Moses know how important for all future generations was his call from God to lead the children of Israel out of Egypt, marshalling them at Mount Sinai to hear God's Law, and taking them to the very edge of the Promised Land? We will never know how much each of these men knew about the far-reaching effects of what God was doing through them. The same is true of Mark and the very important book he wrote.

What was his reason for writing it? Obviously it was to tell people about Jesus, although of course many of them would be already well acquainted with certain facts about him.

First of all, of course, it was the actual proclamation of the good news by its preachers that would tell the hearers something about him, for all authentic Christian preaching has a factual basis in the story of Jesus himself. This preaching would not be at first particularly detailed, and there would be a concentration on the death and resurrection of Jesus. Sometimes perhaps some of the events of his ministry would be included in order to show what kind of Person he was.

Then would come the teaching of converts. We know that this actually began on the Day of Pentecost (Acts 2:42). This would probably include more information about Jesus as a Person as well as more teaching about the meaning of his death and resurrection and some of the practical implications of being a Christian (Rom. 6:17). All this was done orally.

It is not surprising to find so many letters in the New Testament. The task of evangelism was urgent and so the evangelists could not stay long after they had planted churches. Inevitably problems would arise, and what more natural than that the local leaders, unavoidably inexperienced, would contact the evangelists to ask their advice? So the letters of Paul and others were written, their purpose being to deal with particular issues of importance to the churches concerned. Such letters would, of course, build on the oral teaching already given, amplifying and further explaining it, and clearing up any problems that were due to misunderstanding.

It was at about this stage that the Gospels began to be written. Jesus himself is the heart of the gospel, for it is essentially good news about him, and so it was desirable that people should know much more about him. This became even more important when

11

the original witnesses to those facts began to die. After all, if you love a person, you want to know as much as possible about him or her. So it was with Christians and Christ. We can imagine how eagerly they would devour anything that gave them further insight into his life, his character and his teaching, as well as his death and resurrection. It was most important therefore that anything written should be authentic.

The Gospels were in fact based on eyewitness accounts. Luke saw the importance of this if his readers were to be assured of the truth of what was written (Luke 1: 1-4). In oral transmission through a series of human channels things can go wrong, with the danger of minor (and eventually major) departures from strict accuracy. The cultivation of a good memory was encouraged in the Holy Land in our Lord's day. Moreover, if disciples of Jesus who loved him dearly and believed in him as Lord and Saviour had only a vague memory of what he said and did, then nothing can be certain in this world!

It was not, however, all left even to the retentive memories of the eyewitnesses, for Jesus gave his apostles a special promise that exactly fitted the needs of the situation. He said, 'the Holy Spirit ... will teach you all things and will remind you of everything I have said to you' (John 14:26). The Holy Spirit is the great Communicator, and all effective witness to Christ is the result of his work. Jesus called him 'the Spirit of truth' (John 15:26; 16:13), and it was through his work that the apostles communicated the authentic gospel in contrast to all counterfeits (1 John 4:5,6).

Here then, in the Gospels, the Spirit of truth laid a basis for the effective communication of the good news of Jesus not only for the people of the first century but for men and women throughout the entire history of the church. If the gospel was to be proclaimed through future centuries, there would be an abiding need for such authentic written material, and, as we will see, it is probable that from the first the Gospels were intended to be read, not only by the churches that would first receive them, but widely throughout the churches of that day.

3. Two men write a Gospel

Who was Mark? His full name was John Mark and we find Luke mentioning him in Acts 12:12, 25; 13:5,13 and 15:37-39. His mother seems to have been a well-to-do early Christian, for her house was big enough for many Christians to join together in prayer (Acts 12:12).

As a study of these passages will show, he had failed at first as a missionary. He was a member of the team of evangelists who worked together on Paul's first missionary journey, but, for reasons unknown to us, he left the work at Pamphylia in southern Asia Minor, much to Paul's annoyance (Acts 15:37-39). Eventually however he came to be warmly regarded by both Paul and Peter (Col. 4:10; Philem. 24; 2 Tim. 4:11; 1 Peter 5:13). The letters in which he is mentioned were probably all written in the early sixties of the first century, more than a decade later than his defection from the missionary group. It would be most interesting to know what happened in the intervening years and how he came to link up with Paul again and also with Peter, but we have no information about this.

The story of his life is, however, a great encouragement to Christian workers who feel they have failed. Here was a man who was given another opportunity, and what a great work he did! He may not have won many people as a missionary, but we can never estimate how many may have been brought to faith in Christ through his Gospel.

If his mother was a Christian at a comparatively early stage of things, what was he doing during the ministry of Jesus? It is possible that he actually appears at one point in the story itself as he tells it in his Gospel. His account includes the brief appearance of an unnamed character whose inclusion in the story has no obvious purpose (see the comment on 14:51,52). Could this be Mark? Many writers on his Gospel have thought so.

At first sight, the writing of a Gospel by somebody like Mark might seem to raise a problem. After all, the promise of Jesus that the Holy Spirit would quicken their memories was made to his apostles, not to all and sundry, and, even if he was an early disciple of Jesus, Mark was not an apostle. Are there any grounds for extending the relevance of the promise to somebody like him? Yes, there are!

The life of Papias, Bishop of Hierapolis, bridged the First and Second Centuries. He was a companion of that great Christian martyr Polycarp, who had sat at the feet of the apostle John, and he is very likely himself to have heard John. Extracts from his writings are quoted by Irenaeus and by Eusebius of Caesarea, the first great church historian after Luke. Papias said that John (probably the apostle of that name, but possibly somebody closely associated with him) had said that Mark became Peter's interpreter and that he had written down what Peter had preached of the words and deeds of the Lord Jesus. Early writers also say Mark wrote his Gospel in Italy, while others narrow this to Rome. They differ, however, as to whether this writing took place during Peter's lifetime or after his death. If Peter's memories are behind the Gospel of Mark, then the relevance of the promise of Jesus to this Gospel is obvious.

Peter calls Mark, 'my son Mark' (1 Peter 5:13), suggesting that there was a strong spiritual bond between them. This is not a bit surprising, for Peter too was a failed disciple who was restored and given another opportunity of service (John 21:15-17). What experience of the grace of Christ they had between them!

Simon Peter had been introduced to Jesus by his brother Andrew very early in the ministry of Jesus (John 1:41), even before being called from his nets to follow him (1:16,17). He followed him throughout his ministry, and was also present on several occasions when the Saviour had only a few of the disciples with him (5:37; 9:2; 14:33, and perhaps 13:33). It was he who, at Caesarea Philippi, voiced the conviction of the disciples that Jesus was the Christ, the Son of God (8:27-29; cf. Matt. 16:16), the very conviction which was in Mark's heart throughout the writing of his book (1:1).

Peter followed Jesus devotedly, but he refused to accept his teaching that he was destined for a death that would follow rejection by the religious leaders (8:31,32), and, despite his protestations of loyalty to death (14:27-31), failed him in the hour of crisis by a threefold denial (14:66-72). Such was Christ's gracious forgiveness, however, that it was Peter who, on the Day of Pentecost, preached the first Christian sermon (Acts 2).

Peter comes across to us in the Gospel narratives as a vigorous, impetuous character (e.g. see Matt. 14:28; John 18:10; 21:7), who sometimes spoke before he thought (Matt. 17:24-27). No doubt his accounts of events in the life of Jesus would be very graphic, and many of the stories in Mark are dramatically told, as we will see.

There have been some attempts to locate the writing of the Gospel in Galilee or in Antioch, but over the years a majority of scholars has accepted that it was written in Italy, probably in Rome, with Roman Christians as its first readers. Mark 15:21 says that Simon of Cyrene was the father of Alexander and Rufus, and if this Rufus is to be identified with a man of the same name referred to in Romans 16:13 (which, of course, can be neither proved nor disproved), Mark was making a point that would greatly interest Christian readers in Rome. Also he uses some Latin words, such as 'Legion' in 5:9 and 'Praetorium' in 15:16, in addition to which he explains Aramaic words and phrases for his readers in passages like 5:41, 7:11 and 15:34. As we shall see, too, his selection of material and his presentation of it would certainly appeal to Romans.

If, as most scholars think, 'Babylon' in 1 Peter 5:13 is a disguised name for Rome (cf. Rev. 17:9, where the seven hills clearly symbolise Rome; Rev. 17:18; 18:2), then Mark and Peter were in Rome together at the time Peter's first epistle was written. No doubt, as the early church writers suggest, Mark would have learned a great deal about Jesus from Peter's preaching, but there were probably other things Peter would want to tell Mark in preparation for that time when the latter would commit all this material to writing for posterity.

I live in Glasgow, a city with many tenement flats. Some of these are very fine buildings, designed by great architects, while others of course are poorer in quality. Who invented tenements? The Romans! The residential parts of the city of Rome were crammed with tenement dwellings. I imagine Peter and Mark sitting together at a rough table in a small flat, perhaps about the size of a Glasgow 'single end' (a one-room flat), or, if they had family with them, something somewhat larger, the older man talking animatedly and the younger one writing down what he was saying. Over it all, unseen but real, the Spirit of truth was presiding.

It is not surprising then to find that Mark omits a number of events recorded in other Gospels, events which might appear to show Peter in a good light. So Mark does not tell us that Peter walked on the water (Matt. 14:28.29), nor does he record the promise Jesus made to Peter after he confessed him at Caesarea Philippi (Matt. 16:17-19), nor his visit to the empty tomb after the resurrection (John 20:2-7). On the other hand, Mark does record the rebuke Jesus gave Peter (8:32-33), Peter's comment to his Master on the Mount of Transfiguration (9:5,6) and gives a very full account of Peter's denial of Christ (14:66-72). These omissions and inclusions are consistent with the attitude we might expect of a disciple who had failed but had been restored and forgiven by his Lord.

There were probably other sources for Mark's account too. He and Barnabas were cousins (Col. 4:10) and fellow-workers (Acts 15:39), and some have thought the reference to Barnabas as an apostle (Acts 14:14) may suggest he was one of the larger group of missionaries Luke tells us Jesus sent out during his ministry (Luke 10:1ff). If so, he too would have known much about the life and teaching of Jesus and he would have been as eager to share this information as Mark to receive it.

When was the Gospel written? There has been some debate about this. If it was after the death of Peter, this most likely puts it after Nero's persecution, which took place in AD 64 and 65, but probably not long after. If it was written before it, it may have been penned as early as AD 45. Most scholars have been inclined to place its writing in the late sixties.

4. How to tell the story for Romans

The vigorous style and graphic telling of the story have made Mark's Gospel popular in today's church, the church of the television and tabloid culture. It is an excellent Bible book to put into the hands of somebody who is not yet committed to Christian discipleship, but who is interested in Jesus and wants to know more about him.

What did the Romans need and how did Mark present the good news of Jesus to them in a way that related to their concerns?

He gave them facts. They were practical people. There were philosophies current at Rome but they tended to be the more practical ones, not simply speculations about life, but prescriptions for actually living it. They had little interest in theories that could not be translated into practice. Dr Samuel Johnson was once told about a philosophy that denied the existence of matter. Immediately, he kicked a stone, and said, 'I refute it thus!' Whether that was an adequate rejoinder or not, he could easily have been a Roman!

They were also very interested in law, and so were concerned with evidence and how its truth could be established. To them, it would matter a good deal that Jesus was real, and that his cross and resurrection took place in such a way that their truth was accessible to and could be established by witnesses. All this they would get from the Gospel of Mark. The vividness of the account also contributes to our sense that the story had come from an eyewitness.

He gave them action. Typically, the Romans were people of action. They got plenty of it in Mark's book. A glance at the first chapter will indicate how much movement there is in it. 'Jesus came from Nazareth (v. 9) .... At once the Spirit sent him out into the desert (v. 12)... Jesus went into Galilee (v. 14) ... as Jesus walked beside the Sea of Galilee (v. 16) ...' and so on.

This constant activity is often underlined by the use of the word *euthus*, a great favourite of this Gospel writer, which the NIV sometimes translates in different ways, such as 'at once' (e.g. 1:12) or 'without delay' (e.g. 1:20). Sometimes unfortunately it does not translate it at all, as in 1:10. It is true that in Mark's use it may not always suggest absolute immediacy, but what it always does is to give a sense of action, and so it is surely important for it to be translated! In this way, the reader is encouraged to visualize the swift activity that characterizes the whole account.

It has also been pointed out that another of Mark's favourite words, the verb *archesthai* ('to begin'), which occurs about twenty five times, also stresses action. So, for instance, in 1:45, the cleansed leper 'went out and began to talk freely, spreading the news'. The impression gained is that he lost no time in making a start. This verb is particularly frequent in the two chapters which, despite recording the passion of Jesus (and in English the words 'passion' and 'passive' are connected), are actually full of activity (14:19, 33, 65, 69, 71; 15:8, 18). Once more we notice that the NIV does not always render the word.

The fact that this Gospel contains less of the teaching of Jesus than do the others also contributes to the sense of constant action, for teaching not only takes time to give but space to record, and it has the effect of slowing down the action.

He gave them order. This too was a Roman concern.

It is strange that Papias tells us that Mark does not record the life of Jesus 'in order'. What did he mean by this? In the same context there is a reference to Matthew, and it may be that Papias noticed the absence of major blocks of teaching in the Gospel of Mark in contrast to that of Matthew. Perhaps he was referring to such features as the use of a 'flashback' when the story of John the Baptist's death is told in 6:14-29. Another possibility is that he noted some differences in the sequence of events between Matthew and Mark and assumed that Matthew was the more chronologically ordered.

Yet order there certainly is, mostly of a thematic kind. For instance, 2:1-3:6 shows Jesus in debate, as also does 11:27-12:37, while 4:1-34 consists entirely of parables of the kingdom and 4:35-5:43 records a number of miracles in which Jesus rescued people from impossible situations.

He showed them a Man of Power. Like so many people with a strong military interest, the Romans had a great respect for the man who could command the allegiance of others and who demonstrated authority and power.

Jesus is presented in this way. His authority is shown as he commands the winds and the waves, as he calls men to follow him as his disciples, as he drives men and beasts out of the Jerusalem temple. He puts forth power as he heals diseases, casts out demons, raises the dead and then emerges from the tomb himself. Here is a great Leader, whose authority and power were shown in ways that went well beyond those of Julius Caesar or Augustus.

There are points of similarity between the military ideals of the Romans and the messianic ideals of the Jews, for to the Jews the Messiah would be a man of power. Certainly that power was differently expressed in our Lord's fulfilment of the messianic hope than it was in the form that hope took in the Judaism of his day, but the element of power was certainly an important common factor.

Yet it must be said that the Christian message not only relates positively to many of the concerns of its hearers, but it also challenges them deeply. In his Areopagus address, for instance, the apostle Paul is at one with the Epicureans in teaching divine creation of the universe, and with the Stoics in teaching the presence of God everywhere, but he cuts right across them both by proclaiming the resurrection of Jesus (Acts 17:16-32). So, in his Gospel, *Mark showed his readers a Man of Suffering.* What Roman bridegroom would have allowed himself to be snatched away from his bride (2:20)? What great Roman leader would have warned his followers that he was going to the capital city voluntarily to face certain death (10:32-34)? It was not for

19

this that Julius Caesar crossed the River Rubicon. What Roman leader would have allowed himself to be captured, tried and executed without putting up even a token resistance?

So, in its teaching about the sufferings and death of Jesus, Mark's Gospel counters both the triumphalist militarism of the Romans and the triumphalist messianism of the Jews. No wonder the kingdom of God as preached by Jesus and incarnated in him, its King, has been called 'the upside-down kingdom', except, of course, that God's way, so different from man's, is always the right way.

It was our Lord's concept of the style of messiahship that Peter found so difficult to accept (8:31-33). Because of this, it is remarkable that the Gospel of Mark, written under strong Petrine influence, should make the suffering messiahship of Jesus such a leading theme. In its first half the reader is led with the disciples to understand Jesus as the Christ, while in the second half he is confronted first by predictions of suffering and then by the fact of it.

This of course harmonizes with the teaching of Peter's first epistle, where the sufferings of Christ and his glory through resurrection so often occur together and always in that order (1 Peter 1:11; 3:17-21; 4:13; 5:1). Glory for Jesus there certainly was, but never instead of but always by means of his sufferings. This shows how thoroughly Peter's thinking had been transformed by God since the time when he rejected the very idea that Jesus would suffer.

Glory through suffering voluntarily borne! Here is God's own presentation of what it is to serve Him – both in the unique work of the Messiah and also as a pattern for the Christian disciple.

5. A Gospel for all Christians – and through them for the whole world

Was the Gospel of Mark intended only for Christian readers in Rome? By no means! The characteristics of it which would give it a special appeal to those who were Romans in the narrowest sense, that is, who were citizens of the city of Rome itself, would also give it a wide appeal wherever there were Romans and so throughout the whole empire. But we cannot limit it even to them. Bauckham and other contributors to his book have argued that each of the Gospels was intended from the first to be read widely throughout the churches, and that they were intended to be read first of all by Christians and then to be used by them for evangelistic purposes (see page 10).

Does this mean then that we should no longer look for particular themes or emphases relevant to Romans? Not necessarily, but it does mean that we should not interpret the book as if it was intended for them alone.

What would happen to the Gospel after it was written?

There can be little doubt that it would be eagerly sought after, not only in Rome itself, but also in other churches once its existence became more widely known. Because there is some truth in the saying that all roads led to Rome (and therefore also from it) a highly significant Christian document read and used in the church there was sure to become known more widely quite quickly, and copies would begin circulating extensively among the churches. It seems likely that such a wide dissemination was intended by the author himself.

What at first sight is rather surprising is the fact that it soon became quite neglected, being overshadowed especially by the Gospel of Matthew. In fact there were understandable reasons for this. After all, Matthew was an apostle whereas Mark was not. Matthew's Gospel contains virtually everything that is in Mark and it gives a lot of extra material. In addition to this, Matthew emphasises the gospel's link with the Old Testament, and, for a while, the church was very eager to win the Jews for Christ, so that his Gospel would constitute a powerful tool in Jewish evangelism. Eventually the idea began to circulate that Mark was simply an abridgement of Matthew. Rarely does it seem to have been noticed that although Mark is briefer than Matthew, he often gives more detail about the events he does record. For an example of this, compare the records of the feeding of the five thousand in Matthew 14:13-21 and in Mark 6:32-44.

This comparative neglect lasted for a long time, but in the nineteenth century there was a major renewal of interest in Mark, largely due to the fact that it was now thought to be the earliest of all the Gospels, and this century was a period when there was an intense interest in history and particularly in origins.

There is no doubt too that the Gospel has come into its own in a new way today because of changes in western culture and means of communication. Although there has never been a period in history when so much information has been available to readers, and although through the Internet this has become available on the grand scale to large numbers of people, there are many today who read very little, who never even open a newspaper and whose attention span becomes increasingly limited to the 'soundbite'. There can be little doubt that television is chiefly to blame for this. Many books for adults are now difficult to distinguish from those intended for children for both are increasingly characterised by simple language and the incorporation of many pictures. Here is a cultural situation tailor-made for such a book as the Gospel of Mark, in which there is constant action, in which there is swift transition from one event to another, and in which there is a great deal to appeal to the eye of the imagination.

6. Some literary features of the Gospel

It is always interesting to see how a writer develops his theme and how he gives added interest and significance by presenting features that recur from time to time, so that they may be picked up by the careful reader and so may highlight the unity of the whole work. Without doubt, Mark did this kind of thing.

He was very *selective*. At the conclusion of his Gospel, John observes that the whole world could not contain the books that might have been written about Jesus (John 21:25). Obviously Mark, like the other three evangelists, has his own particular points of emphasis, and these determine his selection. Yet it is amazing how little of the life or even of the ministry of Jesus is actually recorded by him. He gives us enough notes of time to enable us to see that when we add together 1:21-38; chapters 4 and 5, 6:30-56, 8:27-9:29 and chapters 11 to 16, these together cover less than twenty days, and yet they constitute well over half the Gospel. Twenty days out of a ministry of over three years and a life of over thirty! It is quite clear from this that his intention was not by any means to give a full record of the life or even of the ministry of Jesus, but simply to select events and sayings that reveal the Person, character, teaching and work of Jesus in a way that would evoke faith and obedience.

Even though his Gospel is the shortest of the four and so he had to be even more selective than the other writers were, it is surprising to find that he often gives *more detail about some particular events* than they do. Undoubtedly he wanted to stimulate the imaginations of his readers, and detail helps in this, for it aids our inner eyes. For instance, he gives the story of the encounter of Jesus with the Gadarene demoniac in twenty verses (5:1-20), whereas Luke takes only fourteen and Matthew as few as seven. This can also be seen if the parallel accounts in Matthew and Luke are consulted in relation to the story of a healing and a raising from the dead in 5:21-43, and that of the feeding of the five thousand in 6:33-44.

He gives us *summaries of the activity of Jesus* during certain parts of his ministry, for example in 1:15 and 39, 3:7-11 and in many later chapters. These are always brief, and are probably given both to balance the strong selectivity of other parts of Mark's book and to indicate how full the ministry of Jesus actually was.

A somewhat similar phenomenon relates to the teaching of Jesus recorded by Mark. It is true that he gives less space, even proportionately, to this teaching than the other three evangelists, but there are *a very large number of brief and memorable sayings,* sentences that stick in the mind and that are deeply thought-provoking, so that the reader of this Gospel may be almost as well placed to grasp the main features of our Lord's thought as those who have read one of the others.

To get you started on studying these, read 1:15 and 2:17. Paradoxically, detailed stories and brief sayings have a similar effect on the reader, fastening on to the memory.

A major feature is *the way he puts two events together to show either a comparison or a contrast between them.* He never spells this out explicitly as a principle he used in his arrangement of the material, but it occurs so frequently that it could hardly be unintentional It is therefore worth looking at in some detail. In 3:20-30, for instance, there is a contrast between the concerned attitude of the family of our Lord, 'He is out of his mind' (v. 21), which presumably arose out of loving concern for him, and the blasphemous suggestion of the teachers of the law, 'He has an evil spirit', (v. 30), which undoubtedly revealed their antipathy to him.

In chapter 5, the stories of the woman with the constant bleeding and that of Jairus and his daughter are interwoven, and this makes the contrast particularly evident. In the woman's case, her approach to Jesus was a very secret one, whereas Jairus was quite public in his appeal to him. There is also a probable contrast between the social standing of the two persons, showing clearly that Jesus was prepared to interrupt a journey to a synagogue ruler's home in the interests of an unknown woman.

In chapter 7, there is a fairly lengthy account of the teaching Jesus gave the Pharisees, the crowd and his disciples on the subject of uncleanness. In this he showed his opposition to some features of Pharisaic casuistry, and he identified the inner cleanliness of the heart as far more important than externals. This is followed immediately by the story of the simple faith of the Syro-Phoenician woman, who was a Gentile as distinct from these Jewish separatists. Other examples of this feature of the Gospel will be pointed out in the relevant chapters of the commentary.

The reader may become aware of *certain themes which are gradually built up* as the Gospel progresses. The most striking is the motif of the death of Jesus. This is introduced first of all as a violent human act (2:19), and the reader becomes aware of a gradual build-up of opposition to him. In the centre of the Gospel Jesus begins to teach that although he would die as the result of human malignity, there was also a divine necessity in his death (8:31, etc). He then goes on to explain its inner meaning as ransom and covenant (10:45; 14:24), before the whole theme reaches its consummation in the event itself and especially in the awful cry, 'My God, my God, why have you forsaken me?' (15:34)

The promise of Jesus in 10:29-31 that disciples losing families for his sake will gain families, appears to build on the concept of a spiritual family introduced in the teaching he gave as recorded in 3:31-35. The teaching about parables in chapter 4, which contains an interpretation of one of them, may be set there as a key for the understanding of later parables. This same passage reveals something of the spiritual dullness of the disciples, which often comes to the fore as the story proceeds further. Jesus gives teaching and rebukes the disciples' lack of understanding after the feeding of the four thousand, in which he makes reference to the earlier feeding of the five thousand.

7. Mark's Gospel and the rest of the Bible

People who begin to read the Bible seriously soon become aware of what is called 'inter-textuality'. This is the fact that there is a unity to the Bible, that its every book exists as part of an amazing corpus of inspired literature. This means that Biblical books need to be studied not only as separate entities, to discover their distinctiveness, but also together, for there is a sense in which these books inhabit each other, not in the way concentric circles do, but in the way different coloured strands may be woven together in a piece of cloth. This feature of the Bible has also been likened to a web in which no gossamer thread exists on its own but always in connection with other threads, or to a beautiful building in which every part is seen to have greater loveliness when viewed in the context of the whole edifice.

All this is profoundly true of the Gospel of Mark. On the

25

face of it this is a simple piece of literature, the story of a great life, in fact of the Supreme Life, told with artless ingenuousness and without any attempt to theologise. So then it might be thought that nothing lies beneath the surface. To take a modern saying out of its usual advertising context, 'What you see is what you get.' There have in fact been some periods in the history of the Christian church when it has been somewhat neglected because of this.

Some years ago another man and I were talking together about art. I mentioned an artist whose pictures I happened to like and asked him what he thought of them. 'Not much,' he said. 'He only painted what he saw and he didn't see very much.' I am not at all sure that he was right. I have looked at the pictures of this artist a number of times since, and I see more and more in them. Perhaps then the one who did not see much was my friend rather than the artist himself.

For a long time, Biblical scholars viewed Mark's Gospel somewhat in this way, but today it is recognised that there is a depth to this book and that it cannot be lightly dismissed. We are used to thinking of Paul and John as theologians, but this is also true of Mark. This does not mean that he interpreted theologically events and teaching that were essentially non-theological, thus introducing distortion. Nor does it mean that he intended his Gospel to be interpreted allegorically rather than literally, even though some scholars have thought, often quite gratuitously, that this was his chief literary motive. Rather we need to recognise that the amazing events themselves, events to be valued because of their historical nature, also cry out for theological interpretation and that the Gospel writer was well aware of this. The statements that Jesus, a Man, was the Son of God (1:1) and that his death was not just the result of human malice but that it was 'a ransom for many' (10:45) are about as theological as you can get.

Mark and the Old Testament

Somebody who reads the Gospel of Mark for the first time is immediately made aware of the fact that the story of Jesus has important links with the Old Testament. In Chapter 1, verses 2 and 3 consist of quotations from the Old Testament. John the Baptist and Jesus are both shown as preaching for repentance, and this is highly reminiscent of the type of ministry the Old Testament prophets had, while the garments of John described in verse 6 remind the reader who knows his or her Old Testament of the clothing of Elijah the prophet.

There are quotations from various parts of the Old Testament, but especially from Isaiah and the Book of Psalms. These are in fact the two books most quoted within the whole New Testament, so that it is evident the writers believed them to be particularly eloquent and extensive in their testimony to Christ. There are many other passages which require a knowledge of particular parts of the Old Testament for their understanding. Why, for instance, is Jesus said to cleanse a leper, when it is obvious that what happened was a healing (1:40-45)? Because of the way the Old Testament views leprosy. When Jesus says, 'Only in his home town, among his relatives and in his own house is a prophet without honour' (6:4), we need to read the Old Testament to find concrete examples of this.

A person's constant reading is bound to affect his or her writing style, through absorbing much from the literature read, largely in an unconscious fashion. Mark, like the rest of the New Testament writers, would have known the Old Testament quite deeply. Some of the narrative parts seem to have affected his own narrative style. This is particularly true of the events concerning Elisha which are recorded in Second Kings. Here we read that time and again God used Elisha to bring blessing to many different people facing a great variety of distressing circumstances. This reminds us of the miracle series in Mark 4:35–5:43 and the constant movement of the Elisha narrative from one story to another is so like Mark's Gospel.

Mark and the other Gospels

Although there is a great deal of common ground between the four Gospels and especially between the three Synoptic ('seeing together') Gospels of Matthew, Mark and Luke, there are significant differences also, for each writer had his own readership, his own emphasis, determining his own selection of material. This is one of the factors giving the Gospels their perennial interest. What is known as the 'Synoptic Problem', a consideration of similarities and differences and of attempts to explain them, has brought a vast literature into being. The discussion is often highly technical and it is outside the purpose of this commentary to deal with the issues in detail. Interested readers are recommended to consult articles on the Gospels in the *New Bible Dictionary,* the *Illustrated Bible Dictionary*, the *Zondervan Pictorial Encyclopaedia of the Bible* or in Donald Guthrie, *New Testament Introduction* or D.A. Carson, D.J. Moo and L. Morris, *An Introduction to the New Testament.*

Whatever the processes which led to the writing of the four Gospels as we have them, Christians believe they were produced under the guidance and inspiration of the Holy Spirit in accordance with the promise of Jesus to his disciples in John 14:26: 'The Holy Spirit ... will teach you all things and will remind you of everything I have said to you.' Two of the traditional authors of the Gospels, Matthew and John, were present when that promise was given, Mark and Peter, as we have seen, were friends, and Luke, a companion of Paul, refers to what was 'handed down to us by those who from the first were eye-witnesses and servants of the word' (Luke 1:2).

Mark contains little that is not either in Matthew or in Luke. Can we then dispense with it altogether? By no means! The account of the life of Jesus given in this Gospel is characterised by great vigour of presentation, by vivid description, and by concentration on essential facts which are at the heart of the New Testament message, the death and resurrection of Jesus. Although formerly people interested in the Christian faith but as yet uncommitted to Christ were encouraged to start their New

Testament reading with the Gospel of John, it is more common today to suggest Mark, and for understandable reasons. As we have suggested already, its vividness means that it is undoubtedly the Gospel for a television and tabloid age

If we compare Mark with Matthew, we find that the latter gives much more of the teaching of Jesus, including some fairly long discourses, notably the Sermon on the Mount. Also Matthew emphasises the Old Testament background to the good news of Jesus. Yet an examination of the teaching of Jesus in Mark's Gospel will show that his terse and memorable aphorisms contain virtually all the themes presented at greater length in Matthew. Also there are quite enough quotations from the Old Testament (beginning in the second verse of the Gospel) to show clearly that Jesus is its fulfilment.

Luke's Gospel is notable for the many parables it gives, some of them distinctive to this book and in many cases among the best-known and best-loved of those told by the Saviour. Yet Mark highlights the importance of concentrated listening and of the spiritual understanding of parables and provides, in his account of the Parable of the Sower, an example of parabolic interpretation from the lips of Jesus himself. Luke gives more information than the other Gospels about the final journey of Jesus to Jerusalem, and thus builds up the reader's awed anticipation of what is to happen there, but Mark's briefer approach means that the crucial events of Passion Week are especially emphasised because they occupy such a proportion of the whole book. Luke gives some fascinating pen-portraits of individuals who come into the story, but Mark can do this too. What a picture he paints of the poor demoniac Jesus met after crossing the lake! Just five verses (Mark 5:1-5) and yet the presentation is unforgettable.

What about the Gospel of John? This is undoubtedly, *par eminence*, the Gospel of the Son of God. In it Jesus gives great fulness of teaching about his divine sonship. Yet this great theme is by no means absent from Mark. In fact the divine sonship of Jesus is stated in the very first verse of that Gospel, and as early as verse 11 it is confirmed from the highest of all sources, by the voice of God himself. No doubt the reader is meant to keep these facts in mind as he proceeds further into the Gospel, and he will note the occurrence of the title in connection with some of the most important events in the life Mark presents. The significance of Jesus is the focus at the beginning of both Mark and John, Mark showing that he is the Son of God and what great power he has, John giving a great number of his names and titles. Both give many of the questions that people asked about him and in both the theme of conflict with the religious leaders is important.

No, we certainly cannot do without Mark.

Mark and the remainder of the New Testament
To explore adequately the thematic similarities between Mark's Gospel and the New Testament writings from Acts to Revelation would require a very large book, or even a series of volumes. I will however make a few suggestions and the interested reader can look out for others in his or her own reading.

The Acts of the Apostles tells us of the birth and growth of the Church of Christ, and in it we read brief accounts of five addresses by Peter. If Peter was for Mark the main source of information about Jesus, we would expect some points of contact between these sermons and this Gospel, and this is just what we find, for Peter's sermon in Acts 10:34-43, preached, let us note, to a Roman centurion and his friends, bears a striking resemblance, brief as the account of it is, to the general outline of the Gospel of Mark.

Mark shows how difficult it was for Peter to accept the fact that Jesus was going to die and subsequently to rise again. It is difficult to read Peter's first letter without noting what a great emphasis he places on the sufferings of Christ and the glory which followed. He had now come to see as central that which earlier he had not accepted at all.

Paul's interest in the cross and resurrection of Jesus and his commitment to these events as the centre of the good news, which comes out clearly and succinctly in a passage like 1 Corinthians 15:3-4, accords very well with the dominance this theme has in the Gospel of Mark from its centre-point in Chapter 8 onwards. Without doubt, Peter would have shared Paul's horror that the Galatian Christians were being encouraged to treat Christ's atoning work at the cross as needing to be supplemented by circumcision and to retreat into a kind of 'Christian' legalism. If Mark had read Paul's letter to the Philippians, with its unsurpassed statement of the humble condescension of Jesus and his ultimate exaltation in 2:5-11, he would undoubtedly have said, 'that is the Jesus I recognise and about whom I have written.'

Mark wrote for Romans and so did Paul. Mark's first verse establishes his purpose of setting forth the facts about Jesus as good news from God and immediately makes reference to Old Testament prophecy. Paul too opens his great epistle with a reference to the gospel of God, says that it concerns God's Son and that it was promised by God through his prophets. Mark presents the great facts about Jesus, focusing on his cross, and gives brief but clear teaching from the lips of Jesus as to the significance of that event. Paul's letter takes the facts about Jesus for granted and expounds their significance at greater length, again with special attention to the cross and the resurrection

The first readership of the Epistle to the Hebrews is uncertain, but it was almost certainly addressed to a group of Jewish Christians who had experienced some persecution. We might therefore expect it to have more in common with Matthew's Gospel than with any of the others. Yet it should be noted that many scholars consider this group to have been domiciled in Rome. It is not surprising therefore to find that the teaching of Psalm 110 is of great importance here, dominating what is said in chapter 7 and referred to in other places in the letter. We recall that Mark gives the comments of Jesus himself on this psalm at the virtual climax of his public ministry (Mark 12:35-37), only a few days before his death.

31

Mark 13 records teaching given by Jesus to his disciples on the subject of the destruction of the temple, teaching which then moves on to embrace also his second advent. The Book of the Revelation brings the New Testament to a close and this too is concerned with what was yet to come. We would expect some links between the two, and we are not disappointed. Mark 13:14 refers to 'the abomination that causes desolation', along with an exhortation to the reader to understand. This is an allusion to Daniel 9:27; 11:31 and 12:11 and the Book of Daniel is an important part of the background to Revelation. In Mark 13:22, for instance, Jesus warns his disciples against false Christs and false prophets. The two sinister beasts which appear in Revelation 13 seem to be a false Christ and a false prophet, and this is confirmed at least for the prophet in Revelation 16:13,14. The warning of Jesus to be alert and to watch, because of the suddenness of his return (Mark 13:33-37), finds an echo in Revelation 16:15.

Some suggested books for further reading, proceeding approximately from simpler to more technical treatments of the Gospel:

S. and C. Danes, *Mark: A Gospel for Today*, Oxford: Lion Educational, 1989.

J. Green, *How to read the Gospels and Acts*, Leicester: IVP, 1987.

R. T. France, *The Man They Crucified*, Leicester: IVP, 1975.

D. H. Juel, *Mark* (Augsburg Commentary on the New Testament), Minneapolis: Augsburg Press, 1990.

R. P. Martin, *Mark* (Knox Preaching Guides), Atlanta: John Knox Press, 1981.

R. A. Cole, *The Gospel according to Mark* (Tyndale New Testament Commentaries), Leicester: IVP, 1961.

J. Sergeant, *Lion let Loose: The Structure and Meaning of the Gospel of Mark*, Exeter: Paternoster Press, 1988.

R.T. France, *Divine Government: God's Kingship in the Gospel of Mark,* London: SPCK, 1990.

W.W. Wessel, 'Mark' in F E Gaebelein (ed.), *The Expositor's Bible Commentary*, Grand Rapids: Zondervan, Vol. 8, 1984, pp. 601-793.

W. L. Lane, *Commentary on the Gospel of Mark* (New International Commentary), Grand Rapids: Eerdmans, 1974.

J. A. Alexander, *The Gospel According to Mark*, Edinburgh: Banner of Truth Trust, 1960.

R. P. Martin, *Mark: Evangelist and Theologian*, Exeter: Paternoster Press, 1972.

NB A very full bibliography may be found in R. H. Gundry, *Mark: A Commentary on his Apology for the Cross*, Grand Rapids: Eerdmans, 1993.

Chapter 1

His Preparation (1:1-13)

God always prepares long beforehand for important events taking place in his world.

Think, for instance, about nature. The clouds gather before the rain comes. There is no ripe fruit until the seed has been planted and there have been months of growth and development. Human birth is the climax of nine months spent in the womb.

The Bible writers were convinced that the God who works in nature is also busy in history. In fact, the latter is where their main interest lies. In his Gospel, Mark records the greatest happenings in the history of the world. These thirteen verses set the scene for us and show us God's processes of preparation for these momentous events.

1. A book with a message (1:1)

What a help it is to know the nature of a book before you start to read it! It means that you can approach it in the right frame of mind. Mark gives us this kind of help when he tells us in the very first verse what his book is. So what is it?

It is really a kind of preaching, for it presents the gospel (the good news) of Jesus Christ, the Son of God. Is it surprising then to find it followed by sixteen chapters of facts? This should not take us by surprise, for every sermon in the Acts of the Apostles majors on facts, all of them, as here, about Jesus or very closely related to him. The message needs to be applied to the hearers, of course, but unless you preach about Jesus and give facts about him you are not preaching the gospel at all in the New Testament understanding of the term.

In every sphere of human life, trust plays an important part. Even in politics, if people are to be challenged to put their faith

35

in a person who is seeking election, they need to know something about that person, particularly his or her character and record. Who Jesus is and what Jesus has done form the strongest possible basis for the most important of all faith-commitments. Luke tells us in his preface that he wrote his Gospel for Theophilus, 'so that you may know the certainty of the things you have been taught' (Luke 1:4). There can be little doubt that this was Mark's aim too.

We are used to the term 'gospel' as applied to a book, but this kind of application of the term was not in use until the second Christian century, so that the word here refers to the contents of the book rather than to the book itself. It is not then simply a biography but a joyful message for the reader about Jesus. One person advising another about a possible friendship will sometimes say, 'Avoid Jack, he's bad news!' Mark is saying to us, 'Get to know Jesus, he's good news! In fact, he's God's own good news.'

Who does Mark show this Man to be?

He is 'Jesus', an individual man, bearing a name shared by many others in his country at this time. This is no surprise, for it was the Greek form of the name 'Joshua', borne in the Old Testament by the man who succeeded Moses and who was sent by God to lead his people from the wilderness into the land of promise. It was also the name of the high priest of Israel when Haggai and Zechariah were prophesying to God's people after their return from Exile (Hag. 2:2; Zech. 3:1). In fact, there is even another Jesus, 'Jesus called Justus', mentioned in the New Testament (Col. 4:11). Like so many Old Testament names, it has a wonderful meaning. In the case of Jesus of Nazareth, this points us to his special work, for it means 'the Lord is salvation'.

He is also 'Christ'. This word is the Greek equivalent of the Hebrew word translated 'Messiah', the person God promised to send to put things right in and for Israel. Many important servants of God had emerged in the long story of God's people. God told Abraham to leave his homeland in Mesopotamia and he led him to the promised land. Moses was used by God to bring the descendants of Abraham out of Egypt and Joshua led them into Canaan; Elijah stood for the true God at a time of great religious crisis. Isaiah transmitted from God to the people many great promises of future blessing through Christ. There were many more. Nobody, however, could be more significant than the promised Christ, and this is who Jesus was and is.

But he is much more. He is the Son of God. As the Christ he was special in what he did, but as God's Son he is unique in who he is. He is, in fact, not only human but divine. So we are not surprised to discover that what he did matters not only for Israel but for every human being. That is why the study of this Gospel of Mark is so important for us today, nearly 2,000 years after the events it records.

Some old manuscripts of the Gospel do not contain the words, 'the Son of God', in this first verse of the Gospel, although they are firmly fixed in the great majority of manuscripts, and they are accepted as genuine by the majority of textual scholars. They seem to be most apt, because this title for Jesus is such an important one in the book. It is particularly at specially important and significant points in the story of Jesus that Mark records its use. These include his baptism (11), transfiguration (9:7), trial (14:61) and crucifixion (15:39). These events bear eloquent testimony to the person and work of Jesus, and the use of this great title at such times shows that his divine status was very important for the work he came to do.

One surprise we have is that the term 'Son of Man' is not included in this verse, for it was a favourite self-designation of Jesus and occurs a number of times in the Gospel, and at most significant points in the story. It has been described as 'a veiled designation of Messiahship' (G.B. Stevens) and it also has some transcendent implications which could be thought of as contained within the expression, 'Son of God'. We will be thinking more fully about this great term later in the Gospel.

Students of literature note that the opening of a book is often of special importance in stressing the book's main purposes and showing the reader what the writer cares about most. For this reason, in reading Mark's Gospel, we must never forget this great opening statement. In every event recorded in the Gospel, Jesus was being revealed as the Christ, the Son of God and this revelation was very special good news from God.

2. The Old Testament Preparation (1:2,3)
Jesus Christ came into the world after many preparatory centuries. God had been guiding his people Israel, and many passages in the Old Testament – both predictions and also events, institutions and persons which prefigured in some way and so anticipated the coming Christ – were fulfilled in Jesus. Mark quotes two of these passages in verses 2 and 3, although, as was the custom among the Jews at that time, he referred by name to the more important prophet only. In this case it was Isaiah, even though the quotation from Malachi stands first on his page. Another example of this kind of thing may be found in Matthew 27:9,10.

Mark uses the expression, 'it is written', which was a technical term for the New Testament writers and is used by them only when they quote from the Old Testament Scriptures. It might be translated, 'it stands written', for it implies not only that something was written in the Old Testament years ago but also that it confronts the living reader as a word from God, with all its power to encourage or challenge.

These Old Testament passages might seem to be about John the Baptist, and of course they are, but only as the forerunner of Jesus Christ, to prepare his way. This means that they are at least indirect witnesses to Jesus himself.

Mark changes the wording of Malachi 3:1, which refers to God, so that it relates to Jesus, 'me' becoming 'you' and 'my way' becoming 'your way'. This too was recognised practice at the time, and it was really a kind of shorthand method of combining a quotation with its interpretation. There is not really a problem here, because it was done simply for convenience and not as an attempt to convince the unconvinced. The first readers of Mark's Gospel were sure already of the deity of Jesus.

This was true for the people of the New Testament as a whole. For instance, in Hebrews 1, the writer takes some Old Testament Scriptures about God and applies them to Jesus, without even feeling it necessary to argue for this way of handling them. One example of this is his quotation of Psalm 102:25-27 in Hebrews 1:10-12.

The quotation from Isaiah 40:3 is interesting, because that chapter of Isaiah soon mentions good news. Its ninth verse reads, 'You who bring good tidings to Zion, go up on a high mountain. You who bring good tidings to Jerusalem, lift up your voice with a shout, lift it up, do not be afraid; say to the towns of Judah, "Here is your God!" ' Roman Christians would know the Book of Isaiah in the Greek Septuagint version, in fact some of them (Jews and also Gentiles who had attended a Jewish synagogue) would have known it long before they became Christians. The Greek word for 'good tidings' in this verse from Isaiah is closely connected with the word translated 'gospel' in Mark's first verse.

'Prepare the way for the LORD' (Isa. 40:3); 'here is your God!' (Isa. 40:9) – how significant such language is! We cannot set any limits to the greatness of Jesus.

3. John the Forerunner (1:4-8)
In the first verse of his Gospel, Mark uses the word 'beginning'. He seems to be saying that the good news began with John the Baptist. Why? Because John kept pointing to Jesus, who was himself the good news. Apart from Jesus, his whole ministry is without meaning.

Simon Peter's brother, Andrew, had been a follower of John the Baptist, as their friend John the apostle tells us (John 1:40-42). Peter was one of his followers too, as we can infer from what he says in Acts 1:15,21,22. Both in that passage and in his later sermon to Cornelius and his friends (Acts 10:37), Peter begins the gospel story with John the Baptist. So we can well imagine Peter talking to Mark and saying to him, 'Start with John the Baptist! That was the real beginning for those of us who became disciples of Jesus.'

It has been interestingly suggested that the word 'beginning' here is used for another reason, and that is that it echoes the first verse of the Bible. Here is Jesus, a whole new beginning to the story of this world. There can be no doubt that in the first verse of John's Gospel Genesis 1:1 is in the mind of the author, for the verses that follow it concern the work of Jesus in creation. We cannot be quite so sure, however, about Mark's intentions. Maybe he did have this in mind – it would have been very appropriate – but we cannot be certain.

John the Baptist, although a character found in the New Testament rather than the Old, was really the last of the old prophets (Matt. 11:13), for, like the others, his task was to prepare for the coming of Jesus. If Jesus is God's Seed, Israel was the soil, and pretty hard soil it was at this time. John's task was to break up the soil, so he spoke to the people about their sins, telling them to forsake them and to be baptized in water. If they were baptized it showed they were in earnest, and that they were looking to God to cleanse away their sins. Mark shows that John's ministry created quite a stir, affecting both Jerusalem and the area round about it.

The word translated 'baptising' here normally meant immersing in water; often, but not always, this was for purposes of cleansing. It is well known, of course, that there has been much debate as to whether other modes of using water, such as pouring or sprinkling, were ever used for baptisms in New Testament times and whether such methods may be legitimately employed in the work of the church today.

Great men and women expect their representatives to dress the part. An ambassador who is down at heel will give the impression he represents a king or president of little consequence. We are somewhat surprised then to see how basic John's clothing was. Surprising as it may seem, however, John's dress did actually represent what he was. It had symbolic significance. It was recognized attire for a prophet (Zech. 13:4). It was especially appropriate for a man who was in many ways the successor of Elijah, who, like John, challenged a king's conduct (Mark 6:17-20; 1 Kings 21:17-26) and called the people to repentance. He too had been clothed in this way; in fact this garb was so characteristic of him that the king was able immediately to recognise him from a report given to him by one of his men (2 Kings 1:8).

What about his food? Like his clothing, it was quite basic. He could find locusts and wild honey in the countryside, and this perhaps meant he could concentrate on the special work God had commissioned him to do without the need to engage in cultivation or to rely much on others to supply his daily needs.

His message about Jesus emphasized how great he was. John felt unworthy even to do the lowly task of a servant for him and so to remove his sandals. In view of this, it is all the more moving to find the apostle John in his Gospel recording an event in which Jesus himself went well beyond the unloosing of the sandals of his disciples by personally washing their feet (John 13).

John contrasted the baptism to which he called people, a baptism in water, with that of Jesus, who would baptize with the Holy Spirit. His words at this time were however intended not only to contrast the baptisms but even more the baptizers. This is made clear to us by Mark, because the way he wrote verse 8, as an examination of the Greek text reveals, places emphasis on the words, 'I' and 'he'. He who baptizes with the Holy Spirit is, without doubt, greater than he who baptizes in water, not only of course because the Holy Spirit is a Person but also because He is God.

Here the whole work of Jesus in renewing and empowering the inner being of his people is briefly stated and promised, for Holy Spirit baptism is essentially inward and spiritual. This promise that came through John the Baptist is mentioned again, and by Jesus himself, shortly before the Pentecostal outpouring of the Spirit (Acts 1:5).

John the Baptist's comment is also a most important reminder that we should never think of the Spirit's work in such a way as to detach it from Christ's, for they are bound together in God's great and gracious saving initiative. The Spirit's work is a consequence of Christ's. This saves us from making the potentially disastrous error of mistaking 'spiritual' experiences which are not Christ-related and Christ-centred for genuine experiences of the Holy Spirit.

4. The baptism of Jesus (1:9-11)

Jesus himself is introduced in verse 9. Here is another comparison with the Gospel of John. John begins his Gospel by reference to the pre-incarnate Word of God and he does not actually identify him as Jesus until verse 17. This means that the reader is given a profound context for understanding who Jesus is before he is himself introduced. Mark does something similar, showing Jesus as the fulfilment of prophecy and as a very great Person. Of course, he does make reference to him in verse 1, but this is somewhat of a general heading.

The New Testament contains four Gospels. Matthew and Luke both tell the story of his birth, Luke adds some facts about his boyhood, while John starts with his life and work with the Father long before he came into the world. It is perhaps surprising that Mark does not begin his story with the birth of Jesus. Instead he starts with his adult life. This is because he wants to stress his special work, which commenced at his baptism, and especially the great events at the climax of his life. As we shall see, his emphasis on the cross is very strong indeed. It is helpful, however, for us to keep in mind that there were thirty silent years of preparation before the events recorded here.

His baptism brought that process of preparation to a climax. Others were baptized because they were sinners. In view of what Mark has just told us about Jesus in verse 8, then, it is most surprising to find him coming for baptism. Matthew records John the Baptist's protest at the thought of administering it to him (Matt. 3:14). Mark, with the strong dramatic sense he undoubtedly had, held the name of Jesus back until the last possible point in his sentence, a feature we discover also in many passages in the Epistle to the Hebrews. This sort of thing is not always easy to bring out in a natural fashion in English translation, but we could render verse 9 somewhat in this way: 'And it happened at that time that there came Someone (that is, Jesus) from Nazareth of Galilee and he was baptized....' How astonishing and how unexpected!

Why then was he baptized? We can see how fitting it was when we find Jesus saying that in this (as well as in all else he did, of course) he was to fulfil God's righteous purpose (Matt. 3:15). An important saying of his, later in the Gospel story, shows clearly that he came to die in the place of sinners (10:45). So, because he was going to bear their sins, he shared the baptism which in their case was an acknowledgement of their sins. His baptism in water foreshadowed the awful baptism of blood which he experienced at Calvary (Luke 12:50).

Some early heretics, known to historians as the Modalists, maintained that the terms Father, Son and Holy Spirit as used in the New Testament are simply different ways of describing the one true God, each appropriate only at certain periods in the Biblical history. In Old Testament times, they said, he was the Father; then, from Bethlehem to the Ascension he was the Son; and now since Pentecost he is the Holy Spirit. In becoming the Son, he ceased to be the Father, and in becoming the Holy Spirit he ceased to be the Son.

This rather naive outlook was an attempt to relate the New Testament evidence and language about Jesus Christ and about the Holy Spirit to the doctrine of God's unity, but it does not square with the Biblical facts. For instance, here at the baptism of Jesus the three Holy Persons participated in one event, so showing that their existence is simultaneous and not simply successive.

Like Matthew, Mark concentrates on what the events connected with the baptism meant to Jesus himself. Three amazing things happened.

First of all, Jesus 'saw heaven being torn open' (NIV). Mark uses the Greek verb he employs here once more in his gospel, in 15:38, where he tells us that when Jesus died for sinners the great veil in the temple, symbolizing the barrier between God and human beings, was rent asunder. Here just before his ministry opens Jesus is being assured that there is no barrier between earth and heaven for him. So, when he died on the cross, he was dealing with a barrier which existed for others but not for himself.

Then, secondly, the Spirit descended on him like a dove. The dove is a symbol of purity, and is so used in Song of Songs 6:9, in the words, 'my dove, my perfect one.' The symbolic use of this bird in this way is due not only to its colour but also to its concern to keep clean. When Noah wanted to know if the waters of the flood had dried up, he sent out a dove from the ark. He knew it would stay out only if it found a dry, clean place for its feet (Gen. 8:6-12). The Spirit of God was of course active in Israel in earlier times, as many passages in the Old Testament show us, but here at last, like Noah's dove, he had found a permanent resting-place. He, the Holy Spirit, had found God's holy Man.

The final event puts the holiness of Jesus beyond doubt. Here we move from visible symbols to words and, in them, to an unambiguous statement: 'You are my Son, whom I love; with you I am well pleased.' God identified Jesus as his beloved Son. We must never forget that his love for Jesus did not take the form of grace, as it does for us who are sinners. Here was a wholly merited favour, for all that he had been and said and done, including his baptism, had expressed his own love, answering his Father's love for him, and his consequent obedience to the Father. In Old Testament days, too, God had spoken audibly, for his voice was heard on Mount Sinai. Then it was to give his requirements; here it is to express his deepest approval and delight.

This is not all though. The words, 'You are my Son', come from a great messianic psalm (Ps. 2:7). This is in fact the key psalm in the messianic teaching of the whole Book of Psalms, because, coming near the start of that book, it alerts the reader to look for the messianic theme as he reads through its pages. The Lord's delight in his Servant on whom he puts his Spirit is found in Isaiah 42:1, which again is a scene-setting passage, for it begins a great series of Servant passages in Isaiah's prophecy that comes to its profoundly moving climax in the picture of atoning suffering given in Isaiah 53. This intensifies the awareness we have already been given in verses 1 to 3 that the later chapters of Isaiah's book are important for understanding who Jesus was and what he came to do.

As we can tell from contemporary and near-contemporary Jewish documents, many in Israel saw no real connection between the Messiah and the Servant. Ultimately, of course, it is God's prerogative to interpret his own Word, and here his voice, speaking from heaven, unites these two Old Testament figures in one great New Testament reality – Jesus himself. He was God's Christ, but he would endure profound suffering in the course of his service to his Father.

5. The temptation of Jesus (1:12, 13)

When God is pleased, Satan is displeased, for his designs are the exact opposite of those that are in the mind and heart of God. He hates to see anybody dedicating himself or herself to the will of God.

In the case of Jesus, of course, this Satanic hatred was particularly intense, for his work would mean the binding of Satan himself, as our Lord was soon to declare (Mark 3:23-27). So the devil tempted him in order to try to deflect him from the pathway of God's will. Mark records the simple fact of his temptation, while Matthew and Luke spell this out for us in more detail (Matt. 4:1-11; Luke 4:1-13).

Mark tells us that it was the Spirit who sent Jesus out into the desert (v. 12). The verb used suggests that Jesus was aware of a strong inward constraint and, because this constraint came from the Spirit of God, this in turn shows that God had a special purpose in the fact that he faced Satanic temptation and overcame it. God does not tempt us, for this is alien to his holy

45

nature (James 1:13-15), but he does not abdicate his sovereignty when evil is on the rampage. The temptations that Satan designs to overcome us God uses to strengthen us, as we face them in the power of his Spirit. What Satan intended as temptation for Jesus, God intended as testing. Satan's motive was entirely evil and intended to thwart God's purpose, but all he actually accomplished was to show how deeply committed Christ was to the will of his Father! In 2 Corinthians 12:7-10, Paul shows his readers how, in his own life, God had used an act of Satan to show him his weakness and therefore to cause him to look to God for strength. So God's sovereignty is at work in such a way that even the evil acts of the devil may be so overruled by God as to serve his purposes. The cross is the supreme example of this.

It is possible that the forty days of his temptation, although of course quite literal, also have some symbolic significance. It was for forty years that the people of Israel were tempted in the desert on their way from Egypt to Canaan, and of course, they failed miserably and, as a result, a whole generation was banned from entering the Promised Land. Like Israel too the very first human beings, Adam and Eve, had been tempted and failed, but Jesus resisted temptation and triumphed over Satan.

Does the reference to wild animals suggest that Jesus is the new Adam, living among the beasts as Adam did in the garden? Or does it perhaps suggest more than this, the fact of his dominion over the animal creation, a dominion given at first to human beings but now only imperfectly exercised (Gen. 1:27ff; Heb. 2:8)? Certainly passages in the Book of Isaiah show us the wild beasts living together in harmony in the coming reign of the Messiah (Isa. 11:1-9; 65:25), which, incidentally, is not easy to interpret unless we think of his kingdom as having some earthly expression after he comes in his Second Advent. It is of course possible that the reference here in Mark is simply a reminder of the hazards of desert life.

Angels attended him during this period. Does this mean he had resources in facing his temptations which are not available to us in ours? Not at all! After all, the Epistle to the Hebrews rather enigmatically tells us that angels have been sent forth to minister to those destined to inherit salvation (Heb. 1:14), just as they ministered to him, salvation's Author. Passages like Matthew 18:10, 24:31 and Luke 16:22 may suggest the nature of their ministry to God's people.

We may find ourselves here reminded of Psalm 91. This is a psalm about God's protection of the godly man, and in it the angels are on hand to rescue him (vv. 11,12). The wild beasts are there too in the psalm (v. 13). In fact, there is even language there that reminds us of Satan, in the reference to the serpent. In view of this, it should not surprise us that Satan, in quoting verses 11 and 12 (Luke 4:10,11), did not go on to verse 13. He probably knows some psychology! He did not want to remind Jesus of the promise, 'You will tread upon ...the serpent'. Remember what God said to the serpent in the garden of Eden: 'I will put enmity between you and the woman, and between your offspring and hers; he will crush your head, and you will strike his heel' (Gen. 3:15).

The temptations of Jesus were real and intense. They show us with great clarity that the idea that we have to yield to temptation before we can help others is simply a lie of the devil. It is just not true, for instance, that we have to experience drunkenness ourselves before we can help people with a drink problem. If two men of equal physical power were to be pushed by somebody else, and one gave in after a few seconds while the other held on for the duration of the assault, which of them more fully experienced the force of the push? Jesus experienced the full force of Satan, but he did not yield. What help he can give us! This is spelled out for us in Hebrews 4:14-16.

6. This passage as an introduction to the whole Gospel

These verses set the scene of the ministry of Jesus for us and careful study of them prepares us for what is to come. This suggests that for Mark, what he gives us here is important not only in its own right but also because of its introductory character, conditioning the reader to look for particular themes as he moves into the remainder of Mark's book.

Here we see that *the book is to be read as good news*. It is therefore a kind of preaching. We discover in fact that not only is the book good news about Jesus when taken as a whole but that so many of its events represent elements in the gospel of God's grace which the New Testament proclaims. Here people are challenged and blessed by contact with Jesus, some of them healed from their diseases (and what greater disease is there than sin?) while others are liberated from evil powers that have taken possession of them. All these point us towards aspects of God's salvation in Christ. Here too are miracles that feature the impact of Jesus on the physical world, for instance his miraculous feedings of multitudes and his ability to walk on water. This feature points suggestively in the direction of the supreme manifestation of his power over the physical world in his resurrection from the dead.

Then there is the importance of the Old Testament, viewed as prophetic and anticipatory of Christ, and brought to its final stage in the ministry of John the Baptist who, although belonging to the New Testament, was really, as we have seen, the last in the great line of prophets under the Old Covenant. There is so much in the subsequent story that reminds us of the connection between Christ and the Old Testament.

Here too we see the importance of repentance. The gospel of Christ challenges the whole outlook and lifestyle of the world, even of the religious world, and requires a complete reorientation in the life of the man or woman to whom it is presented. Here is no mere 'easy believism', and the disciples were certainly to discover this when he challenged them to take up the cross and follow him (8:34).

Of course, the chief emphasis of the book right from the beginning is on Jesus himself, the Christ, the Son of God, the One who would baptise with the Holy Spirit. In the preached gospel of Christ, people are called to put their trust in him, and for that trust to be meaningful there must be teaching that focuses on him. This is what the Gospel does from its beginning to its end. The supreme worthiness of Jesus is already made clear to us in these verses. Not only so, but in the temptation by Satan, the theme of opposition to him is introduced, that opposition which would come to its climax in the story of the cross.

Jesus as the Son of God and his cross as God's great saving act. These are the themes of the preached gospel and of Mark's written Gospel too.

Some questions for personal reflection

1. John the Baptist had a deep sense of unworthiness when faced with Christ and yet he preached with considerable authority. Do I see that these are in fact consistent with each other and, if so, what does this say to me about my own position as a member of God's family?

2. What can I learn from our Lord's temptations about what temptation is and about how to face it?

Chapter 2

His Works (1:14-45)

Mark 1 is one of the busiest chapters in the New Testament, and it gives us quite a selection of the kind of things Jesus was doing early in his ministry and which he continued to do. Here he is marked out as unique at his baptism, after which we find him preaching, gathering followers, teaching, casting out evil spirits, healing, praying and cleansing a man with leprosy. Anybody reading it for the first time is likely to be struck with awe at the activities and the power of this Man, and would see at once that there was something special about him.

There is constant movement in the chapter. 'Jesus came from Nazareth in Galilee and was baptised by John in the Jordan' (1:9); 'he was in the desert' (1:13); he 'went into Galilee' (1:14); he 'walked beside the Sea of Galilee' (1:16); he 'went to Capernaum' (1:21); 'he travelled throughout Galilee' (1:39). Here was a most active life in which he must have encountered great numbers of people and quickly become well-known, especially in the northern part of Israel, which was known as Galilee.

This comes out too in Mark's use of one of his favourite words. This term occurs only once in the New Testament outside the Gospels, but Mark uses it constantly, especially in the first half of his book. It is used eleven times in this one chapter, the same number as all its occurrences in the seventy-three chapters of Matthew, Luke and John together. That is striking, but we need to note that Mark uses it much more in this chapter than he does elsewhere. Why is this?

Perhaps he is telling us something at the start and doing this so forcefully that all he needs to do later is to remind us of it from time to time. In fact, this kind of technique seems t` characteristic of his Gospel. Here Mark wants us to understand that Jesus was an intensely active Person, constantly on the move, constantly at work, constantly bringing the power of the gospel and the authority of the kingdom of God to bear on every situation he found. If this is the point he is making, he has made it most persuasively.

What is that word? It is the Greek word *euthus*, translated in a number of different ways in the NIV, as it is in a number of English versions. In verses 12, 18 and 43, it is 'at once', in verse 20, 'without delay', in verse 23, 'just then', in verse 28, 'quickly', in verse 29, 'as soon as' and in verse 42, 'immediately'. In three places (vv. 10,21,30) it is not translated at all in the NIV, but in fact it has exactly the same basic meaning in all eleven verses. Mark is underlining for his readers the fact that the life of Jesus at this time was one of constant activity.

This vivid sense of activity also shows itself in many of the active verbs we find in our present passage. Jesus proclaims (v. 14), walks (vv. 16, 19), teaches (vv. 21,22), gives orders (vv. 25, 27), heals (vv. 31, 34, 42), drives out demons (vv. 34, 39) – and prays (v. 35).

Here is something to ponder: could the last of these activities be the key to all the others? After all, the others are all connected with his activities among people, while this is about his fellowship with God, and it was to serve God – largely through his ministry to people – that he came into the world. The picture presented to us is not simply one of ceaseless activity but of effective ministry, and many a Christian worker has discovered to his or her cost that they are not identical. A Christian may be extremely busy, working almost ceaselessly at some task or other, yet to little avail. Why? Because there is little dependence on God. Our Lord's concentrated time with his Father in the earl᎒ ᴍnings, seen on one occasion in this passage (v.35) and ᴇd in Isaiah 50:4, shows us that in his earthly life ᴏf God needed prayer. So there can be no question ᴅ of it.

1. The Person he was

The name 'Jesus' dominates this early section of the Gospel, as it does the whole book. As we saw in our last chapter, this is a human name. It is earthed still more when he is called, 'Jesus of Nazareth' (v. 24; cf. v. 9). Not only was Nazareth not heaven; it was not even of much distinction on earth, even in his own land. To call him 'Jesus of Nazareth' is to give him a title which would not even be a status symbol, let alone a divine appellation.

Jesus was born in Bethlehem and he would die and rise again at Jerusalem, but the New Testament never calls him 'Jesus of Bethlehem' nor 'Jesus of Jerusalem'. This is surprising, for either would have been appropriate, as they were both specially associated with King David, and he was the Son of David (10:47,48). 'Jesus of Capernaum' would have had less messianic suggestiveness than Bethlehem or Jerusalem, but it would have been apt, for, as we will see, he seems to have made this busy fishing port his base during his Galilean ministry. Instead he is identified by the name of a most insignificant place, one not even referred to in the Old Testament. In fact, it seemed to one of the disciples, Nathanael, a most unlikely place to associate with the Messiah (John 1:46). He really had no time for the place at all. 'Nazareth! Can anything good come from there?' He should know, for he came from Cana (John 21:2), and you could walk from one to the other in the space of three hours or so.

Our Lord was, however, more than simply 'Jesus of Nazareth'. He was 'the Holy One of God' (v. 24). This phrase was uttered by an evil spirit, but it was true. The Bible word 'holy' is very eloquent. Basically it means 'set apart' and especially 'set apart for God'. So used of a person it can also signify 'the set-apart one', 'the unique one', 'the one who is different'. Jesus was in fact all this, because, as we have seen already, he was and is the Christ and the Son of God, and these titles certainly imply that he was set-apart by God and that he was unique in his relationship with God.

Don't forget then, as you read this section of Mark's book,

and in fact the whole Gospel, that the person so often simply called 'Jesus' is actually what the Gospel's first verse says he is, 'Jesus Christ, the Son of God'. Jesus – so human! The Son of God – so divine! The Holy One of God – so perfect! This is the Person who did all the wonderful things described in this passage.

2. The message he proclaimed

The ministry of Jesus opens with a reference to his preaching (verses 14,15). This establishes the importance of it for his ministry. In fact there is a reference to it even in the few verses that occur before the entry of Jesus into the story, for John the Baptist too was a preacher.

What is preaching? Today it conjures up a picture of a church building, a seated congregation, a raised pulpit. Actually this stereotype does not express at all well what the Bible calls preaching. Certainly the Lord Jesus preached in the synagogue buildings of his day, but he also declared God's word in the open air. While it is true that it is from the same root as the Greek word for a herald and so possesses connotations of official appointment, it is doubtful if we should restrict the word to proclamation to a group. Some are called to the regular task of public proclamation, but to tell somebody about the Saviour and to call that person to trust him is to proclaim God's message and so is to preach in a broad sense. This is something every Christian can do.

This passage contains references to synagogues and to the fact that Jesus preached in them (vv. 21, 29, 39), apparently quite frequently. How was he able to do this? We know that such preaching was by invitation and that those who presided at the synagogue services might invite either a suitable member of the congregation or else a visitor from elsewhere. Paul too had many an opportunity afforded to him by this custom, as see, for example, in Acts 13:15 and 17:2,3. Of course, it always presupposed the goodwill of those who controlled a local synagogue.

The synagogues which are so familiar a part of the scene in the Gospels seem to have originated in Babylon during the exile when the Jews got together to pray and to study the Scriptures, especially the Mosaic Law. In recent years archaeologists have discovered an ancient synagogue at Capernaum, the town which was central to our Lord's Galilean ministry. Although a little later in date than the New Testament period, it may well have been built on the site of an earlier one and possibly even one where Jesus himself worshipped and preached.

What qualities did the preaching of Jesus have?

It was joyful (v. 15).
It was good news.

Imagine the reaction of the first hearers! For over four hundred years the people of Israel had been longing for the day when God's kingdom would come through his Messiah. They had been waiting without any new word from him, for there seem to have been no prophets between Malachi and John the Baptist. In terms of British history and its relationship to our own day, this would mean a wait beginning in the reign of the first Queen Elizabeth. Now Jesus came to tell them that the long wait was over; the kingdom's coming was imminent. What joyful news!

When we compare verses 14 and 15 with verse 1, we learn that Jesus was both preacher of the gospel and the heart of that gospel. As Mark will show, in his unfolding of the fact and significance of the death of Jesus, especially in 10:45 and 14:24, it is certainly true, as has been said, that he came 'not only to preach the gospel but that there might be a gospel to preach'.

As we read the Acts of the Apostles we see that the gospel continued to make those who received it rejoice, for, as Luke tells us, 'the disciples were filled with joy and with the Holy Spirit' (Acts 13:52), and Paul reminds the Thessalonian Christians that, despite the severe suffering they experienced at the time of their conversion, they had 'welcomed the message with the joy given by the Holy Spirit' (1 Thess. 1:6). The gospel message still brings joy today.

It was authoritative (vv. 22, 27).
The scribes, 'the teachers of the law' as the NIV calls them, were
the chief religious teachers of the day, but their method of teaching
involved much quotation of earlier scribes. The Talmud, in which
rabbinic and scribal teaching was collected and given written form,
shows many examples of this feature. The people quickly saw the
contrast. Jesus was speaking as the Son of God, and the authority
of his teaching could not be missed. The religious teachers of the
day spoke from opinion or out of an ongoing tradition; but he spoke
with divine authority. This is why we too must listen to what he
says, as the divine Voice from heaven was to make clear (cf. 9:7).
In him we are addressed by none other than the very Son of God.

It was patient (vv. 21,22).
This is implied in the word 'teaching', for it was not a once-for-
all proclamation but a patient course of instruction in God's
truth. This is in fact stressed in the grammatical form used in
verse 22, for Mark uses a type of expression that always
emphasises continual action. As we shall see later, he illustrated
this teaching in parables, which are stories with spiritual
meaning. Good and effective teaching almost always involves
illustration. We will also see that even then people sometimes
misunderstood him, including those who knew him best and
had listened to his teaching most frequently. This will raise
questions for us about what sin does to our minds, which is an
aspect of our involvement in sin that is often overlooked. Are
we capable of thinking straight about the things of God without
a work of his grace taking place in our thought-processes?

It was challenging (vv. 15,17).
His preaching stated facts, as all preaching must, but it went
beyond this. Preaching needs to combine exposition and
application, with its imperatives firmly based on its affirmatives.
If the two are divorced, this is not Biblical preaching. It was
said of Samuel Rutherford's preaching that his doctrine was all
application and his application all doctrine, and this made it

true preaching. Jesus certainly combined the two, for he not only affirmed that the kingdom had come near but, in view of this, he called his hearers to repent and believe the good news. This then was preaching that challenged the wills of his hearers. Jesus took issue with their whole way of life. They were to repent, which means a radical turning away from sin. They were also to believe the gospel.

Even at this early stage in his ministry, it was made clear that this would mean people accepting God's kingdom and so acknowledging his right to govern their lives. The kingdom of God, in its essence, is not territory but authority over persons. It is God's rule. There is of course a sense in which it is always true that God possesses authority over every human being, whether they acknowledge it or not. The authority of the supreme King does not depend on its recognition by his subjects, but he has every right to expect that recognition and the surrender of their wills to him which is its necessary consequence. At this time, however, the kingdom was near in a very special sense, for the King himself, the Lord Jesus, was now in their midst and was calling rebels to repentance. Later it would be made clear that acknowledgement of the kingdom meant accepting the King. Already he showed his right to command by calling four fishermen to follow him (vv. 16-18), which, as Mark shows, secured a ready response.

It was essential (vv. 37,38).
Already he had healed many people and expelled demons from those possessed by them. Because of this, he was a great attraction. People are always interested in those who have proved they can offer something which will improve their quality of life, especially if it is free.

Mark gives us what appears to be the record of one day's activity (vv. 21-34), and at the end of it, he tells us, the people brought to Jesus all the sick and demon-possessed. 'The whole town gathered at the door, and Jesus healed many who had various diseases. He also drove out many demons' (vv. 33, 34).

Many a preacher would have been sorely tempted to stay in a situation of such obvious blessing. Here God was clearly at work. Jesus however moved on to other towns. This was because he knew that the main point of his ministry at that time was preaching. 'That is why I have come' (v. 38), he said. Nothing, not even his healing and exorcising ministry, must be allowed to overshadow the proclamation of the good news. This reminds us that Mark's introduction to the Galilean ministry in verses 14 and 15 appears to identify its central feature as gospel proclamation.

This underlines the fact that Christianity is first and foremost a message, a fact which also emerges clearly in the Acts of the Apostles. We need to grasp this. No other activity, no matter how important, must be allowed to put the proclamation of God's message into the background. There are doubtless many good things a Christian church can do, but it must never surrender the central importance of the preached word.

3. The power he exercised

If Mark was writing his Gospel for Romans, it is not surprising that he should bring out the power of Jesus in many of the events he was recording, for power interested them greatly. John the Baptist had already stressed the power of Jesus the Christ. 'After me will come one more powerful than I' (v. 7), he had said. Perhaps one reason why Mark records these words is that he would soon give many illustrations of that power, as he certainly does in the section of the gospel we are now considering.

Of course power has potential both for blessing and for danger. Think of any source of physical power – fire, electricity, gas, water, steam, nuclear energy – and you will see this straight away. 'Don't play with fire!' children are warned. Yet how good to come home to its warmth on a bitterly cold winter's evening!

For the right exercise of power it is not only wisdom that is needed, but goodwill. A source of power in the wrong hands is a fearful thing. That is why there has always been so much concern about the character of a person who has great power, especially now if his finger is on the nuclear button. In the Books of Kings verdicts are given on the various monarchs of Israel and Judah and these verdicts relate very much to their influence on others, for good or ill, for the true God or for paganism, because they had power to affect the religious and moral quality of a whole nation. There can be no doubt too that Mark's Roman readers would know their history well enough to recall examples of both helpful and anti-social uses of power.

Here in Mark's book we read about the use of power by the wisest Man the world has ever seen, a Man who is the very incarnation of God's holy love and infinite wisdom. How reassuring it is to know that today it is he who is on the throne of the universe, the place of ultimate power! What do we see him doing with his power in this particular passage?

He used power to *liberate* people and so to open up new life for them.

Like the other Gospel writers, Mark was aware of the existence and activity of beings he describes as demons (v. 34) or as evil spirits (vv. 26,27). The word translated 'evil' here (*akathartos*) really means 'unclean' and this sharply differentiates these in character from the Holy Spirit who descended on Jesus at his baptism (vv. 8-10). Here then are two spiritual realms in conflict. Jesus the Son of God, was filled with the Holy Spirit. Some of those he met were possessed by unclean spirits. It would be a mistake for us to think of evil simply as the opposite of good. It is not only different from good; it is antagonistic to it, and we see that very clearly here.

In the case of the man in the synagogue (vv. 23-27), the power of the unclean spirit was seen both in its possession of him and also in the violent way it shook him at its shrieking departure. We see from this that we cannot doubt either its power or its malignity. We see something too of the reality of the possession in the way the man oscillates between the singular and the plural when speaking of himself (v. 24).

The result of the spirit's encounter with Jesus was however never in doubt. His command, 'Be quiet!' (v. 25) really means

59

'Be muzzled!' It is also employed in 4:39, there in connection with his stilling of a storm. Paul uses the same word when he says, 'Do not muzzle an ox while it is treading out the grain' (1 Cor. 9:9). A muzzle can prevent either eating or biting. In either case, the animal has been put under control. The evil spirit's power to harm the man had been decisively broken by Jesus, who showed in this his complete mastery of this situation.

Some commentators do not accept the reality of demonic possession and see the actions of Jesus in such passages as this as evidence that he accepted the (sometimes mistaken) beliefs of his day. Quite apart from problems this approach raises for the Christian who believes in both the deity and the veracity of Jesus, it often shows the influence of a rationalistic philosophy which, if taken to its logical conclusion in a complete denial of the supernatural, would destroy the entire Christian faith.

In today's western culture, however, there is a resurgence of belief in the supernatural. People who never enter a church eagerly read their daily horoscopes, and the use of ouija boards and tarot cards is widespread. Then there is the whole New Age phenomenon and Satanism. All this holds dangers for the participant and it is banned in the Old Testament (e.g. in Deuteronomy 18:9-14). So then it is out of bounds for the Christian. If its contemporary prevalence has a positive feature, however, it is that at least it bears testimony to a retreat from rationalism on the part of many.

Here then is a strange anomaly! Many non-Christians now accept a supernatural dimension to life while some in the churches are hesitant about it or even deny it!

Many missionaries have for years been aware of the demonic dimension of evil, for they have encountered it in their work and it is only too real to them. It is not only the overseas missionary today who needs to be aware of Christ's power over evil spirits, however, but Christians in the lands of the west as well. Remember though that Christ's power to liberate is not limited to this demonic realm, but that he can free from every thrall those who put their trust in him.

He used power to *heal* people and give them wholeness.

Mark tells us that Jesus healed people who had many kinds of diseases (vv. 32-34). Just before this, he gives us a concrete example in the story of Simon's mother-in-law and her fever.

Here we meet a general feature of Mark. He is very interested in people and not just in the mass, but in particular individuals. So often he turns the spotlight on one person in his or her encounter with Jesus. In this, he had certainly sat spiritually at the feet of Jesus and learned his attitude to people. Any society that treats people simply as so many statistics has badly lost its way.

Not only was Jesus concerned for one person, but he did not dispense healing at arm's length. He grasped her hand and raised her up. Ever afterwards she would recall the strong grasp that conveyed healing to her fevered body. As we shall discover, there are many examples of physical touch in the healing stories recorded by Mark.

Can Jesus heal people physically today and do so in a direct way? Of course he can. There can be no doubt about that. We can be sure of it because Jesus is God and does not change. We can be sure of it through particular Scriptures, for we see many examples of healing in the church's story in the Acts of the Apostles, and James makes it the basis of exhortations in his letter (James 5:14-16). Moreover there are well-authenticated examples of it from the story of the modern church.

We must be careful though. Many exaggerated claims have been made, and these can bring the gospel of Christ into disrepute, for it is only truth that glorifies God and carries conviction. Also we should not discount the wonderful God-given advances in medicine and surgery. God in Christ healed this woman of a fever, and it is the same God we should thank for modern medicines that deal with fevers. He is the God both of the natural and of the supernatural. Whether a person's healing takes place through natural means or supernaturally, he or she has the same Person to whom to express gratitude.

He used power to *reconcile* people, bringing them into God's presence.

Mark tells us the story of the cleansing of a leper (vv. 40-45). The fact that this is called 'cleansing' shows us that there is an added dimension here that takes the event beyond a healing. In the Old Testament ritual law, leprosy was a special kind of disease, for it produced ritual uncleanness, which involved exclusion from the house of God, the tabernacle or temple (Lev. 13:1-46; Num. 5:1-4). This did not of course mean that the person with leprosy was denied the possibility of salvation. But it did mean he or she could not join with others at the house of God for worship. The psalmist may have felt a little like a leper when he found himself excluded, whether through distance or through exile, from the house of God in Jerusalem (Pss. 42, 43, 63, and 84).

Leprosy was not in itself a sinful condition, although it could be inflicted in certain instances as a punishment for sin. We see this in the stories of Miriam (Num. 12) and of King Uzziah (2 Chron. 26: 16-23). It had symbolic significance, for it pictured the exclusion from God's presence that results from sin.

To be restored to wholeness, to be 'cleansed', must have been a wonderful experience for this leper. The first century Christian preacher, reading this story in the newly-minted Gospel of Mark, may well have used it to proclaim that in Christ God has broken down the barriers that keep human beings from God. So these events, utterly real as they were and literally as they were to be understood, also symbolized an even greater activity of his grace, the way Christ's gospel liberates us from sin, gives us spiritual wholeness and reconciles us both to God and to others. It could even be the case that so many miracles are recorded in the Gospels not only to show the power and compassion of Jesus, but also to serve as illustrations of his gospel. They have certainly been used for this purpose by Christian preachers of every time and place.

The leper was sent to the priest, an officer of the ritual system within which the exclusion operated, to be examined and also to make an appropriate thank-offering. There were regulations covering this and they are set out in Leviticus 14:1-32.

We no longer have a worship system after the style of the tabernacle or the temple. We are however excluded from God's presence in a much deeper sense and for a much more serious reason. It is because of our sin. We are the spiritual as well as the natural children of Adam and Eve, who were themselves excluded from the tree of life and from the Garden of Eden, for they had become separated from God through their disobedience (Gen. 3; Rom 5:12-21). The glorious news of the gospel, however, is that Christ has destroyed that barrier by taking our place at the cross and carrying our punishment. 'He died the righteous for the unrighteous, to bring you to God' (1 Peter 3:18).

Jesus gave the man 'a strong warning' (v 43). He was to tell nobody. Why not? Because Jesus did not want to be known as a mere wonder-worker. We can understand the feelings of the man and his desire to make public what had happened, but we should not try to excuse him, or we might start excusing ourselves for disobeying commands of God we do not fully understand!

4. The interest he aroused

Jesus was quite a phenomenon in Galilee. Mark records the amazement of the people. Was this caused by the teaching he gave or by the way he cast out demons? It was evidently both (vv. 22,27), and when he also began to heal, this too brought people to him in great numbers (vv. 32,33,37).

So everything about Jesus was remarkable. The supernatural dimension was present all the time, but it is important to remind ourselves that this is true of the natural dimension also. Certainly he was the Son of God, certainly too he was filled with the Spirit, but all the time he was human. His compassion (v. 41) was divine but it was felt in a throbbing human heart. You see, you cannot separate certain aspects of his ministry from the rest and say that in these he was remarkable while in others he was not. You cannot separate his acts into two categories, some divine and some human. He was always both and his deity and his humanity were seamlessly joined in one Person, the One who performed all the actions.

One evening the whole town gathered about the door of the house where he was staying (v. 33). Was this an isolated case? No, for Mark tells us that as a result of the testimony of the leper to his cleansing, Jesus was mobbed whenever he tried to enter a town openly (v. 45). Were all these people committed to him? By no means! There can be little doubt that many were interested only in securing the physical blessings he could give, and others would be captivated by his consummate storytelling.

This section opens however with an encounter of Jesus with four men whose names we now know as members of his team of twelve apostles. He called them to follow him (vv. 17, 20; cf. v. 29). Later he was to make it clear that following him could be a very costly business, perhaps involving even death (8:34 ff.). Later still, as John tells us, he told Peter that, as far as he was concerned, his death would certainly come through martyrdom (John 21:18,19).

We should not imagine, however, that there was no cost for them in their response to him at this time. Fishing on Galilee's lake could be a lucrative business. We know that there were facilities for salting the fish, and salted fish from Galilee was on sale not only in the streets of Jerusalem but even in Rome. These men were probably doing pretty well.

Jesus used their trade as an analogy for the spiritual work to which he was calling them. He would make them fishers of men. His words also make it clear that expertise gained in fishing was not simply transferable to spiritual work. They needed instruction and empowerment from him to do it adequately. There is an important lesson here. There are ordinary human skills, such as teaching and management abilities, which might seem just what is needed for effective Christian work. We need however to recognise that work for Christ can never be effectively done unless we receive from, learn from and depend upon him.

It is notable that the very first disciple mentioned here is

Simon (1:16), later known also as Peter (3:16). Not only so, but he is mentioned four times altogether in the chapter. This is most understandable and even to be expected if Mark is recording in his Gospel the eye-witness testimony of Peter.

Mark's account of the call of those first disciples certainly bears all the hallmarks of the eyewitness. It was a most significant day in Peter's own life, and its every detail must have been etched on his mind. In telling the story to Mark, he remembered that he and his brother were actually fishing at the time of their call, while James and John were still preparing their nets. Not only so but the eye of his imagination recalled the picture of their father Zebedee and his hirelings in the boat. This would serve to underline something of the cost for his two friends; it was no small thing to leave both business and family, for this was at a time and in a culture where family members usually stayed in the same area and worked at the same job all their lives. This shows how effective the call of Jesus was. These men had of course met Jesus before this, as we see from John 1:35-42, but it is certainly impressive that they made such an immediate response.

They were not to know it, but the change of lifestyle for them was to be not only permanent, but increasingly demanding. Their response of course was not simply an expression of obedience, although it was that, but like Abraham's many centuries before, it was an act of faith as well (cf. Gen. 12:1; Heb. 11:8-10), for there is no indication that Jesus told them at this time what to expect. Then as now, to obey Christ's call is to trust him with the consequences of it.

One feature that often puzzles readers of this Gospel is the exhortations to silence which Jesus gives from time to time (1:25, 34; 3:12; 5:43; 7:36; 8:30). They are certainly not what we might have expected. They have interested scholars too and have been the cause of some speculation. About a hundred years ago, W. Wrede put forward the view which has come to be known as 'the Messianic Secret'. He thought all these commands were related in some way to the messianic identity of Jesus.

Wrede held a somewhat sceptical view of the historicity of some of the Gospel material, and so he maintained that this feature of the Gospel of Mark was not authentically historical but was the early church's way of explaining why Jesus seems to have said so little about his messiahship.

A number of features of Wrede's view need to be challenged, but basic to it is the idea that the Gospel accounts have been 'doctored' by the early church, so that they do not give a straightforward account of what actually happened. There is no need whatever for such scepticism, particularly as other very reasonable explanations of this feature of the Gospel can be given.

There were probably two reasons for this command. The first is that Jesus wanted people to recognize who he was by observing him and coming to personal faith, not simply accepting the opinion of others. This probably accounts for his command to the demons to keep silence (v. 34). The other is that, as Messiah, Jesus exercised much power to heal and to cast out demons, and he did not want to get a reputation that was dominated by these healings and exorcisms. We see this in the story of the cleansed leper (vv 43-45). His ministry of teaching could have been seriously hindered if the people came to him simply for the acts of power.

5. The importance of prayer to him

There are various ways in which a writer can emphasise a point. For instance, he can do it by repetition. This is how Luke demonstrates the importance of prayer for Jesus. He shows him praying at many of the most important times in his ministry. Mark must have been just as much aware of the importance of prayer for Jesus, but he makes the point differently. There is the fact that he makes reference to prayer at a very early point in the ministry (v. 35). He also shows its importance for the Master by indicating how very early he left the house to pray. He shows too that he did this at a time of intense busyness in his life. Could he have indicated any more effectively how vital Jesus felt prayer was to him?

We do not of course know the content of his prayers here. It is surely of significance though that they were followed by a move, and that the main purpose of the move was to enable him to continue his ministry of preaching.

Prayer and the ministry of the word of God. These were of central importance to Jesus. No wonder the apostles also gave a place of prime importance to them (Acts 6:4)!

What about you?

Some questions for personal reflection

1. To tell somebody about the Saviour and to call that person to trust him is to preach, for preaching means 'proclaiming a message'. If this is true, do I ever preach?

2. The cleansed leper was able now to worship with others at God's house. Think of some individual Christians with whom you would never have had fellowship unless God had reconciled both them and you to himself, and give him thanks for them.

3. The lifestyle of the disciples changed when they began to follow Jesus. What difference has discipleship made to my lifestyle?

Chapter 3

His Conflicts (2:1–3:35)

What is it that makes a compelling story? Almost invariably, it is conflict. This is one of the major factors in literature produced in every age and clime. This conflict may be of various kinds, and may not by any means always be physical. At times it may even be entirely within the mind and heart of one person. It is not easy, however, to think of a story that grips the mind but from which this element is absent.

It is part of literature because it is part of life. The work of God, truly done in God's way, always involves it. Ask the minister who is not prepared to wait for people to come to church but goes out in Christ's name to invade and attack Satan's strongholds in his district. Ask the woman who gives a bold witness for Christ in her place of work. Ask the missionary who, in a place dominated by another religion, presents Christ's claim to unreserved and exclusive devotion. It is of course what we should have expected, for it is exactly what we see in Scripture. It is in fact one of the many reasons why the whole Bible story is so gripping.

This element emerges very early in the Word of God. Genesis 3 shows us the wiles of the serpent and Genesis 4 the murderous hatred of a man for his brother. There is conflict between the Lord and false gods, as in the story of the Exodus (Exod. 12:12), in the clash of Baal-worshipping Jezebel and God's prophet Elijah (1 Kings 16:29-21:29) and in the overthrow of the gods of Babylon when God sent Cyrus the Persian against the Babylonians (Isa. 46:1-2).

This conflict theme reaches its climax in the incarnate life, death and resurrection of Jesus. Here was the supreme work of God and it was bitterly resisted at every step by Satan and his agents. Who did these agents turn out to be? Deeply immoral men? Servants of false gods? No, they were worshippers of the one true God. They were, in fact, the religious leaders of the nation. We are so used to this that we no longer feel how utterly astounding it is. Not only so, but we recall that these men possessed and diligently studied the Scriptures in which the promises of God which came to be fulfilled in Jesus were recorded.

Certainly some of the Sadducees, who were priests, may have treated religion largely as a means to an end, with motives like status, power, comfort and financial gain far too prominent in their outlook. In their case, it was not only Jesus who saw through them, for the people as a whole had come to despise them. The teachers of the law and the Pharisees, however, were different. Undoubtedly there were hypocrites among them, although this word, so often used of them by Jesus, especially in Matthew, need not imply that their whole religion was a sham but simply that they liked to put on a show for the observers. Many would be deeply sincere, with a high degree of dedication to the Law of God as they understood it. Yet they emerged as bitter adversaries of Jesus.

Why? This section of the Gospel tells us. It reveals the many-sided nature of their opposition to him and enables us to see what lay behind it all.

Mark here concentrates on conflict, and this theme dominates the whole section. It was of course to come to its ultimate climax in Jesus' life in the Passion narrative, but an intermediate climax point is reached in 3:6 with the beginnings of a plot to kill Jesus. So early in his ministry? Yes. The popular idea of a 'Galilean springtime' of the ministry of Jesus is only a half-truth. Certainly in these early days the people flocked to see and hear him, but at the same time bitter enemies were plotting against him.

Various other characters appear, and in three of the five stories the disciples feature. Do not miss this fact. They were there while Jesus gave his teaching and they witnessed many of his acts of power. The readers of the Gospel get used to their presence in the story and so are in this way prepared for important events concerning them which Mark will go on to record. In their work after the resurrection and Pentecost, their role as witnesses of the facts about Jesus was to be a vital one, and so the ministry of Jesus was a very important preparation time for them.

Each conflict story here contains an important statement or question from Jesus, usually at the end of it. This is a feature too of chapter 12, with its Day of Questions, a chapter so reminiscent of our present passage. There, in fact, the importance of his words is underlined still more, as we shall see, by the way the day ends – not with his response to their queries but by his own challenging question.

The areas of conflict were all about relationships of one kind or another. This is true in literature because it is true in life, and most of all in the Life above all lives.

1. Jesus and God (2:1-12)

In 1:21, we get the impression that Jesus arrived in Capernaum shortly before the Sabbath. Now in 2:1, Mark says, 'When Jesus again entered Capernaum, the people heard that he had come home.' It seems that this bustling fishing town was the centre of his wide-ranging Galilean ministry. A straightforward reading of 1:29-34 certainly gives us the impression that Simon and Andrew's home was the setting for a healing ministry that went on well into the evening. It also looks as if it was from their house that Jesus set out early in the morning to find a place for prayer (v. 35).

Had the family moved there from Nazareth at some time? This is not impossible, but it is much more likely that it was a centre Jesus chose deliberately. Did he lodge at Simon and Andrew's house regularly when he was in town? Possibly he did, although we cannot be sure. The translation 'come home', which occurs in so many modern English versions instead of the more literal 'in the house' assumes this, and some versions, such as the NRSV and NASB, translate the same way in Mark 3:20, although the NIV does not.

71

Why then did Jesus make Capernaum his centre? The Gospels do not tell us, but it is worth noting that Nazareth was much more remote from the wider world. Also whatever may have been their relative sizes, there would have been much more of an urban feel about Capernaum. From the latter salted fish was despatched far and wide. Here was a place with plenty of contacts with the wider world.

What a consummate story-teller Mark was! The tale of the paralytic is presented most graphically and yet with such an economic use of language that it is all over in twelve verses. If you were at Sunday School as a child, you may well have a clear mental picture of it, drawn by your imagination when you first read or heard this story.

The first four verses set the scene: a one-storey flat-roofed house crammed with people, with seats found for some respected religious leaders who were present, and folk still trying to get into an already full building. The same kind of crowded scene is pictured by Mark in 4:1, although this time in the less claustrophobic setting of the open air.

Love is resourceful and often shows skill in improvising when the well-being of the one loved is threatened. In their eagerness and determination to bring their disabled friend to Jesus, the paralytic's friends climbed the outer stairway and, as Luke tells us (Luke 5:19), removed enough of the thatch and tiling from between the wooden rafters to make way for him on his sleeping mat.

The man and his friends were, of course, very much aware of his physical incapacity, but Jesus saw a deeper need than healing and he told the paralytic that his sins were forgiven. It is important to notice that, far from avoiding conflict with the religious leaders, Jesus, in saying this, actually provoked it. As a result, conflict between Jesus and the religious leaders was initiated on his own terms, and this raised the vitally important question of his identity.

This question is a leading theme of the whole Gospel of Mark. The author has shown us this already in his general heading in

1:1 and also in 1:11, where Mark's own estimate of Jesus as
'Son of God' is confirmed by God himself. The reader should
not therefore be taken by surprise when he comes to this passage.
The identity of Jesus must always be given a central place in
Christian witness, and this means that the church can never avoid
controversy. In our multi-cultural and multi-religious society
we might be tempted to soft-peddle it, but we cannot do so and
be true to our Lord himself.

The teachers of the Law asked, 'Who can forgive sins but
God alone?' Were they right? Of course! 'Sin' is essentially a
religious word. An offence against me I may forgive, but a sin
can only be forgiven by God, because by definition it is
committed against him. They said this, of course, because they
did not recognise who Jesus was.

'Which is easier....?' asked Jesus. At a superficial level, of
course, it was easier to pronounce forgiveness, because this is
an invisible blessing whereas healing can usually be seen.
Certainly in this case the healing of the man was evident for all
to see. At a much deeper level, of course, healing is easier, as
forgiveness affects the whole being and life-history of a person
and even that person's eternal destiny, not just the functioning
of his or her limbs. In the case of this man, the greater, invisible,
spiritual blessing of forgiveness was confirmed by the lesser,
physical blessing of healing.

In 2:10, Jesus uses the term 'Son of Man'. We often find
him employing it later in the story. It was obviously important
to him. What does it mean? In the Old Testament it often simply
means 'man', with suggestions of frailty. Psalm 8:4 is a good
example of this: 'What is man that you are mindful of him, the
son of man that you care for him?' The two clauses of this verse
are clearly in parallel, saying the same thing in different words.
In one important vision in Daniel, however, the prophet saw
great beasts, representing pagan kings and kingdoms, rising up
from the sea and securing great power for a time. Then, in
contrast, he saw 'one like a son of man', 'coming with the clouds
of heaven' and receiving from God a kingdom that was both

universal and eternal (Dan. 7:13,14). Because of this passage, the phrase, without losing its emphasis on humanness, came to have also much more exalted connotations.

Because the emphasis in this Marcan verse is on the authority of Jesus and not simply his humanity, it seems more than likely that Jesus here identifies himself with the great figure in Daniel. The Christ, the Son of David, both in the Old Testament and in inter-testamental Jewish thought, was a kingly figure, with a kingship bestowed on him by God, and Mark has already used that title of Jesus (1:1). The Son of Man figure too was kingly, as the Daniel passage shows, with an authority that was universal and eternal, the kind of authority we normally associate with God alone. So then the power to dispense forgiveness could surely not be excluded from it and so from the role of Jesus as the fulfilment of it.

So then Jesus was special, not only in his work but also in his Person. He could do divine things for he was the Son of Man and the Son of God.

2. Jesus and sinners (2:13-17)

Jesus continued to call disciples. Where would you expect God's great Messiah to gather followers? Probably among the priests in the temple or the teachers in the synagogues, among those whose whole lives were concerned with the worship of God and the word of God. But did he? No! First of all he called the manual workers, men with hands roughened by physical toil and who smelled of fish. Somebody has said that God must be very fond of ordinary folk, because he created so many of them. Here is even stronger evidence. It was ordinary folk Jesus first called to follow him, and the same ordinary folk were later sent out to spread his gospel and establish his world-wide church. It is mostly ordinary folk who do this still. Paul, commenting on the Corinthian church, says, 'not many of you ... were influential, not many were of noble birth' (1 Cor. 1:26).

Next he called a 'middle-class' man. Still surprising, but just a little less so? No, this was more, not less surprising. The fishermen were at least pursuing an acceptable trade, but this man was a hated and despised tax-collector! Tax-collectors have never, of course, been popular in any society, although their work is important if a society is to function properly. The attitude of the Jewish people towards them was not however based chiefly on the fact that they were commissioned to collect money from them. Rather it was because of their links with the hated Gentile power that was occupying their land. As an employee of the Gentile Romans, Levi, called Matthew (meaning 'gift of God') in Matthew 9:9, would be regarded by the Jews as perpetually unclean. No self-respecting rabbi would have anything to do with him. Incidentally, his ready response to the call would have had considerable financial implications for him, as his office was extremely lucrative.

To make matters worse, Jesus joined Levi at table with other tax-collectors and assorted disreputables, the kind of people the ostracised tax-collectors would often associate with. In the culture of the times, a meal with another person betokened acceptance and friendship even more than it does in our own. For many observers, that would have ruled Jesus out of account not only as the Messiah, but even as a man of God. You can almost hear them saying, 'A man is known by the company he keeps.'

Here then we see in an actual event a kind of acted parable of the gospel. Christ accepts sinners who receive him, and welcomes them to fellowship with him at his table. Christian readers, both in the first century and today, would be reminded of the later institution of the Lord's Supper for the disciples. Levi (or Matthew, of course) was to be there at that supper when Jesus presided over it. Many if not all his disciple-companions at the Last Supper had a better social standing in their community than he and his friends; nevertheless they were sinners too. This would remind those early readers of the Gospel, as it reminds us, that God accepts us on the basis of his own unmerited favour, and not through any imagined righteousness of our own.

In Jesus, God's own healing was coming into a sick world. A doctor cannot be blamed if sick people ignore his skill, refusing even to recognise their need of it. The terms, 'righteous' and 'sinners' (v. 17) represent the valuation the people concerned placed on themselves, and of course the valuation the Pharisees put on the tax-collectors and their friends. This was vividly illustrated by Jesus in one of his parables (Luke 18:9-14), and also just as clearly (when we take its context into account) in the story of the Prodigal Son and the Elder Brother (Luke 15:1,2, 11-32). Without doubt the Pharisees were just as sick as the tax-collectors, but they assumed the role of the healthy. How self-deceived they were!

Awareness of our need is all-important. Self-righteousness bars the door to the Saviour.

3. Jesus and contemporary Judaism (2:18-3:6)

The Pharisaic approach to the Old Testament was largely Law-centred. We cannot altogether fault these men for this. It is evident to any reader of Old Testament Scripture that the Law was important. God gave it at a very important time, soon after he had liberated Israel from Egypt. He gave it to people without a full legal system of their own, for they would have been living under Egyptian law for many generations. Also it was given in circumstances of great solemnity (Exod. 19,20), from the top of a great mountain and with all kinds of awesome accompaniments. Moreover, much of it was basic for later stages of God's revelation recorded in Old Testament Scripture. Its importance had been reaffirmed by Ezra after the return of the people from Babylonian exile (Neh. 8). The Old Testament links two of the three Pilgrim Feasts (Deut. 16:16, 17), the Passover and Tabernacles, with the people's history, with the Exodus and the Wilderness Wanderings respectively. It is not surprising that the Jews themselves later decided to celebrate the giving of the Law at the remaining feast, the Feast of Pentecost.

The Pharisees concentrated on it and tried to show its relevance to contemporary life. This was not in itself undesirable and is the sort of thing modern Christians should also be deeply concerned with. The Word of God should never be regarded simply as ancient literature, for it is God's living Word. To show its relevance was laudable and undoubtedly required a great deal of careful thought from them.

Unfortunately, their interpretations and applications of the Law, which at this stage were still oral, had come to be regarded by many as of equal authority with the Biblical Law itself. Some were even saying that this oral Law was given to Moses on Mount Sinai and had been passed down through the generations to the present day. Tradition can be useful – after all, we can always learn from the past – but we should never give it a status that effectively removes it from criticism. This is something that those of us who are getting older need especially to remember, although it can happen to younger people too. It can in fact stifle real spirituality if it blocks the living power of the Word of God.

In recent years, some scholars have been looking again at what we may learn about the Pharisees of the New Testament period from contemporary documents, and it has been suggested that they were not as legalistic in their outlook as we tend to think. Whatever may be said of the best of the Pharisees or of their greatest leaders, however, there can be little doubt from the witness of the New Testament about them that many of their local representatives, the kind of folk Jesus met so often, taught that the Law is so all-important that salvation depends on keeping it. In theory the leaders of the Pharisaic movement may have held that God's gracious covenant is even more important than the Law, but this certainly did not get through to those they taught, and among whom legalism and self-righteousness were fostered.

We see from the Sermon on the Mount that Jesus accepted God's Law, the written Law of Moses (Matt. 5:17-20), and in no way did he question its importance. What he did reject was the legalism which had taken all the joy out of religion.

In this situation, what was it that Jesus came to bring?

He brought joy (2:18-22).

Fasting finds some place in the Old Testament, although the Day of Atonement was the only compulsory fast prescribed in the religious calendar (Lev. 16:29, 31, where self-denial probably means fasting). Other fasts were added by the Jews during the Exile (Zech. 7:5; 8:19), as part of their mourning for Jerusalem and its temple, now in ruins, and many of the Pharisees fasted as frequently as twice a week, as the Pharisee in the parable was at pains to remind God (Luke 18:12)! We are not told why John's disciples fasted. There was an ascetic side to John (Luke 7:33) and they probably modelled their lifestyle on his. There could of course have been a special reason for it now, for he was in prison and they would be deeply concerned for him (cf. 1:14).

The words of Jesus here cannot be taken as a total rejection of fasting, but they demonstrate that he was concerned about its appropriateness in certain circumstances. There are times when it is apt and times when it is not. He makes his point by means of a little parable, based on a familiar situation, but with a twist in its tail. A wedding is a time of joy. Of all occasions for feasting, this is perhaps the one that crosses cultural frontiers most effectively. Wedding customs may vary, but feasting is an element common to all. The imagery of the wedding feast enters into the symbolic imagery of the New Testament and especially of the Book of the Revelation, and it continued to have the association with Jesus that he gave it in this passage. Jesus, surrounded by his disciples, was clearly the Bridegroom in the parable. The discerning listener would perhaps pick up an allusion to the Old Testament picture of God as the Husband of his people (Isa. 54:5; Jer. 31:32). He was not simply making a point about fasting, but a point about himself.

The unexpected twist in the parable of course is about the violent snatching away of the Bridegroom, which would change the whole emotional atmosphere of the occasion. Here is the first reference in this Gospel to his death, a theme which would dominate the second half of it. Verse 20 may owe its first verb to the influence of the Greek version of Isaiah 53:8, which says that 'by oppression and judgement he was taken away'. It clearly indicates a violent death. In the event, the human cause of it emerged as the criticisms of the religious leaders (which provide the context here) came to be hardened into bitter antipathy and a determination that Jesus should die (3:6).

He also brought satisfaction (2:21-28).
Again he clothes his thought in two quickly-sketched word pictures, so apt, so memorable. When the patched garment was washed, the shrinking influence of water on the new cloth would ruin the garment, and the gasses released from the new wine as it fermented would burst the skin bottles already stretched during earlier fermentation processes.

The new cloth and new wine of the gospel of Jesus had and have enormous potential to beautify and to refresh. Nothing could be more satisfying. As we have already seen, though, the religious leaders of contemporary Judaism had devised structures that proved totally inappropriate when this message encountered them. The gospel could neither be added to the Law nor confined within it. Legalism and the good news of God's grace in Christ were never meant to go together.

This does not mean, of course, that the Christian has no respect for God's Law nor concern to keep it. Christian concern, however, is not legalistic, nor does it express craven fear. Rather it springs from a deep love that embraces God's will because we are eternally grateful to him. After all, the Old Testament itself shows in what a joyous spirit godly people can embrace the Law of God. We see that most clearly in Psalm 119, the great psalm of the Law (Ps. 119:14-16, 24, 47,48, 97, 103, etc.).

There have been attempts from time to time to drive a wedge between the teaching of Jesus and that of Paul. Read Paul's letter to the Galatians, however, and you will see how misguided this is. The teaching of that epistle about Christian freedom under the grace of God is really an expansion of the kind of teaching given here by our Lord. Paul was being completely true to the teaching of his Lord in offering, in his preaching and teaching, an acceptance with God that is independent of human effort.

After these two little parables we see the reaction of the Pharisees when the disciples picked ears of corn to satisfy their hunger on the Sabbath day. The Law of Moses forbade working on the Sabbath, and reaping was included in this. Clearly normal reaping is work, but how should reaping be defined? The oral tradition specialised an exact definition of such things, and it had in fact declared what the disciples were doing to be reaping. So this brought them condemnation from the Pharisees.

What could Jesus do in such a situation? Redefine the Law? But this would have played into the hands of his critics, for it would have led simply to an argument about casuistry. His real difference of outlook from them was not just a matter of indicating the scope of the Law. There were, in fact, some differences among the Jews on such matters. What he was concerned about was a much more fundamental issue than that.

As always, he showed great wisdom in the way he handled the situation. He took the opportunity to emphasise something that the legal experts constantly overlooked, and that can be overlooked today: the Law was intended for the blessing of men and women. Its prescriptions are important, but their importance lies in the good, the real good, of people, people like David and his companions, people like Jesus, the greater David, and his disciples. There are circumstances where human need must be the over-riding consideration, although we must be careful not to make this an excuse for departure from standards.

There is a problem in verse 26, in that Ahimelech, not Abiathar his son, was high priest at the time to which Jesus was referring, although both were involved in the incident that is in view here (1 Sam. 21:1; 22:20). Several explanations have been attempted. Perhaps it is best to recognize that the phrase used does not really mean anything as definite as 'in the days of', but simply 'at' or 'upon'. It is identical with one used in 12:26, where the NIV translates 'in the account of the bush'. The Jews divided the books of the Old Testament into sections, rather larger than our chapters, so that in these two passages the expressions probably mean 'the Abiathar section' and 'the bush section'.

The punch-line is to be found in verse 28. Whether these are the words of Jesus or the author's comment at the end of the story, as some commentators think, is less important than the actual meaning. There is an implicit claim here by or for Jesus, that he is really the Lord of all human life, and therefore Lord of the Sabbath, which was actually made for man.

If that is true, can he be any less than God?

He also brought healing (3:1-6).
By this time, the antagonism of the religious leaders made them try to get Jesus to incriminate himself. The oral tradition gave permission for medical help to be given to a sufferer if his or her life was in danger. Clearly this was not the case here. What would Jesus do?

He did not wait for them to react. Instead he took the initiative and once again moved discussion away from casuistry. His question made them face an important general principle and their hypocrisy was exposed. Jesus was angry. Anybody can be angry at unacceptable conduct, but it is only holy love whose anger expresses deep distress for the self-destructiveness of sin.

The Herodians are not a party known from other sources. Clearly they were supporters of the Herod family, who owed their royal status to Roman support. Because of this, there can be no doubt at all that the Pharisees, 'the separatists', would regard them with intense disapproval. They may perhaps have feared that Jesus would prove 'politically incorrect', just as the teachers of the law and the Pharisees regarded him as religiously incorrect. How significant then that these two groups, who would certainly regard co-operation with each other as quite unthinkable in all normal circumstances, came together in opposition to Jesus and were together plotting his death! It can still happen that people who are daggers drawn are united in their opposition to Jesus and the gospel.

4. Jesus and his disciples (3:7-19, 31-35)

As we see especially in the Gospel of John (John 2:4; 7:6, 8, 30; 8:20; 12:23; 13:1; 17:1), Jesus had a strong sense of divine predestination as far as the events of his own life were concerned. The time would come when he would walk forward into the hands of his enemies, but that time was not yet. So he withdrew, presumably away from the town, to the lake (3:7).

At this point, Mark shows us the great crowd that was attracted to Jesus and followed him. The bulk of it was of course composed of Galileans, because they were comparatively local, but it was swollen by others from the south (even as far away as Idumaea, which lay beyond Judaea), from Transjordan and from the old Phoenician cities of Tyre and Sidon. All this too without modern means of communication!

Mark's language seems to suggest that the whole region was represented, but there is no reference to Samaria. There were distinct barriers between the Jews and the Samaritans, a hybrid race, a mixture of Jews and Gentiles imported from the Assyrian empire hundreds of years before. They had a slightly unorthodox form of the Old Testament religion. Perhaps they were absent because they would not be welcomed in Jewish territory and might well have been afraid to come.

The importance Jesus attached to preaching (which we saw in 1:38) shows up again when he used a boat as a pulpit, a device he was to repeat (4:1). This withdrawal from healing in order to preach showed which he regarded as the more important. The modern church too needs to be committed to his scale of relative values.

Mark writes not only of the crowd but also of 'his disciples'. Who were they? Not simply people who flocked to him as to a phenomenon, because Mark distinguishes them from the crowd. The term is often used of the Twelve but is appropriate also for a wider number, those who had some measure of commitment to Jesus and his teaching.

The Twelve were to be given special training so that they might act as his apostles. The term 'apostle' means 'sent one', and these men were in fact sent out by Jesus both during his ministry and after Pentecost. They were to be the founder members of a church committed to mission. Modern interest in group dynamics has focused largely on small group work and many a church has developed a house-group system. A group of twelve makes educational sense, for it is about the maximum number that can derive full benefit from the close contact with a teacher which such a group affords. Of course the number twelve is also symbolic, representing the twelve tribes of Israel (Luke 22:28-30; Rev. 21:14). Here, in the wisdom of Jesus, a practical issue and important symbolism could be combined.

The Twelve were called authoritatively, appointed and sent, but they were also to spend time with Jesus. This fellowship was fundamental to their calling, which had no meaning apart from relationship to him. This gives added sadness to the comment that closes the list. The treachery of Judas was committed against the background of years spent in the close company of Jesus.

Three were given nicknames, Simon and James and John. Jesus was to make comment on Peter's name somewhat later (Matt. 16:17,18), but no explanation is given of the nickname of the two brothers. What does it mean? Perhaps it was given because they were fiery-tempered, as we see in the incident recorded in Luke 9:51-56. On the other hand it may reflect the nature of their ministry, as prophetic and with judgement as a leading theme. If John wrote the last book of the Bible, we can certainly see the appropriateness of the latter in his case.

It is amazing that Matthew, the tax-collector, who had worked for the Romans, and Simon the Zealot, who had been dedicated to their violent overthrow, should find themselves together in the same close-knit group. What a testimony to the reconciling power of Jesus! Later Jesus sent them out two by two (6:7). Did these two ever minister together? How we would like to know!

At the end of chapter 3, the focus of attention is again on disciples. For Jesus the most important relationship was not natural but moral. This reminds us of John 8, where he identifies Abraham's children as those who are like him and members of God's family as those who love Jesus himself because he came from God. Perhaps Paul had some of this teaching in mind when, in Galatians, he asserts that it is not Jews as such, but believers, whether Jews or Gentiles, who are the family of Abraham (Gal. 3:6-9).

The context here is the assertion of the natural family of Jesus that he was 'out of his mind' (v. 21). Jesus took the opportunity to teach the lesson that there is a family of God and that those belong to it are in obedience to God's will. John follows his master by making the same point in his first epistle (1 John 2:3-5).

It is still obedience that most clearly demonstrates relationship to Jesus.

5. Jesus and Satan (3:20-30)
This whole section we are considering in this chapter is about conflict, and, without doubt, the greatest enemy is Satan. There is comparatively little about him in the Old Testament. Just as in the Book of the Revelation it is in the second half that we become particularly aware of his malign presence and activity behind the scenes, so it is when we move out of the Old Testament into the New. Our awareness of Satan becomes that much greater.

The reference to Judas Iscariot at the end of the list of our Lord's disciples (v. 19) precedes this passage. This man, whose name is now synonymous with treachery, was eventually to be controlled by Satan (John 13:27) in the betrayal of Jesus. It is not surprising then that Mark goes on to outline other dimensions of opposition to Jesus and what he stood for.

These verses contain two evaluations of Jesus that are profoundly disturbing, for they show how greatly the people concerned had misunderstood him. The friends and relatives of

Jesus (v. 21), think him mad, but the teachers of the Law go far beyond this in dubbing him Satanic (30). This leads to a warning against the 'eternal sin' against the Holy Spirit.

A family often finds it difficult to come to terms with the popularity of one who has suddenly become prominent. In the case of Jesus, the family reaction seems extreme. Remember though that he had moved straight from the carpenter's shop into a many-sided messianic role. They did not find this easy to handle.

The second evaluation was made by people whom Mark calls, 'the teachers of the law who came down from Jerusalem'. This looks very much like an official investigating committee, probably acting on reports relayed to them by the local Galilean Pharisees and possibly urged by them to come, as they found it difficult to deal with Jesus.

What then was their verdict on Jesus? 'He is possessed by Beelzebub! By the prince of demons he is driving out demons...He has an evil spirit.' Beelzebub, first of all the name of a pagan deity, Baal Zebub, the god of Ekron (2 Kings 1:2, 16), was now used by the Jews for Satan. Our Lord's use of the kingdom and house (i.e. household) analogies, plus their phrase 'prince of demons', shows a shared awareness of a king and kingdom of evil. Jesus' comment exposes the irrationalism of their comment.

The further analogy of the strong man bound assumes conflict. Strong powers are facing each other. It is Jesus, of course, who would thus immobilize Satan, for the story's background is his own casting out of demons. In terms of the analogy, this must be the robbing of Satan's house.

Do not focus so much attention on verses 29 and 30 that you overlook the glorious statement in verse 28: 'I tell you the truth, all the sins and blasphemies of men will be forgiven them.' How wonderful! Here is a gracious promise from God to be set alongside passages like Isaiah 1:18 and Jeremiah 31:33,34, Hebrews 8:11,12 and 10:14-18, and many another. So, in the part of the Gospel we are considering in this chapter, Jesus first pronounces forgiveness to an individual (2:5), and then makes a general comment on the whole matter of forgiveness.

The importance of the context of verses 29 and 30 cannot be over-stressed. Here men were face to face with the supreme revelation of God, Jesus Christ. They had probably come on a fact-finding mission, so that they were making no snap judgement. They apparently knew that Jesus had been driving out demons, so that they were aware of his work. He had, of course, crossed their fellow-Pharisees. Apparently they had come so to identify the Pharisaic outlook with God's will that one who questioned it must be of the devil. Their values were now opposite to God's, for they attributed to Satan what was clearly a work of God.

Jesus does not actually say they were committing this sin. Perhaps he was warning them not to do what they were near to doing. To reject his claims and call his work Satanic is an eternal sin, its consequences beyond calculation. Immediate and full repentance is the only hope in such a situation.

Some questions for personal reflection

1. Has my stand for Christ ever involved me in some form of conflict? If not, is it possible that my stand is not clear enough to those with whom I come into regular contact?

2. If I am involved in some kind of house group, fellowship group or discipleship group, to what extent am I there as a receiver and to what extent as a giver? Should I be giving more?

Chapter 4

His Parables (4:1-34)

Everybody loves a story.

It all starts when we are small children, and most of us never really grow out of our early delight in a tale well told. Many an adult would admit that one of the good things about being parents is that we can at last find a good excuse for reading again the stories we so much enjoyed as children!

A story may hold us, so that we cannot put it down, and this whether it is 'Cinderella' or Wuthering Heights', whether 'Winnie the Pooh' or 'War and Peace'. In many cultures of the past, and some still today, the storyteller in the market square is a familiar figure. With the contemporary growth of street festivals in our cities, this figure could well be on the way back even in our own land.

A strange thing about stories is that the best of them continue to grip us even after we have heard them times without number. Try to shut the book of familiar stories before the end and Tommy or Mary will cry out, 'Oh, don't stop! We've got to hear what happened!'

Can truth be served by fiction? The answer must be 'Yes!' Stories that are fictional can still be true in a very important sense. A credible tale about an admirable character may teach truth, for it may teach lessons about courage or fidelity or even godliness. This is one reason why, in every culture, great fiction has been used in education. The Greek philosophers knew this when they employed the tales of Homer to illustrate the ideas they wanted to promote. Truth is often best understood and recalled through the concreteness of a tale. The twists and turns of a book's plot may teach us something about the twists and turns of life, its characters may show us the importance of moral decisions. It is a method appropriate in every culture. Of course, stories can also convey untruth dressed up as truth, and do so in a way that will stay in the mind. That is why we should be concerned about the stories our children read or hear or see.

The Saviour knew well how powerful a story well told can be. Most people know that his characteristic method of teaching was the parable. But what are parables? They are fiction used in the interests of truth, God's truth.

1. The Method

'Parable' means 'something placed beside', so it is a story placed alongside a truth to illustrate it. The Bible is a perfectly true book, the Word of the God of truth, inspired by the Spirit of truth, finding its great theme in the One who is the Incarnation of truth. Most of its stories are of course true in every sense of the word, not only true to life but also conveying accurate historical and biographical information. When it does contain fiction, this is presented with no pretence that it is historically true.

The prophet Nathan told David a most moving story (2 Sam. 12:1-7) and the Spirit of God used this to secure a spiritual result. Isaiah actually sang a story (Isa. 5:1-7), at first in dulcet tones and then with an increasingly sombre note, and when it ended his listeners found that, despite the fact that it was fiction, they were actually in the story. It was really about them! We will see an outstanding example of this kind of thing when we come to Mark 12, for one of the parables of Jesus recorded there is like a further edition of Isaiah's parable in which the same story is taken further on and powerfully applied to contemporary listeners. The rabbis also often conveyed their message by the use of the parabolic method. This means then that the hearers of Jesus would be familiar with the method.

The Saviour told a great many parables. All those recorded by the Gospel writers are fairly short, although it is not impossible that we have some of them in abbreviated form, while some occupy no more than a verse or two in one of the

Gospels. This chapter contains a major cluster of them, but we have come across some brief ones already. In chapter 2 we found a tale about a special event, a wedding, and two from the ordinary life of the home, about mending clothes and bottling wine. In chapter 3 there was the disunited kingdom, the divided household, the violent robber. Of course, some of these are hardly more than imaginative language, extended metaphors. But they stick in the mind.

A preacher whose sermons consist of nothing but a string of stories deserves the criticism he will get from those who love the Scriptures and long to be fed from them. Nevertheless there is plenty of room for the well-told story, the modern parable, as an illustration of truth within the context of an exposition of God's Word today. Some preachers have been somewhat disconcerted to find that many of their listeners recalled their children's addresses when most of their sermons had been forgotten. Are there lessons to be learned from this?

The stories told in chapter 4 were appropriate for a largely agricultural community. Even the towns of Galilee would have been mostly typical country towns, their relationship to rural communities being quite essential to them. Many of us who preach in places of large and concentrated population will need to seek parables for the city, and yet, as we will see, without the least necessity to abandon those recorded here from the lips of Jesus.

Were all four parables told on the same occasion? We cannot be sure. Only the first of them is given an actual setting in the ministry of Jesus. Mark enables us to picture the scene, with Jesus in a boat on the lake and the people strung out or perhaps even massed along the water's edge. The fact that three of the four parables are about seed may suggest they were told on the same occasion, so that the later ones are almost like extensions of the first. On the other hand, they may have been brought together in this chapter simply because of similarity of theme. We will assume that they do all belong to the same occasion, although little depends on this.

2. The Matter

Here then we have a sequence of four tales, all of them simple in conception and presentation. Despite what we have just said about the need to find parables appropriate to our culture, it should be noticed that although knowledge of the cultural background yields much extra insight, these stories, like most of those told by the Saviour, need remarkably little translation from one culture to another. This is because he so often talked about things that are part of life everywhere. Agriculture is basic to virtually all communities, so that the stories are universally appropriate. Even in schools located in depressed inner-city areas whose children may rarely or never see the countryside, a teacher will often plant a few seeds in a pot or on a piece of damp flannel in the class-room and get the children to follow the stages of their growth.

The first story is universally known as the parable of the sower, although it might better be called 'the parable of the soils', for it is the condition of the soils that is the focus of attention. Jesus told the whole story first of all, before interpreting it to the disciples. With a story, this is usually a better method than trying to show the meaning on the way along. Tell the story in its own terms first of all, and then, if it seems desirable to do so, point out its lessons, otherwise the attention of the listeners will flag.

Next the Speaker took his hearers from the field into somebody's home. The average one-roomed house of Palestine would be fully illuminated by its central lamp, as Matthew 5:15 ('it gives light to everyone in the house') clearly indicates. Of course, as Jesus indicated in that passage in Matthew, the whole effectiveness of the lamp depends on its position in the room, in a place where nothing obstructs its light.

The great potential of seed, spelled out in verse 20, becomes the basis of two more parables. For this reason, we should not forget the importance of the seed, even in the first parable. The condition of the soils is vitally important, but without the seed there could be no crop at all.

Seed scattered shows amazing vitality if, of course, as the first parable has shown, it gets into good ground. The farmer does not have to have a degree in biology to do his work effectively. In fact even if he did, it is questionable if he would be able fully to understand the awesome mystery of plant growth. His job is to sow and then prepare for the harvest. No doubt there are intermediate activities of a useful kind, but Jesus concentrates here on the two vital elements – the sowing and the reaping. In a fascinating passage, Isaiah ranges more widely over the whole process of crop management from ploughing to threshing (Isa. 28:23-29) and draws lessons from this for his listeners. This shows that, under the guidance of the Spirit of God, the same basic illustration may be employed to emphasise different truths

In the last of the parables, it is the great potential of a single seed that is the focus of the story. Some have objected to the words of Jesus here because there are seeds smaller than the mustard seed and plants larger than the mustard bush. This is a most wooden interpretation, and it misses the fact that hyperbole is an accepted mode of speech in every language. Jesus was simply saying, in a vivid manner, that this seed is very small and yet how great a bush comes from it! Some in the Holy Land grow as high as ten feet. As Paul says, in Romans 1:16, the gospel of Christ is powerful.

3. The Meaning

One feature common to all these parables is their simplicity. In fact, Jesus was pointing out nothing that was not perfectly obvious. Everybody knows that seed needs good soil, grows of itself and can produce great results. They also know that a lamp needs to be visible to be effective. Yet a story based on obvious facts can still be compelling to listen to, and the message may be all the more effectively conveyed. If the physical facts are obvious, there is perhaps a hidden implication that the spiritual facts ought to be just as clear to the listener. No wonder many Christians are able to testify that real discipleship for them began in childhood when the Spirit of God used these and other parables to bring them into the light of Christ!

In this whole passage there is considerable stress on the importance of understanding. It is not simply that Jesus underlines the need for the parables themselves to be understood, but also that some of them have *understanding* as their actual theme. He called for maximum attentiveness in his hearers (4:3, 9, 23, 24) and Mark's comment also stressed the importance of understanding (4:33,34). If you look up all these verses, you can hardly fail to see how greatly this is stressed in the whole passage.

At the beginning, there is a most striking call for attention. In verse 3, Jesus says, 'Listen! See!' It is a pity that most English versions (including the NIV) fail to translate the second of these words. Far from being redundant, it adds emphasis. It is not impossible that both words were intended literally. Could Jesus see from the boat a farmer scattering seed in his field and was he drawing the people's eyes to the scene? Possibly. If so, and if all the parables in this passage were uttered on the same occasion, we can see the value of staying with the seed analogy for three out of the four parables. On the other hand, 'See!' might have been an appeal to the eye of the imagination. When the words of a story engage with our experience (and how can we understand them unless they do so at least to some extent?) then they normally present pictures to the imagination.

Now Jesus calls for attention with both sight and hearing once again, for a literal translation of verse 24 would be, 'See what you hear!' Whether seen physically or imaginatively, with the outer or inner eye, however, the audience needed insight into the meaning. The farmer, the seed, the soil, the plant, the fruit, the house, the lamp, were all examples of analogy; each one stood for something else, for a spiritual truth.

The parable of the sower which began with such an unusually strong call for attention ended on the same note, for Jesus says to the crowd, 'He who has ears to hear, let him hear' (v. 9)! These words occur again after the story of the lamp (v. 23). We find him saying this elsewhere (e.g. in Matt. 11:15 and Luke 14:35) and his words in Mark 8:18, ('Do you have eyes but fail to see, and ears but fail to hear?') simply put the challenge into the form of a question instead of an exhortation. The expression also occurs in the Book of the Revelation, in each of the letters to the seven churches (e.g. in Rev. 2:7, 11). Its presence there is very apt, for the whole book is dubbed, 'The Revelation of Jesus Christ which God gave him' (Rev. 1:1), in other words it is as much the teaching of Jesus as are the parables here.

Here then we see that physical hearing is not enough. There must be reflection on the stories, because none of them is told as an end in itself, none is intended just to entertain; far from it. Paradoxically though, the story form which can be so illuminating to the spiritually receptive, can be the reverse for the unreceptive. Such people may enjoy it simply for itself and never discern the deeper meaning. A radio transmitter may be perfectly in order, but we may not get the message because there is something wrong with our receiving sets. It is a sobering thought that you or I may remember a preacher's illustration, but not what it illustrates.

The stories are simple and clear, but their understanding requires a spiritual dimension in the outlook of the hearer. This is what is meant by 'the secret of the kingdom of God' (v. 11), which is the spiritual reality presented in many of the parables, whether this is explicitly indicated or not. True spiritual hearing is needed for conversion and forgiveness, but, as verses 11 and 12 indicate, this has to be given by God. These verses do not, of course, mean that forgiveness is denied to those who truly seek it, but rather that, beneath true seeking, there is always prior divine activity. It is God in his wonderful grace who takes the initiative.

The quotation in verse 12 is from Isaiah 6:9,10. In its original context it is God's word to the prophet at the time of his call. He must preach the word God has given him to declare, but he is left in no doubt that many of the people will reject it. The Book of Isaiah gives a salutary example of this in its very next chapter, for there we read of Ahaz and his hypocritical rejection of God's message through Isaiah.

It is a law, an awesome principle of the inner life as God has constituted it, that truth that is meant to illuminate and liberate will, if repeatedly rejected, harden the heart and moreover that this happens because God intends this should be so. It is our responsibility to accept his word, to co-operate with his laws of hearing. If we do not, we have only ourselves to blame, the selves we have become through our failure to respond. Paul brings out the same truth in 2 Corinthians 2:14-16 and, as you will see if you consult this passage, by a kind of parable of his own.

Jesus tells his disciples that the secret of the kingdom of God has been given to them (v. 11). How can it be described as a secret when it was in fact the theme of our Lord's public preaching (1:15)? Because by their God-given faith in Jesus they had begun to understand a most important truth, that the kingdom promised in the Old Testament had drawn near in the presence of Jesus among them. This means then that they had the key to the interpretation of the parables, even though at times they could be very obtuse, as we see in verse 13. The questions of Jesus here and the concern they show suggest that there was a degree of culpability in their failure to understand.

In verses 24 and 25, Jesus takes up the theme again. His words here follow on from the parable of the lamp. The room that contained the lamp, the bed and the bowl would also contain some vehicle of measurement and he draws a lesson from it. It is rather like the law of sowing and reaping to which Paul refers in Galatians 6:7-9. We receive new understanding according to the measure of faith we bring to the truth we hear or read, although the phrase, 'and even more' recognizes God's generosity. If we do not bring faith to our listening, we will lose even the small measure of understanding we may have. In the Epistle to the Hebrews, the writer comments on the attitude of the people of Israel to God's word during the period of the wilderness wanderings, and he says, 'the message they heard was of no value to them, because those who heard it did not combine it with faith' (Heb. 4:2). His great concern was that those to whom he was writing that great epistle should learn something from this that would influence their own attitude to God's word.

One further point may be made from this passage in relation to the interpretation of the parables of Jesus. We should not imagine that every single detail was intended to have a distinct spiritual interpretation. The reference to the farmer sleeping and getting up (v.27) adds little if anything to the main point of the parable, but it does add extra vividness to the story, and this was probably its purpose. We should also note, however, that it was not a distracting feature that would take the minds of the hearers in some irrelevant direction.

Verses 33 and 34, as well as verse 2, indicate that Mark has simply made a selection from the parables of Jesus, and also that this was the Saviour's normal method of teaching. They were used in his public preaching and the explanation of them was clearly a major part of his private teaching of his disciples.

4. The Message

The *parable of the soils* is interpreted in some detail by Jesus and shows realistically that the hearers may be heedless, rootless or fruitless. There is nevertheless the clear anticipation of fruit when the word is thoroughly accepted.

Already in this Gospel there have been two references to Satan. It was he who tempted Jesus after his baptism (1:13) and he referred to him in refuting the allegation of the Jerusalem scribes that he was possessed by Beelzebub (3:22-30). Verse 15 recognizes Satan's evil activity when the word is preached, a theme Paul was to take up in the opening verses of Ephesians 2, for 'the ruler of the kingdom of the air' there is a reference to him. The same writer also alludes to the activity of Satan in opposition to his ministry of the Gospel (1 Thess 2:18). Such opposition shows that Satan is aware of the power of the word and also his concern lest it should produce fruit. Sometimes then the word is merely heard and has no spiritual effect at all.

Next Jesus deals with those who receive the word and react to it emotionally. Their rootlessness presumably means that there is minimal understanding and particularly that the will has not been committed to the truth conveyed in the word. Lacking such commitment, they cannot face trouble or persecution, which will seem a contradiction of their joy and so perhaps a denial of what they would themselves regard as the chief value of the word – its power to bring gladness to the heart. This shows that they are still essentially self-centred rather than God-centred in their outlook. This is not, of course, to deny that joy comes when the word is truly and deeply received. The illustration of the wedding feast in the previous chapter (2:19) clearly implies this.

It is not simply unpleasant circumstances that can have negative results when the reception of the word has been superficial, but the attraction of other things, the worldly motives that have never been subdued under the influence of the Holy Spirit. The worries and desires may well be the result of the deceitfulness of riches. The rich man worries as to whether his financial enterprises are going to succeed or fail. As Ecclesiastes 5:12 says, 'the abundance of a rich man permits him no sleep.' He discovers too that the craving for more does not go away even though his wealth has put him well beyond the threat of poverty. The persecution and the deceitful promise of material things, so reminiscent of the original temptation recorded in Genesis 3, also clearly come from the devil. Here then we are again made aware of a sinister figure in opposition to Christ.

According to the NIV, the fruitful 'accept' the word (v. 20), whereas the rootless 'receive' it (v. 16). This translation reflects a difference in the Greek verbs used by Mark here. The one in verse 20 is distinctly stronger than the other. The change from one to the other is unlikely to be purely a matter of stylistic variation, for Mark as a writer does not seem over-concerned about this. Clearly the word of God has penetrated to a deeper level in the fruitful. The exhortation of Colossians 3:16, 'let the word of Christ dwell in you richly', is somewhat reminiscent of this. Such rich indwelling of the word surely implies the engagement of the whole personality with it. Early in the same letter Paul wrote of 'the word of truth, the gospel that has come to you. All over the world this gospel is bearing fruit and growing, just as it has been doing among you since the day you heard it and understood God's grace in all its truth' (Col. 1:5,6).

The parable has major implications for the preacher. Preaching needs to go to the heart of the matter (which, it has been said, is the matter of the heart), so that it is not simply doctrine unrelated to life nor simply a call to find our happiness in Christ. There needs also, on the preacher's part, to be prayerful dependence on the Holy Spirit. Paul stresses the role of the Spirit in preaching in 1 Corinthians 2.

The parable, starkly realistic as it undoubtedly is, also contains encouragement for the Christian preacher, for it clearly implies that, along with disappointments, there will be fruit from the faithful preaching of God's word. Another encouragement emerges from a small linguistic point. The Greek word for 'seed', like its English counterpart, can be used in its singular form either as a true singular or as a collective. So, we do not normally say that we have bought a packet of seeds, but rather a packet of seed. Also, however, like English, the word can be employed in the plural, and when this occurs in a context where it has also been used collectively in the singular, it can have the effect of underlining the plurality somewhat. Most English translations do not bring out here the fact that in verse 8, for the first time in the passage, a plural word is used in connection with the seed. It is encouraging to find that this applies to the good ground.

No interpretation is given of the other three parables, but there is much in that of the soils to help us interpret them, because of the emphasis it places on receptivity and also because it uses the analogy of the seed, which is central to two of the others also. Probably Mark puts it first in this passage so that it may furnish an interpretative key to the others. This is probably

97

implied in the words of Jesus in verse 13, which may also suggest that this parable was a particularly simple and straight-forward one.

The *parable of the lamp* shows that God does not intend his truth in Christ to be hidden. The spiritually unresponsive may fail to understand it, but eventually it will be declared openly. He uses the same analogy, in a different context, in the Sermon on the Mount (Matt. 5:14-16), although there it has a somewhat different application. Here is another characteristic of his teaching, for he used many aphorisms, brief and pithy sayings that stick in the mind like burrs. In some cases he did this in different contexts and with somewhat different applications. This is another way in which the Christian communicator may emulate him, for basic truths of great importance deserve terse, forceful and memorable expression.

The *parable of the growing seed* is the only parable peculiar to Mark's Gospel. Like that of the sower, it encourages the preacher both in his work of sowing and also in his dependence, for every significant event in addition to the actual sowing and reaping takes place out of sight and is due to divine activity.

The *parable of the mustard seed* shows the great vitality of the kingdom and its message. Most commentators take the reference to the birds to be simply a way of stressing the size of the tree and therefore the great potential of the seed, tiny as it is. A minority see a sinister meaning in them, comparable perhaps to the reference to Satan in the parable of the sower and to the farmer's enemy and the weeds in another parable recorded in Matthew 13:24-30. This seems unlikely however in view of the fact that the vitality of the seed is very much in view in two other parables in our context here, and that this one can easily be interpreted in the same way.

The phrase, 'kingdom of God', is common to the two final parables. We have already encountered it in the preaching of Jesus (1:15). The modern literature on this expression is immense. It is widely agreed that it means 'the reign of God' rather than 'God's territory', that the emphasis is on his reign over personal beings, and, in the New Testament, over his church, so implying acceptance of his rule by his people. As thus used in the New Testament, it is presented sometimes as inaugurated by Jesus the King at his first advent. Probably, as the commentary will argue, this is in view in 9:1. Sometimes we see men and women entering it through repentance and faith or in the new birth (Mark 1:15; John 3:3,5), so that this means it is a present reality or at least a future one into which entry is secured in the present. Sometimes it is unambiguously future, as consummated at his second advent (Mark 14:25; Luke 21:31).

In the kingdom of God then there is a sowing, a growing, a reaping. All three stages in the history of the kingdom as taught in the New Testament are present in the parable of the growing seed, for the seed here is not the gospel planted in the heart of an individual, but rather is the kingdom itself, planted by Jesus, growing over the years and coming eventually to completion. Of course, the kingdom grows through preaching and conversions, although this parable does not go into this. The mustard seed parable too shows the three processes of sowing, growing and reaping.

One feature common to two of the parables is not interpreted by Jesus. Who is the farmer who sows the seed? Are we meant to ask this question? Possibly. If so, the farmer is undoubtedly Jesus himself. He had come into Galilee as the Sower of the seed of the gospel (1:14,15). In the Gospel of Mark the theme of the kingdom eventually becomes intertwined with the story of the cross, for it was through his death for sin that Jesus inaugurated the kingdom. As somebody has truly said, 'O'er hill and dale he sowed his seed, till, on that last bare hill, he sowed himself.' That is why Paul can call the message, 'the word of Christ' (Col. 3:16), for he is its great theme.

Of course, the Gospel later shows Jesus calling his disciples to do what in fact he himself did. They did it first of all within the context of his earthly ministry (6:6-13). Then, after his resurrection, they were sent out to preach the word everywhere (16:15-20; cf. Matt. 28:18-20). We too are to sow the seed and we can take much encouragement from the teaching given here. If we do our work faithfully, God will be at work, bringing about his own purposes through the word, just as Isaiah, who was earlier warned of the sparse results of his preaching, later heard God say, 'As the rain and the snow come down from heaven, and do not return to it without watering the earth and making it bud and flourish, so that it yields seed for the sower and bread for the eater, so is my word that goes out from my mouth: It will not return to me empty, but will accomplish what I desire and achieve the purpose for which I sent it' (Isa. 55:10,11).

Some questions for personal reflection

1. Is there some situation with which my friends are familiar and which I may use to illustrate the gospel so that they can understand it better?

2. The gospel may have deeply penetrated my heart, but is this also true of the messages I heard (or preached!) last Sunday? What is the proof of that penetration?

Chapter 5

His Miracles (4:35–5:43)

Writing a history book is not just about putting facts down on paper. The historian cannot possibly write down everything nor would there be any point to such an exercise. He or she concentrates on things that are really significant. Nobody needs to know what Napoleon had for breakfast before the Battle of Waterloo – unless, of course, it gave him indigestion and diverted his attention from military tactics! So selection is the name of the game.

A little thought will show how important this then becomes. Two histories of the same period may be very different. So, for instance, one may be written by a military historian, and will concentrate on battles and generals, on strategy and tactics, while another may be the work of an economic historian, who is interested in the growth of industries, in the reasons for inflation and recession and the effects of import licences. Then there are political histories, social histories, and so on.

What about the Gospel writers? They too needed to choose. What is so important in their case is that their minds and therefore their pens were guided by the Spirit of truth. Jesus himself promised the apostles that the Spirit would remind them of everything he had said to them (John 14:26), and of course Peter would make this information available to Mark. We find that the Holy Spirit guided each Gospel writer in his selection of material in such a way that each book is different, each records information particularly important for its first readers, and yet the four together produce a wonderfully balanced and harmonious picture of the Life of lives.

Mark is more highly selective than either Matthew or Luke. We suspect this to be the case, of course, as soon as we notice how brief his Gospel is compared with theirs. In this section we get special confirmation of this. As we consider this passage and especially the language of 4:35 ('that day'), 5:1 ('they went across the lake'), and 5:21 ('when Jesus had again crossed over by boat to the other side of the lake'), it looks as if Mark is presenting us at this point with just two or three days in our Lord's ministry. When we consider how much Jesus did in that short time, it makes us realise how long the Gospel might have been if each period had been treated in a similar way. No wonder then that John, who wrote a somewhat longer Gospel, says 'Jesus did many other things as well. If every one of them were written down, I suppose that even the whole world would not have room for the books that would be written' (John 21:25)!

1. The purpose of the miracle stories

If so much could be written, why then were these particular stories recorded and why are they brought together into one part of Mark's narrative? This is worth thinking about.

1. To preach the gospel

It is interesting that these four miracles follow four parables. How then are we to understand these events? Should we take them literally or are they really acted parables?

In fact, there is no need to choose. Each of these events is recorded as historical fact, and so has the importance of something that actually happened at a particular place and a particular time and in the lives of particular people. It is also true though that each is also like a parable of the gospel, for it shows the saving power of Jesus, that power which found such concentrated and yet costly expression in his death on the cross, which, although seeming to be a place of weakness was actually 'the hiding place of God's power' (James Denney). Both the parables and the miracles of Jesus illustrate his gospel, the parables from fiction and the miracles from fact.

The Old Testament has much to say about salvation. Its use of terms like 'save' and 'redeem', however, is almost exclusively related to some sort of physical deliverance, from disease or death (Pss. 6:4; 69:1), or social salvation, from enemies (e.g. Exod. 15:13; Ps. 7:1), rather than salvation from sin. It is true that there are some exceptions, such as Psalm 51:14, 'Save me from bloodguilt, O God, the God who saves me,' and Psalm 130:8, 'He himself will redeem Israel from all their sins.' Such exceptions as these however only serve to underscore for us how predominantly physical most of the Old Testament references are.

When we turn to the New Testament we discover that all this is reversed. What was formerly the exception now becomes the general rule, for the greatest Saviour/Redeemer has come, and his work is to deliver us from the greatest danger of all, sin which leads to eternal death, and from the greatest of all enemies, Satan. It is interesting though to find that there are still some examples of the Old Testament type of word-use. Luke 1:71 in the Benedictus (the song of Zechariah, father of John the Baptist), for instance, makes reference to salvation from enemies, and in Luke 18:42, a story in which a blind man is given sight by Jesus, the word which the NIV renders 'healed' is literally 'saved'. So, taking the two testaments together, we can see that our great and living God is the Saviour of the whole person.

Do not forget that Mark has shown us the nature of his Gospel at its start. In 1:1 he indicates that his book is a proclamation of good news in Jesus. Not far into the book, in 1:14,15, he tells us the nature of this good news. At this point he shows Jesus coming to tell his listeners that the Old Testament promises of the kingdom of God had been fulfilled, that the kingdom was now at hand, and that those who heard his message of the kingdom needed to respond in repentance and faith.

Why then are so many miracles recorded in this book, a book which tells us the good news of Jesus? Why too are there so many also in the other Gospels? One of the main reasons is undoubtedly to further the progress of the good news in the hearts of the readers.

Here we can see something of what the kingdom is like, the kingdom Christ came to bring through his first advent and which will be brought to its great consummation when he comes again. In that final stage of the kingdom all the suffering that has come into human life through the Fall into sin will be finally done away with for those who are Christ's (Rev. 21:1-5). What we have in the miracles of Jesus is a plain indication that the power of God's kingdom is already at work, and, in the healing miracles, that he is concerned for the salvation of the whole person.

There is something else. So often in the Bible spiritual truth is taught to us by way of physical analogies. We are told that God is a Rock, and so we learn that he is a firm Foundation for life or a Place of Refuge as we face life's storms. He speaks of himself as a Shepherd and from this we learn his care for us. These are just two examples taken almost at random. By using this same principle of analogy, we discern in the physical miracles the great spiritual truth that Jesus came to save us from sin. Not only so, but this happens through actual events, just as Christ's atonement for our sins was a very specific saving event, the event of Calvary.

So then the spiritual insight so insisted on and so emphasised in the parable section of chapter 4 enables us to see something deeper in the miracles also. This is true even though Mark does not spell out their 'sign' character in the way that John does in his Gospel (John 2:11; 20:30,31). To understand the parables, the disciples needed to have ears to hear (4:9); to discern the significance of the miracles we need to have eyes to see. Both the discerning ear and the discerning eye come from the God of grace.

2. To exalt Jesus and to show his power

In this section, as in the whole Gospel, Mark draws our attention to Jesus himself. He is the central character and all the other people who come into the story, no matter how important they are in their own eyes, in the eyes of others, or even to the narrative itself, are subsidiary to him. Everything that happens is calculated to elicit from the reader the question, 'Who is this?' (4:41). In a sense, this is not really a different purpose from that of preaching the gospel, because the gospel is Jesus (1:1; cf. Acts 8:35; 9:20, 22). Yet we need to spell this out quite specifically, because it is so easy, and so tragically mistaken, to turn what is wonderfully personal into something abstract and impersonal. The gospel is not just an idea or a 'thing'; it is a Person. There is no 'salvation' that can be abstracted or detached from the Saviour himself.

The miracles recorded in this section, very different as they are, nevertheless have something important in common. Each of them portrays the utter helplessness and consequent hopelessness of human beings. Feel the cumulative force of words and statements like these: 'drown' (4:38), 'No-one was strong enough to subdue him' (5:4), 'instead of getting better she grew worse' (5:26), and, most sombre of all, 'dead' (5:35). The weakness and inability of the people concerned takes different forms and relates to varying needs. In every case, however, the coming of Jesus into the situation, with his compassion and his power, brings deliverance.

Here then we can see how wide is the range of his power to bless, and we, the readers, are encouraged to put our trust in him. If he was able to meet such diverse needs, then there is no doubt that he can meet our own.

(a) Deliverance from Danger (4:35-41)

The way this story is told gives us an unmistakable impression that it is based on the experience of an eyewitness. Of course Peter was there, and Mark would learn it from him. Given Peter's personality, we can perhaps imagine how compellingly the story would be told. Notice how graphic the account of the events is and what evidence there is of attention to detail! He went with the disciples 'just as he was' (v.36), meaning presumably that there was no delay while other things were dealt with, and the fact that there were other boats with him as well. These two details are important for their very lack of seeming relevance, for they bear testimony to the detailed nature of the account Mark was given.

The Sea of Galilee is subject to sudden fierce squalls, and this is briefly but vividly brought home to us. Galilean fishing boats were not large, and this has been confirmed to us by the discovery of a very ancient boat in that region in modern times. They had both sails and oars but a really fierce squall would present major problems to the occupants. It is true that the lake is not particularly large (twenty-one kilometres long and never more than eleven kilometres wide), but even a few hundred metres of turbulent water will present a great threat to human life.

Some of the disciples were very experienced seamen and were masters of the skills needed when catching fish on the Sea of Galilee. On this occasion, however, they are impotent, their skills inadequate and unavailing. To whom do they turn for effective help? To a Man of the land rather than of the sea, the Carpenter of Nazareth! Can we imagine such a thing happening with respect to anybody else but Jesus? In the NIV, the word 'Jesus' occurs in verse 38, although it is not present in the Greek. This is not inappropriate, for it is the translators' way of making clear for readers of the English text that the story is actually about him. In the original however what occurs is an emphatic pronoun. So Mark is saying '*He* was in the stern' and this gives a little more emphasis to his presence there than the simple use of his name would have done.

It is interesting to notice that Jesus uses the same command to the sea as he directed to the demons (cf. 4:39 with 1:25). The verb Mark uses on each of these occasions, translated 'Quiet!' or 'Be quiet!' really means 'muzzle' (another example of the use of analogy) and shows the absolute power of Jesus in each case. Some have even suggested that the use of the same word shows that there were demonic influences at work in the storm, that it was a manifestation of Satanic antipathy to Jesus. Job 1 is quoted as a somewhat parallel case in the Old Testament. We cannot be sure that this was so, and the linguistic evidence, although interesting, must be deemed inconclusive.

When he had calmed the raging squall, Jesus challenged the disciples to trust and also to ask themselves why they were so fearful and lacking in faith (vv. 40, 41). Far from making them excessively introspective, however, this served to emphasize for them the greatness of the wonderful Person who had performed such a miracle. From questions about themselves, they were led to ask questions about him. Faith is elicited and grows as it considers its Object.

The obedience from others secured by a person of strong character may be considerable. In the case of Jesus, his ability went further still, and encompassed even the natural elements. This raised for the disciples, and it raises for us, the deepest of questions about the One who possesses such power. When Mark tells us, in verse 41, that they were terrified, this was clearly no longer fear of the sea, for by now it was calm, but rather a trembling awe in the presence of Someone who could exert such great power. Whoever could he be? The question asked by the disciples is echoed in different forms many times over as the Gospel proceeds (e.g. in 6:2; 7:37; 8:27-29). Many centuries have passed since this Gospel was written, and yet that question will not go away. As the Gospel story unfolds, we will see how it comes to be answered.

(b) Deliverance from Demons (5:1-20)

Here is a drama in four scenes, featuring in turn the man (1-10), the swine (11-13), the townspeople (14-17) and the man again (18-20).

The location was the Decapolis (5:20), which was an area beyond the lake and, as its Greek name indicates, associated with ten Greek cities that were there. They were organised as ten small independent city-states on the standard Greek model, but they now owed allegiance to Rome.

The manuscripts of the Gospel of Mark give various names for the people of the region. They were either Gerasenes,

Gadarenes or Gergesenes. Gerasa was a big town some distance to the southeast of the lake and important enough to give its name to a large district. Gadara was a smaller town nearer the lake, and Gergesa a village on the lakeside. So any of the three names would be appropriate and it really makes little difference. In fact, the reading 'Gerasenes' is the best attested in the manuscripts.

Mark places considerable emphasis on the total inability of others to control this man. In this way he stresses the special power of Jesus. Here the One who was stronger than Satan (3:27) demonstrates his superior strength.

The man's reaction to Jesus was clearly a mixture of attraction and fear, and this reflects the fact that he was demon-possessed. One side of this reaction is shown in his deep sense of need and in the fact that he ran to Jesus. Because he recognized who he was, he fell on his knees and addressed him as Son of God. The other side revealed itself in the fact that he did not just speak the name and title of Jesus but yelled it out at the top of his voice, perhaps, it has been suggested, in an attempt to exercise spiritual control over him. In the same aggressive way, he commanded Jesus not to torment him. Soon there was a change of mood and the truculent attitude was succeeded by one of pleading. In this way and in the use of 'my' and 'we' in the same sentence (v. 9), Mark is demonstrating the demon-possessed condition of the man.

The name, 'Legion', a Latinism, was of course based on the term used for the formidable Roman army division of 4000 to 6000 men. Perhaps the man had seen such a legion tramping through the countryside and, fearing it, could find no better designation for himself, because he was tormented by so many demons.

The man said to Jesus, 'Swear to God that you won't torture me!' The reference to torture may reflect the fact that the demons were anticipating their future judgement. Another possibility is that the man may have been afraid that their expulsion would be a traumatic experience for him.

'The Most High God' was a title for the true God often used by Gentiles, and it is found both in the Old Testament and in the New (Gen. 14:18ff; Num. 24:16; Dan. 3:26; Acts 16:17). This is very apt in this particular story. The fact also that there was a herd of swine nearby is confirmation that this was basically Gentile country, for the eating of pork was strictly forbidden to Jews (Lev. 11:7,8).

The activity of the demons in the herd would give the man and any observers convincing evidence that the demons had actually left him. How deeply this would impress him and them! As the account tells us, those who saw this event began to spread the news everywhere in that district.

This miracle has sometimes been criticised. It is true, of course, that every part of the universe, including the animals, has value, for it is created by God, but human life is of the highest value. The reaction of the townsfolk shows a wrong sense of values. We can be sure that it was motivated, not by love of animals, but by concern about a lost source of income. Their reaction anticipates the opposition which the preachers of the gospel encountered and which Acts records (Acts 13:8; 16:18ff; 19:23ff).

In verses 19 and 20, the use of the words 'Jesus' and 'Lord' is most interesting and significant. In his Gospel, Mark shows people addressing Jesus as 'Lord', but he does not normally use this term himself in the narrative framework he provides until after our Lord's resurrection. At this fairly early place in his narrative, however, he is giving his readers the clear hint that the great title 'Lord', with it overtones of deity, was perfectly appropriate for Jesus even before the resurrection.

The so-called 'Messianic secret' has been the focus of a good deal of scholarly interest and speculation over the years. Why did Jesus counsel silence about himself on a number of occasions? Our present passage may well be the key for our understanding of this, for the events recorded in it took place in a largely Gentile area. Among the Jews at this time there was a good deal of misunderstanding of the Messiah and his vocation.

It was widely held that he would be a military figure and many hoped that he would lead an army against the hated Romans. If such a view of Jesus were to become widespread among the Jews, it could upset the programme of ministry which was God's plan for him at this stage of things, for instance by stimulating Roman antagonism to him. There was, however, little danger of such misunderstanding in Gentile country, and so the man is told to tell what had been done for him.

(c) Deliverance from Disease (5:21-34)

Styles differ somewhat from one writer to another. One interesting feature of Mark's style is to be found in the fact that he sometimes links two stories very closely. He does this in 3:20-35, with the stories of the family of Jesus coming to take charge of him and the story of the comments about him made by the teachers of the law. He also does so in 11:12-25, with the accounts of the cursing of the fig tree and the cleansing of the temple. He does the same kind of thing here with the story of the daughter of Jairus and that of the woman with the constant bleeding.

As a synagogue ruler, Jairus would have been a Pharisee. He must have been desperate, for the decision he made to move towards Jesus, at least on this occasion, would have meant swimming completely against the tide that was flowing amongst the Pharisees and teachers of the law (cf. 3:6, 22).

The interruption must have distressed Jairus greatly. The woman with the constant bleeding certainly had a distressing problem, for quite apart from any physical repercussions, this was a condition that would render her perpetually unclean (Lev. 15:25-30). With so many people coming for healing, nobody could blame her for wanting relief from her own condition. Despite this, Jairus might well have chafed at the delay. Distressing as the trouble was, it had been with her for many years, but was not fatal, whereas his daughter was dying.

Mark emphasizes the persistence of the woman's malady and not only the helplessness of the sufferer, but also that the remedies of the physicians were less than effective. Not only so, but she could get no more help from them as her money had run out. It has been pointed out, a trifle facetiously, that it is Mark, and not Doctor Luke, who gives this adverse comment on her encounters with the physicians!

Was there an element of superstition in her idea that contact with the clothes of Jesus would get healing for her? Possibly. It is rather like the idea of *mana*, a word used by students of religion for the idea that something of a person's power, particularly that of an eminent person, is transmitted to his or her possessions or clothing or to bodily parts like hair or nail clippings. Perhaps this was what this woman thought. Yet there must have been in her heart an element of true faith in Jesus himself, for what matters most about faith is the Person towards whom it is directed, the One in whom trust is placed. Her faith may have been imperfect, but it was real faith nevertheless.

His realization that power had gone out from him has special interest. For one thing, there is no suggestion in the language employed that he was simply a human channel for divine power, because Mark says that the power went out *from* him and not that it passed *through* him. It appears he was the source of this power, even though on another occasion he could be described as its channel (Matt. 12:18,28). The two facts belong together in the profound and awesome mystery of his divine/human Person. Then there is perhaps here a suggestion that his healing ministry was not without cost to him. Matthew makes the same point in a different way by relating it to the great prophecy of his sufferings and of its costliness in Isaiah 53 (Matt. 8:16, 17; cf. Matt. 12:15-21).

There is something else here that we could easily miss. This woman was healed, but were there no other sufferers in the crowd around Jesus? We must realistically face the fact that we can have close contact with Jesus at some level (in this case physical) without ever benefiting from that contact if faith is absent. After all, Judas Iscariot was very close to Jesus for a long time. Jesus himself identified faith as the element in her attitude which had led to power being available to meet her

111

need. Now she was face to face with Christ. Even if her faith had been imperfect, with an element of superstition mixed with it, she would go away remembering not so much his clothes but his face and his words, and her gratitude would be to him rather than to those who let her get close enough to touch his robe.

There are two passages in Acts (Acts 5:15; 19:11,12) where even the casting of a person's shadow or contact with aprons or clothing had healing power. Again, there must have been a real element of faith in Christ amidst the superstition on such occasions.

The word of Jesus to the woman, 'Go in peace!' (literally, 'Go into peace!') is significant in two ways. First of all, the word Jesus used signifies far more than the 'peace' of the English rendering. It is an immensely rich word, suggesting wholeness. So a diseased body meant that the person was less than whole. The gospel is concerned with the body as well as with the inner person. This is made clear to us in the Biblical doctrine of the resurrection and also in the teaching of the Book of the Revelation about the ultimate abolition of pain (Rev. 21:4). Also the use of this kind of expression by Jesus may be the basis for the fact that so often, in the opening greetings in the epistles, peace, as well as grace, is said to emanate from Christ as well as from the Father (e.g. Rom. 1:7; Titus 1:4). Now not normally visible but exalted to the Father's right hand, he is still the great source of peace, not just for particular individuals, but for the whole company of his believing people.

(d) Deliverance from Death (5:35-43)

The three miracles we have so far considered in this chapter all show Jesus, in his power and compassion, coming into situations of human helplessness and hopelessness. At least one of these cases (the storm at sea) may have been life-threatening, but life had not in fact been extinguished. 'While there's life there's hope!' To make the absoluteness of the power of Jesus abundantly clear, therefore, Mark shows that power operating in this situation of ultimate human hopelessness.

The word 'sleep', in the way Jesus uses it in this story, was probably based on Daniel 12:2, 'Multitudes who sleep in the dust of the earth will awake.' Clearly the reference in Daniel is to resurrection, and it is evident that it refers to the body, not the soul. The use of this particular analogy may well have been based on the fact that those who encounter a newly dead body may think at first that the person is asleep. Of course, the term also suggests a temporary condition and so is well fitted in a context where resurrection is in view.

The actual words of the Aramaic *talitha koum* (v. 41) probably meant 'Get up, my little lamb!' originally. They would have been remembered by those who were present in the house because of their great tenderness, as well as their association with a wonderful miracle. Ever practical, Jesus indicates that because her life has been restored, the child needs food again. In their excitement and joy, the family may have been in danger of forgetting that.

3. To stress the importance of faith and discipleship

Notice that all but one of the four miracle stories makes reference to faith (4:40; 5:34, 36) and that the exception (the Gerasene demoniac) implies that the man had become, at least at some level, a disciple of Jesus (5:18-20). If we see these stories as preaching the gospel and exalting the power and compassion of Christ, we should learn from them also that we need to respond in faith to him.

2. The presuppositions of the miracle stories

Every author has his presuppositions, things he takes for granted and which therefore colour his view of things. Sometimes he is fully aware of them, sometimes at least partly unaware. This is why it is so important, when studying a book on a subject that really matters, to look for any hidden assumptions, because these may deeply affect the arguments used by the author. Some commentators, for example, never discuss the possibility that the Biblical miracles really occurred in the way they are presented. Every other possible explanation is canvassed except the one that credits the account itself with truth! To assume that miracles just do not happen is a massively important presupposition with a profound effect on the interpretations offered to the reader.

What presuppositions were in the mind of Mark? As he was a Christian writer of the first century, accepting both the Old Testament and the revelation in Christ, we can be relatively sure of these. Here are some of them:

1. This is God's universe

The one true God is absolutely sovereign over the universe he has brought into being. He is incomparably great and everything is subject to him. He has control over all the phenomena of the universe – the world of nature in all its manifestations, supernatural beings (for he created the angels), and human beings. All his activities, therefore, including any miracles, demonstrate his sovereignty. In this Gospel, and very markedly in this section of it, God the sovereign over nature and personal beings, both supernatural and human, shows his power in all these realms.

2. This is a universe affected by sin

In Genesis 1 and 2, the world is created as a perfect environment for human life, but, as a result of sin, as Genesis 3 shows, the environment as well as human life is affected. There is still order, but a principle of disorder now operates too. In this section of Mark's Gospel, winds and waves are not supportive of human life but are potentially destructive. Supernatural beings shouted for joy at the creation (Job 38:7), but in this passage we see evil spirits operating to bring disorientation and disintegration to a human personality. Disease is a negative feature of human life and death the ultimate evidence that things have gone wrong. 'You will die' (Gen. 3:3, literally, 'dying you shall die') was God's warning to the human beings he had created.

The miracles of Jesus here are all performed in the context of a universe affected by sin.

3. God is planning a new creation

This is evident within the Old Testament. To take just one of its prophetic books, the last two chapters of Isaiah promise the coming of a new heaven and a new earth, and there are earlier passages in that book (especially chapters 11 and 35) where the picture presented certainly seems to show the original conditions of Eden restored, with animal life brought back into order. The righteousness and peace that God will bring into human society is therefore reflected within the animal kingdom also. Even plant life is shown in all its power to provide beauty and food and shelter for human beings.

This Old Testament hope appears again in the New Testament. In Revelation 21-22, the effects of the Fall are removed, and this includes the curse (Rev. 22:3), sorrow, crying, pain and death (Rev. 21:4,5). It is no coincidence that some of these features are found in the Gospel narrative, in the story of Jairus' daughter, for instance.

4. Jesus comes to bring the power of the new creation into the old

In the Gospel of Mark we see Jesus dealing with many of the effects of the Fall, at least temporarily, and particularly in this section of the Gospel. Some of these features would afflict these people again and death would overtake them all in the end, but, for a glorious interlude, some radiant beams from God's new creation shone on them during and by means of the ministry of Jesus.

Here then is what the theologians call 'realized eschatology'. In other words, features of God's new age for his creation, promised in the Old Testament, which is to come in its fullest form at the Second Advent, have already entered the human story through the first advent of Jesus. Here in operation already are what the Epistle to the Hebrews calls 'the powers of the coming age' (Heb. 6:5).

In his book *Miracles*, C.S. Lewis promoted the idea of a distinction between miracles of the old creation and of the new. Those of the old creation are chiefly those in which God does, usually more speedily, what he is already doing within this fallen world. We will see a striking example of this in the next chapter. New creation miracles, however, introduce the powers of the coming age, and raising the dead certainly belongs to this category.

Now this prompts some questions for our minds. We may accept the fact that God in Christ still works miracles in our day and age. Should we then expect them to occur as comprehensively and as frequently as they did in the ministry of Jesus? There we never read of a case of physical need which was not met fully by him, and in most cases immediately.

It is worth remembering that the Bible gives some examples of the use of natural means for healing purposes (Isa. 38:21; 1 Tim. 5:23) and that there have been great advances in medical knowledge, every one of them making use of materials to be found and techniques learned within the world as God has given it to us. We should not deny the providence of God in the history of medicine by rejecting all medical means of healing. The God of the natural and of the supernatural is one God.

The most terrible of sin's effects on the human race in this world is death. In fact, this is the one especially stressed in the Genesis account of the Fall. In New Testament times, there are of course examples of the raising of the dead, not only in the ministry of Jesus, but also in his name through the apostles. Clearly death has not been done away with completely for Christian people as yet. But when Christ comes again, this last enemy (1 Cor. 15:26) will be utterly vanquished and every lesser enemy with it.

Hallelujah!

Some questions for personal reflection

1. To what extent do I think of the gospel as a Person, the Lord Jesus Christ, and to what extent abstractly as 'salvation' or 'justification' or 'redemption'? Can I bring the two types of thought together?

2. If I came to Christ as a helpless sinner, am I now more conscious of my helplessness than I was then – or less?

Chapter 6

His Communicating (6:1-44)

In Chapter 4 we examined the parables recorded in Mark 4, and gave some thought to the way truth is communicated by telling stories. So much in that earlier chapter of Mark's book brings into focus the vital power of the word of the gospel. At the point we have now reached, this Gospel deals again with communication, but in this case not so much its dynamic or its means, but rather its authority and its costliness. We need reminders of all these factors.

In the New Testament, different terms are used for preaching or proclamation on the one hand and teaching or instruction on the other. The distinction between these two activities is real but not rigid. Both are concerned with communication and their difference is largely a matter of style. The characteristic posture of the preacher is a standing one, he is a herald. As Luke says, 'Then Peter stood up with the Eleven, raised his voice and addressed the crowd' (Acts 2:14). On the other hand the typical teacher, basing his posture on the style adopted by the Rabbis, sat down to teach. The Sermon on the Mount is introduced by the words, 'Now when he saw the crowds, he went up on a mountainside and sat down. His disciples came to him, and he began to teach them' (Matt. 5:1,2). No doubt Jesus often taught like this, especially in informal situations.

Both activities require authority and knowledge in the communicator, but the emphasis in preaching is more on the former, while in teaching it is more on the latter. As far as the hearer is concerned, he or she needs both to understand and to make a commitment of his or her will to the truth, but in preaching it is the commitment which is most in view, while in teaching it is the understanding.

This passage uses both terms (vv. 2, 6, 12, 30, 34). The people of Israel in the time of our Lord's earthly ministry heard the good news of the kingdom proclaimed by him and they were called to respond to the preached word in repentance and faith. There was, however, much that needed to be explained to them clearly and plainly, so that their commitment could be on the basis of real understanding. This was largely due to the fact that at that time there was so much misunderstanding as to what the Messiah would do when he came and also about the kind of response God was seeking from the people themselves. The teaching was largely done in the synagogues and if the synagogue teachers had misapprehensions about these things, as they had, those taught by them would be seriously in need of re-education.

1. Jesus the supreme Communicator (6:1-6)

As we have already seen, Mark 5 concludes with the story of Jairus and his daughter. We do not know where this family lived, neither can we be absolutely certain whether Nazareth or Capernaum is intended by the phrase, 'his home town' used by Mark in 6:1. You might like to read again the comment on 2:1 in Chapter 3 of this book. Because of the detailed reference to the family of Jesus, however, it is most likely that the reference at this point is to Nazareth. Already we have seen how amazed the people of Capernaum were when Jesus taught in the synagogue there (1:22), and this amazement was all the more to be expected in the place where he had grown up.

What the people of his home town fasten on now are his wisdom and his miracles. The special miraculous works he performed were in fact undertaken in pursuit of his messianic vocation. John clearly implies that no such miracles occurred prior to the start of his ministry (John 2:11), which was inaugurated by his baptism. During his childhood, the Lord Jesus will have been outstanding in character, for his sinlessness embraced the whole of his life, but in other ways he would have seemed less remarkable to the observer. The apocryphal

Gospels tell stories supposedly coming from his childhood but which are completely unworthy of him. Are we really expected to believe that he made model birds from clay and gave them life for his own amusement? Worse still, are we to accept the story that he miraculously struck down other children who annoyed him? These stories lack the ring of truth, for they do not square with the character we know from the canonical Gospels.

This passage gives us the fullest information we have about his family. The absence of reference to Mary's husband (the Joseph or Joses referred to in verse 3 is clearly of the same generation as Jesus), suggests that he may have been dead by now. Certainly he makes no appearance in the Gospels at all after the stories of the nativity in Matthew and Luke. The tradition that he was considerably older than Mary may therefore be correct.

Luke also gives us the fullest account of the teaching Jesus gave at Nazareth and he tells us that his teaching was rejected there (Luke 4:16-30). Its content challenged the deepest prejudices of the hearers. Here we see that there was another reason for his rejection there, namely his familiar origin and probably his unremarkable family. The proverb, 'Familiarity breeds contempt', never had a sadder illustration.

Mark tells us that, with a few exceptions, 'he could not do any miracles there' (v. 5). Does the phrase 'could not' seem a strange one in application to the Son of God? Is this a denial of his power? This is quite an inconceivable conclusion to draw from a remark in a Gospel by Mark of all people, for no Gospel writer emphasizes the power of Jesus more than he does. We should remember that there is more than one kind of impossibility. On this occasion it was moral; it was not morally fitting for them to receive this blessing. Unbelief so often bars the door to vital blessings from God.

Why was he amazed at their lack of faith? Perhaps because of the very fact that they were such close acquaintances. Surely they had noticed something remarkable about his character, something to make them think very deeply! What a privilege to live in the very town where the Son of God had been reared for something close to thirty years! Perhaps for some of them this had meant rubbing shoulders with him almost every day of life.

Remember though that we too have privileges. All of us in the English-speaking world have access to the whole Bible. Our Christian bookshops are able to offer it to us in many modern translations as well as in the classic Authorised or King James Version. Some of us know the Bible quite intimately. Most of us are within reach of a church where the gospel of Christ is clearly preached, and many of us have had the great privilege of a Christian upbringing. How amazing, how appalling, how inexcusable, if we too are without faith!

From his home town Jesus went out on his itinerant teaching ministry again, continuing the pattern because he was moved still by the same motive as we find in Mark 1:38,39, 'That is why I have come.'

2. Communication through his disciples (6:7-13)

The twelve disciples have already been appointed apostles by their Lord, which means, of course, that his intention for them was that they should not only learn but work for him as his representatives (3:13ff). They now begin a new stage of their 'on the job' training.

They were sent out two by two. Why? Their Jewish hearers would understand that it was not just for company. It was of great importance that their message was taken seriously, and the principle of two or more witnesses was an important one among the Jews. There needed to be corroboration of evidence. This principle was in fact derived from the Old Testament, as we see from Deuteronomy 17:6 and 19:15. Jesus makes reference to the same principle in John 8:16-18, and so it is not surprising that he acted on it in sending out his messengers.

Do not miss an important implication of this: their preaching was based on facts. It is really only facts that can be the subject of such witness. There was much Jesus had yet to tell them, but already they could testify to the fact of Christ, which they were to proclaim so simply and yet eloquently after Pentecost (Acts 2:32; 2 Peter 1:16-18; 1 John 1:1-4). Authentic Christian preaching always involves testimony to the great fact of Christ. This means then that it must have content as well as practical application. If it lacks either, it is not preaching as the New Testament understands it.

It is clear too that the conditions of their work, as established by Jesus, left room for faith. Before going out on their travels they were to provide themselves with the essentials of life but no more. If we think of the ultimate ministry to which Jesus sent them after Pentecost we can see at least one reason for this. In this wider ministry they would encounter many difficulties and would have to trust God in the midst of them all. Here they were serving an apprenticeship in the life of faith.

In this passage Jesus allows them a staff, but in Matthew 10:10, set in a passage which is largely parallel with this, this is prohibited. How can this be explained? The simplest and probably the true explanation is that the staff here is probably a simple walking stick whereas the account in Matthew is most likely to refer to a cudgel for defence.

Clearly their lifestyle was to be frugal. Hospitality to strangers was an important part of the culture of that time and place. It would therefore be customary to offer hospitality to travelling preachers and quite right to accept it. If offered a place to stay, Jesus told them they were to remain in that home throughout their residence in the town. There was to be no question of looking for greater comfort elsewhere.

It was not only in the Holy Land that the travelling preacher was a familiar figure in those days. The market places of the wider world into which the apostles and other preachers went after Pentecost often heard the voices of strangers from other lands advocating, in Greek, some new philosophy or the latest religion. This we can infer from Paul's experience at Athens, recorded in Acts 17:16-21, but there is plenty of independent testimony to this. The friars and Lollards of the Middle Ages took these instructions of Jesus to his apostles as their model, as has many a missionary since. Cultures change of course, and with them acceptable styles of living, but it is always a bad testimony to the world when Christian preachers abandon commitment to a simple and frugal lifestyle and go in pursuit of comfort for its own sake.

Verse 11 clearly implies that, like Jesus himself (as we have already seen in verses 1 to 6), the apostles would not always find the message of the gospel welcomed. Their mission however was urgent, and so they were told not to linger in a place that gave them a hostile reception. There could well be places further on that would give the message a better hearing. It was a custom among Jews to remove dust from their sandals when returning to the Holy Land from Gentile territory. This makes Paul's even more comprehensive act, shaking out his whole apparel, which Luke tells us about in Acts 18:6, very solemn, and, as it was done in relation to Jews, not Gentiles, it would administer a very sharp shock to those who saw it.

The authority the Twelve were given included exorcism as well as preaching. This was already mentioned in Mark's record of their original appointment by Jesus in 3:15. They also had a healing ministry. The reference to anointing with oil shows us that James was following the example of Jesus when he encouraged the use of this in praying for the sick (James 5:14). In fact the ministry of the apostles was really an extension of that of Jesus himself. In this way, all they did demonstrated the coming of God's kingdom, that kingdom which was already active through the words and deeds of Jesus. In and through them the powers of that kingdom were making an impact on the world.

The gospel emanates from a God of great power and just as great compassion. These two divine attributes were revealed in what they did as well as in what they said. Whether or not they find the same expression today (and God is free to use his servants in any way he determines), these two qualities should be evident in all a Christian preacher does in the service of his Master.

3. The cost of faithful communication (6:14-29)

At first sight, this passage may seem like an intrusion into the narrative and to be totally out of place at this point. In actual fact its inclusion just here could hardly be more appropriate. What it does is to show us very clearly that Mark was concerned with themes and not simply chronology in his arrangement of his material. It would have been very simple and natural for him to give the story of John the Baptist's martyrdom in chapter 1, in the early part of which John is an important figure. It would seem that he has deliberately placed the story at this later point in order to underline the cost of faithful preaching. Chronology is not however abandoned, for, in verses 12 to 16, Mark links this story to the sequence of events in the life of Jesus.

Apparently some of the people were saying, 'John the Baptist has been raised from the dead, and that is why miraculous powers are at work in him' (v. 14). This seems almost incredible in view of the fact that Jesus and John the Baptist appeared together to public view at the time of our Lord's baptism. We should however remember how limited were the means of communication at that time. What had happened in one part of the country might be quite unknown elsewhere. The various opinions of the people about Jesus are mentioned again in 8:27-30, where we will consider their significance.

Josephus, the Jewish historian who was a younger contemporary of Jesus and the men of the New Testament, says that the event recorded here took place at Machaerus, east of the Dead Sea, a town rebuilt by Herod's father and favoured because of the hot springs located nearby.

Later on, Jesus was to link Elijah's ministry very closely to that of John the Baptist (9:11-13; cf. Matt. 17:11-13). The story of John told here reminds us in some ways of that of Elijah, especially those parts of the earlier prophet's ministry which are recorded in 1 Kings 18 and 21. Like Elijah, John did not hesitate to confront a king and his wife and to insist that they face their wrongdoing.

Herod was half-Jew and half-Edomite, and he was never

really accepted by his Jewish subjects, for they recognized that their kings should not only be Israelites but also be from the tribe of Judah. The Maccabean rulers who came to power in the second century BC had not been Davidic. At first they did not claim regal powers, but after they were treated as kings their dynasty had deteriorated in character. The Herod family, who replaced them, had marriage links with them. The Herod of this story, known as Herod Antipas, was a son of Herod the Great, who was in power at the time of our Lord's birth.

The marriage of a man to his brother's wife while he was still alive was in clear breach of the Law of God recorded in Leviticus 18:16, and this was why John had challenged Herod in the way he did, for he stood in the authentic line of prophecy which went back to Moses and recognized the authority of the great revelation which was given to Israel through him. Was the dancing-girl Salome, who was the daughter of Herodias by her previous marriage to Herod's brother, Philip? We cannot be sure, but she may well have been.

How genuine Herod's respect for John was is not easy to say. To recognize somebody as a man of God and yet keep him locked up in prison, even ostensibly as protective custody, is hardly evidence of a strong commitment to the will of God! Herod may perhaps have imagined he would escape the punishment of God so long as he saw John came to no actual harm.

Herodias was nursing a spirit of revenge and she awaited her opportunity. At last it came. Herod played right into her hands. In order to use him as her tool, she had probably studied his weaknesses and turned them to her own advantage, very much as Lady Macbeth did with her husband in Shakespeare's play, and as Jezebel did too in the story of Naboth's vineyard (1 Kings 21). Herod's wrong sense of values is shown in the almost unbelievably irresponsible offer he made as a reward for a dance (vv. 22,23). It is the kind of thing a man might do after imbibing too much wine at a banquet. His concern for his own reputation is shown in the fact that, no matter how reluctantly, he allowed John to die rather than be shamed before his guests.

The story recorded here is almost like an anticipation of the crucifixion, for in both cases there was a gross miscarriage of justice by those who should have been its guardians. Remember that Herod was also a guilty party to the death of Jesus (Luke 23:7-12). The context of the present story as Mark presents it to us is the opposition shown to Jesus and also the expectation that his disciples would find that some of their hearers would refuse to hear their message (6:3-6, 11). Soon Jesus would be predicting his death (8:31ff) and the story of his life would move on swiftly to Calvary. Here then, in his selection of material from the story of Jesus and that of his predecessor, Mark is preparing us for what lay ahead.

Jesus was, of course, going to tell the disciples that they too must take up the cross and follow him (8:34), so it is important for us to remember that the story of Herod and John told here is set in the context of opposition to the disciples as well as to Jesus.

4. Feeding five thousand plus (6:30-44)

This event is recorded in all the Gospels. In fact, apart from the supreme miracle of the resurrection of Jesus, it is the only miracle to be found in all four. We are surely right, in view of this, to assume that the Gospel writers saw it as having quite special significance, especially when we realise that they were all very selective in the accounts they gave of the life and work of Jesus.

Verse 30 makes a connection with the mission of the Twelve recorded earlier in the chapter, and shows the story of Herod and John in the intervening verses to be a parenthesis. This robs these verses of none of their importance; in fact, it could even suggest that Mark was concerned that an important event should be recorded even if placed out of its chronological sequence.

Verse 31 shows that it is right sometimes to leave a place of need for a time of rest, which was also in this case a place of prayer (v. 46, cf. 1:33-36), so as to return with greater effectiveness. The Christian life needs that balance. There is no doubt that some Christian workers are just too busy and need to spend more time in rest and prayer, no matter how urgent the tasks facing them might appear to be.

Here Mark makes two references to teaching (vv. 30, 34). These, plus the fact that the story is recorded in close connection with 6:1-29, suggest that the author may well, like John, have seen a symbolic meaning in the feeding of the people. Jesus the Shepherd (v. 34), out of a compassionate heart, teaches the shepherdless throng and in this way feeds people with the bread of life. We see how profound the analogy of teaching and feeding was when we see the way it is developed in John's account of the same event, as recorded in chapter 6 of his Gospel, where he links it with teaching of Jesus about the fact that he is the Bread of Life. In this way, John shows that Jesus fed the people not only with his spoken word, but by the breaking of his body, which was to become the living Word of God to them (cf. John 1:14).

In an event recorded earlier, the disciples had been unable to control their boat (4:37), and Jesus had rescued them by his word of power. They now discover the power of Jesus in another realm of felt inadequacy. The Christian life is very much the story of a series of inadequacies discovered in experience and met by Christ's abundant provision. We should notice that, in taking the loaves and fishes, Jesus looked up to heaven and gave thanks (v. 41). The work of Jesus was always in harmony with and in dependence on his Father.

Mark's God-given talent for storytelling reaches a very high point in this story. We are made aware of the excitement and eagerness of the people (v. 33), we can see the huge crowd assembled like a great flock of sheep and seen by Jesus, with compassion, when he landed (v. 34), the disciples discussing the situation with him (v. 35-38) and the scene as the people sat down in large groups. Readers living in temperate climates may wonder why Mark says that the grass was green, but of course a little experience of warmer climes and their frequently parched grass quickly shows the reason. What Mark says indicates that the event probably took place during or shortly after the rainy season. He also uses colourful words about the groups of people sitting down. He appears to be suggesting that, in their ordered rows and variously-hued garments set against the background of the green grass, the people resembled a series of vegetable-plots.

What a lot of numbers there are in this story – five, two, twelve, five thousand! In this way Mark's account stresses the miraculous nature of what happened. There was so little food available at the start, and this is emphasized quite especially when the numbers of the loaves and fishes are repeated (v. 41). Then comes a reference to the quantity of the leftovers and finally the large size of the crowd. Mark's dramatic sense comes across even in such a detail as the use of the masculine 'men' (v.44), so that the reader's imagination is left to conjure up a picture of a vast crowd of family members along with the adult males. This means that to call this miracle, ' the feeding of the five thousand', although this is the standard term for it, is somewhat misleading. There must have been considerably more people fed. In all these different ways, Mark shows a concern that the readers should grasp what a very great miracle Christ performed on this occasion.

Whatever would the author have said if he had heard the suggestion of a modern writer that many of the people had in fact brought food with them, that they greedily kept it for themselves, and then were shamed by the generosity of the boy mentioned in John 6:9 into sharing it with others? Quite apart from any other consideration, this suggestion does no justice to the fact that Mark constantly seeks to show how very powerful Jesus was.

In our fifth chapter, we noted the distinction C.S. Lewis made between miracles of the old and new creations. In a miracle like that of turning water into wine (John 2:1ff), Jesus was doing quickly what the Father does, more slowly. Our present story is the record of an outstanding old creation miracle. Through the ordinary processes of nature, both in the plant and animal worlds, represented by the loaves and fishes, God has set natural processes that make for multiplication by reproduction. Here then Jesus is one with God the Creator and is working, not at cross-purposes with him, but, as always, in line with his great purposes.

What lessons are the readers of the Gospel meant to learn from this story? At least three.

We learn from it that Jesus has power in yet another realm beside those already featured in the Gospel so far, so that in this way his greatness comes ever more clearly into view. Mark never tires of exalting his Lord and showing his readers his great power.

If there is anything parabolic about this miracle, as there surely is, then we see too that teaching people the gospel of Jesus is like giving them food, for both are quite indispensable, the one to our physical life and the other to our spiritual.

It is also evident from the story that we should show compassion for people in the whole range of their need, physical as well as spiritual. It is true that the spiritual need is the deeper, but Christian compassion should find many-sided expression. How can we harden our hearts to the poor, the sick, the oppressed, and claim to have the love of God in those same hearts?

Some questions for personal reflection

1. Jesus was amazed at the lack of faith of the people of Nazareth. Is my faith in him amazing for its weakness – or even its absence?

2. The disciples had a frugal lifestyle. Are there good reasons why I might opt for a less comfortable one than I have just now?

3. If Christians should show compassion for people in their physical as well as their spiritual needs, with what specific challenge does that present me?

Chapter 7

His Widening Ministry (6:45–7:31)

Few men in modern times have had as much influence on the history of ideas as Immanuel Kant from Königsberg and Søren Kierkegaard from Copenhagen. Turn up the index to any book on philosophy and many books on theology and you will find plenty of references under their names. Because of their wide influence, you might expect them to have been widely travelled. It is therefore a great surprise to discover that both of them were quite exceptionally reluctant to venture outside the cities that gave them birth and where they lived for virtually their whole lives. There was so much movement in their minds and so little of their bodies.

How different it was with Jesus! The story of his life is full of physical movement, and this strikes us particularly in the Gospel of Mark. If Jesus of Nazareth had lived after the invention of printing, like these two philosophers, or in today's era of the radio and the television, would he have moved around so much? We do not know, of course, but it is difficult to imagine him as a sedentary communicator, simply telling his parables over the radio or giving them in some audio-visual form on a television screen.

This does not mean, of course, that Christians should not use modern means of communicating the gospel when the opportunity is afforded to them. Yet we have always to remember that there is more to communication than passing on ideas. They can be easily conveyed through literature, the microphone or the screen, but compassion is a dimension of communication between people that is most effectively expressed through personal contact. Research has shown what a very high factor personal friendship or involvement with a group of warm-hearted Christians is in the way the Holy Spirit conditions people to take the gospel seriously.

On the assumption that the events recorded in this Gospel from 4:35 to 6:53 have been recounted in roughly chronological order (for no historian normally attempts to record sequence with absolute strictness), Jesus can there be seen moving around the northern environs of the Lake of Galilee, from Bethsaida in the northeast to Gennesaret, which was in the west. The reference to the country of the Gerasenes, as we have noted in commenting on 5:1, is a very general geographical reference. The main centre of Christ's preaching prior to the period recorded in this section of the Gospel appears to have been Capernaum (1:21; 2:1), which was also on this part of the lake shore. In addition, there are two references to the lakeside in 3:7 and 4:1.

The impression we tend to gather from all this is that a great deal of the activity of Jesus was confined to a series of towns strung out along the lakeside, where the two extremes were perhaps not more than a dozen miles apart. Yet Mark has given us some strong hints that this would be a misreading of the situation. In 1:39, he says that Jesus travelled throughout Galilee. He also says that he went round teaching from village to village (6:6). Also 6:56, where Mark says, 'wherever he went – into villages, towns or countryside', seems to imply a fairly wide-ranging itinerary.

At this next stage of his ministry, we get the impression that there was distinctly more movement away from its lakeside centre. He was apparently still based in Galilee, but he was moving further towards the east and north than hitherto. In this section this is evidenced in 6:53-56; 7:24, 31, and we see it also later on in 8:27. The reference to his movements in 7:31, 'Then Jesus left the vicinity of Tyre and went through Sidon, down to the Sea of Galilee and into the region of the Decapolis,' maps out an itinerary which may well have been close to a hundred miles, depending on the precise route taken.

We may see this as an anticipation of the wider ministry Christ's church would engage in after Pentecost, and of course the apostles, who were travelling with him at this time and who were therefore getting used to a good deal of travelling, were to form the nucleus of that church and to be its first evangelists.

1. Walking on the water (6:45-52)

At the conclusion of the feeding of the five thousand, we read, 'Jesus made his disciples get into the boat' (6:45). Why is it that Mark uses such an unexpectedly strong verb? It means, quite literally, 'compelled'. It is worth noting that Matthew also uses it in his account of the same event (Matt. 14:22) and that everywhere else in the New Testament it signifies compulsive force, either physical or argumentative. For instance, Paul uses it when he says that, before his conversion to Christ, he tried to force Christians to blaspheme (Acts 26:11).

Perhaps the explanation may be discovered in John 6:15. There John tells us that the people Jesus had just fed intended to force him to be king. There they said of him, 'Surely this is the Prophet who is to come into the world' (John 6:14). In doing so they were referring to the promise of God that he would raise up a prophet like Moses (Deut. 18:15-18). According to Jewish tradition, the new Moses to whom this passage refers would repeat the miracle of the manna, giving bread from heaven. If Jesus was indeed that prophet, the people would think, he should be King.

If there was a danger that the disciples would support this move, we can understand the concern of Jesus to get them away from that scene as quickly as possible. This would line up this passage with those where the 'Messianic Secret' theme appears (see the comment on 5:19-20), for it was so important that the nature of his mission should not be misunderstood. If he was not a military Messiah, neither was he a universal provider.

At another significant point, too, the Johannine and Marcan accounts coincide, for immediately after telling of the plan to make him king, John says that Jesus went to the mountainside alone (John 6:15), while at the corresponding point Mark says he went up a mountain to pray (6:46). If we can assume that

John knew Mark's Gospel, there seems to have been no studied attempt by him, and certainly not an artificially contrived one, to make his account of the life of Jesus fit that given by Mark, and so such correspondences are worth noting when they do occur.

It is well known that Luke in particular shows Jesus at prayer in several crisis situations, but it is also true that Mark does this to some extent, especially at times when success (1:35; 6:46) or the approach of suffering (14:32-36), might constitute a temptation to him to abandon his determination to carry his commitment to God's costly will right through to the cross. In this he provides an example to his people, showing us the special need for prayer at times when we encounter temptation.

Here once more (cf. 4:35-41) Jesus shows his Lordship over the elements of wind and water, but in a quite different way. On that earlier occasion he had done what God often does, that is, he transformed a situation by a change in the weather. Now, however, he does something never seen before and quite unlike anything seen in the old order of things. Here then is another example of a new creation miracle (see pages 115-16), for it anticipates the conditions of his resurrection body. That body, as we can see in Luke 24: 31 and 36, was not limited in the way human bodies are under present earthly conditions. Could there be any stronger evidence than we have here that the powers of the future kingdom were already at work through him, its King?

Mark tells us the feelings of the disciples. First of all, they were terrified because they thought him a ghost. His words immediately calmed their fears, just as the words of a parent will calm a child who faces something new and seemingly threatening. The disciples knew Jesus well enough to find his presence totally reassuring. They knew his voice and all they needed to know was that what they had taken to be a ghost was in fact their beloved Master.

Then came their amazement, for not only had he been able to walk on water, but his entry to the boat brought about a calming of the wind. Mark's comment in verse 52 shows us very clearly that the various events of the life and ministry of Jesus were intended to elicit and encourage faith, just as John also implies (John 2:11) and then states (20:30,31). The disciples should not only have learned both his power and his love through the feeding of the five thousand; they should have realized too that these were permanent qualities of his nature. To grasp this would mean that they could trust him in one situation after another, in fact in any situation at all.

Mark's words, 'their hearts were hardened', may well reflect some comment of Peter, uttered when communicating the facts of this story to his Gospel-writing friend. He knew from experience, as we will see in Mark 8, that the hearts even of disciples like himself need continual softening by God himself if they are to receive spiritual truth.

2. Miracles at Gennesaret (6:53-56)

This passage is short, but Mark has wonderfully captured the atmosphere of hustle and bustle here. With a few deft strokes of his pen he stimulates the imagination of the reader so that he or she peoples the scene with little groups moving swiftly from place to place, going into their homes and bringing their sick relatives and friends as quickly as they can to where Jesus was.

It is interesting that Mark tells us that the sick were placed in the marketplaces. They were probably the largest open spaces in the towns, but this perhaps also reminds us that the chief purpose of Jesus before the Passion was to preach (cf. 1:38). The marketplaces would be the main gathering-points of people in the open air. Here he would get access to crowds.

It was however as a healer that he most interested the populace of Galilee at this time. In fact, Mark tells us that all who followed the example of the woman with the issue of blood (5:25-29) and touched his clothes were healed. In this way, he reminds us again of the power of Jesus, and also of his compassion, for of course we can be certain that healing was not obtained from him without his permission, and that reveals his loving concern for the people.

Perhaps this was the high point of our Lord's popularity in Galilee, especially as a healer. A hundred years ago, it was common for some writers on the life of Jesus to refer to 'the Galilean springtime' of his ministry. A passage like the present one lends some credibility to such a phrase, but we should not forget that Jesus had already indicated that he was aware that his ministry would come to its close in violent action against him (2:20). There may have been some facile optimism in the minds of his disciples, but it was never in his.

It is not surprising then that at this point Mark goes on to describe a further encounter of Jesus with the religious leaders, who had already begun to plot his death (3:6).

3. The tradition of the elders (7:1-23)

Again there is a reference to a religious deputation from Jerusalem, for such is mentioned in 3:22. Was this a second visit or is it rather evidence that there was now a more or less permanent group of Jerusalem Pharisees and scribes resident in Galilee to monitor the situation? This seems quite likely. After all, Jesus was now a major phenomenon on the Galilean scene, and he needed to be watched constantly. Already, as we have seen in Mark chapters 2 and 3, there had been clashes between Jesus and the Pharisaic party over the latter's interpretations of the Law. This is again the issue which led to confrontation.

The NIV quite appropriately indicates the parenthetical nature of verses 3 and 4. Mark here gives an explanation of Pharisaic custom for the benefit of his Roman readers. Present-day readers of the Bible quickly realise that they and the Bible-writers belong to different cultures. Part of the task, therefore, of the modern Christian preacher or teacher is to make enough cultural comments on the Bible, as an ancient and eastern book, to enable his hearers or readers to understand references alien to their own culture.

This passage is about ceremonial and not merely physical uncleanness, for this was considered most important at this time. Mark gives some indication of the influence of the Pharisees when he makes reference to 'the Pharisees and all the Jews'. Every place of any size in Israel and also in other lands where there were Jewish communities had its synagogue, and here the Pharisaic outlook on things was taught to the ordinary Jewish citizens. No wonder Jesus found it necessary to spend time in dealing with Pharisaic teaching, for it was very much part of the mental furniture of most of his hearers.

'The tradition of the elders' was a body of oral interpretations of the written Law. This had grown up over the years, and it was designed to show its application to changed and changing conditions. The Law was originally written for a community and in an era somewhat different from the period of later Judaism. This material arose because of a very understandable desire to take the Law with due seriousness in its application to the contemporary world. Those of us who are concerned for the application of the Bible to modern life ought to sympathise at least with the motives that lay behind the development of this teaching.

The trouble was that these interpretations and applications came to have the same status as the written Law itself for the Pharisees and those influenced by them. This kind of thing can still happen today. Cherished traditions can become so merged with Scripture in the minds of church-goers that they come to have some authority in their own right. In the case of the tradition of the elders, however, it was even said that they were delivered to Moses at the same time as the written Law, and of course there is not a shred of evidence for this.

This constantly growing body of material was later given written form in the Talmud. The Mishnah, the most ancient and important part of this written tradition, has a long section on the subject at issue here, the matter of ceremonial uncleanness. It was obviously considered to be of much importance.

Jesus objects here to certain specific traditions, and in doing so clearly opposes the whole business of elevating such traditions to equal status with the written Law, given through Moses by divine inspiration.

His quotation of Isaiah 29:13 has important implications. This passage was part of a prophecy directed against the sacrificial externalism that was prevalent in pre-exilic Jerusalem. At that time there was an excessive emphasis on sacrifice, as Micah 6:6-8 and many other passages clearly show us. This was to come to its climax at the time of Jeremiah, when there was feverish activity in the temple courts, no doubt to try to convince God that the people were truly repentant and that there was no need to punish them through the Babylonians who were battering at the city gates. Our Lord's quotation of this passage from Isaiah makes us aware of the fact that he saw clearly that the legal externalism of the Pharisees was exactly the same in principle. God is never impressed by religious observances that do not express the heart's devotion to him.

Despite all recent attempts to present the Pharisaism of the New Testament period in a better light, we cannot set aside the evidence of the Gospels and therefore of a passage such as the present one. Here we see that all was not well with them as our Lord encountered them in the course of his ministry. In fact, he did exactly what the prophets had done when they came face to face with the sacrificial externalism of their day, as we see in passages like Isaiah 1:10-17: he elevated the moral above the merely ceremonial.

His words in verse 9 are ironical. The Pharisees who showed such concern for the Law had in fact devised ways of evading some of its clear injunctions when it suited them. Once again Mark gives an explanation for his readers. This time it is a translation of the Aramaic word, *Corban*. In fact, what had thus been declared by a man to have been given to God was not necessarily removed altogether from use by the person making this declaration. So the practice was open to serious abuse by those who wanted to evade their responsibility to care materially for their parents.

We should note the attitude of Jesus to the Old Testament shown here, for it is most significant. For one thing, he quoted from Isaiah in full confidence that his readers would recognize that these ancient words had application to their situation many centuries after the death of Moses. He did not have to argue for such an application. Although the way human nature manifests itself from one century to the next may change, that nature itself does not change. The word of the prophet exposing the hypocrisy of the men of his day was equally applicable to the people of our Lord's day – as it is also to ours!

Notice too how he sets 'the commands of God' over against their traditions, which he calls 'the traditions of men'. What were these commands of God? Not simply those of the Decalogue (the Ten Commandments) announced in such awesome fashion from Mount Sinai (v. 10a, cf. Exod. 20:12), but also those given slightly later (v. 10b, cf. Exod. 21:17; Lev. 20:9). These are 'what Moses said', and yet they are 'the commands of God'. What an elevated status for words spoken by a human being!

This means then that for Jesus the written Law has abiding worth as God's word, while the oral traditions completely lack such a standing. Today there is a widespread concern to distinguish God's word from the traditions which have become associated with it in many minds, and this, although uncomfortable for some of us, is good. The Reformers did not think of the Reformation as a single event, but rather they thought in terms of the constant reformation of the church of Christ by the Word of God, and this should be our outlook too.

Now Jesus called for the attention of the crowd. He had something of major importance to tell them. What was this? It was to the effect that it is the inner life, and its manifestation in words and deeds, that matters. The emphasis the religious leaders had been placing on matters of food and drink was directing people away from the really essential issue, the condition of their hearts. Stress on secondary issues always carries that danger.

On an earlier occasion, the disciples had asked Jesus to explain parables to them (4:10), and at that time he had expressed amazed concern at their lack of understanding (4:13). Here again

139

they show spiritual dullness. They use the word 'parable' of this utterance of Jesus, when in fact he had spoken to them quite plainly. 'Are you so dull? Don't you see ...?' he asks them. His explanation in verse 19 again takes up obvious facts. It is the heart that matters, as Isaiah too had clearly seen (vv. 6, 7).

If Peter's memories of the ministry of Jesus are the basis of Mark's Gospel, this passage must have been particularly significant for him. After all, we can assume that he was one of the disciples who had asked for the explanation and he had heard what Jesus had said. Yet despite this, when at a much later time he had seen a vision of a sheet with some 'unclean' animals in it, he had sharply reacted against it (Acts 10:9-16). 'Tell me the story often, for I forget so soon.' Most of us are in no position to criticise Peter, for often God has to teach the same lessons again and again to us also. His patience is to be marvelled at.

4. The Syro-Phoenician woman (7:24-31)
The journey to Tyre took Jesus beyond the bounds of the Holy Land proper. This was one of the two great cities of Phoenicia, the other being Sidon. Mark tells us earlier that people from that area had heard about Jesus and had come to swell the crowds who were drawn to him (3:8). Now he was to pay a personal visit to their own land.

The reason is not given to us. His concern to keep his visit secret here is unlikely to have any connection with the 'Messianic Secret' (see comment on pages 109-10), which was related not to the fact that he was in a particular place and wanted this fact to be kept secret but rather with the possible misinterpretation of his mission in political and military terms. Perhaps he went there for rest and prayer.

How apt for this event to be placed after 7:1-23! Paul, with whom Mark had worked for a time, taught that God accepts Gentiles simply by grace and not by works of the law, as we see confirmed in Luke's record of the Jerusalem Council recorded by him in Acts 15. Mark here emphasizes that this woman was a Gentile. She is described by him as 'a Greek born in Syrian Phoenicia'. By this he seems to be saying that her language was Greek and that she was not an emigrée Phoenician, such as were the North African descendants of the ancient Carthaginians, but rather was born in the Phoenician homeland. Matthew 15:22 uses an old and very broad term, 'Canaanite', indicating that she was a descendant of Israel's ancient enemies. So both have indicated that she was a Gentile, although in somewhat different ways.

Here then is somebody whose every designation shouts aloud that she is not a Jew – yet she was blessed by Jesus! This is a foreshadowing of Pentecost and beyond that the great ingathering of the Gentiles through the mission of the church of Christ.

Our Lord's apparent rebuff to her stimulated her faith. This was surely his intention, for divine love has many ways of securing its aims. Sometimes he allows us to reach desperation point to give our prayers new urgency and depth, and this certainly happened on this occasion.

The Jews often referred to Gentiles contemptuously as 'dogs', for the dog was not then the much-loved domestic animal that it is among us today, but a scavenger of the streets. Children did, however, often play with the puppies, which were brought into people's houses. Jesus used the diminutive, which would be appropriately translated 'puppy dogs', when he spoke to the woman. In this cultural context, this expression had connotations of the home rather than of the street. This unexpectedly softer language would take her by surprise, but it did more than that – it gave her hope, and her faith blossomed.

After giving his account of this event, Mark plots the course of a journey by Jesus which took him first northwards and then to the southeast, terminating eventually in the Decapolis area where we have seen him already in 5:1-20. Again we can see how selective Mark's account is, for he tells us nothing about the ministry of Jesus in Sidon.

Some questions for personal reflection

1. If compassion is best conveyed through personal contact, how might that affect my life this week?

2. Am I bound by religious traditions that work against my obedience to God's word, and if so what are they? Remember that they may not in fact be irksome but might even seem comforting.

Chapter 8

His Observers (7:32–8:21)

The course and style of our Lord's ministry made him a public figure. Like many great teachers, he gathered a group of learners around him, but unlike most of them he spent a great deal of time moving among crowds of people and not only teaching but doing many other things for people that brought blessing into their lives. As we have seen, he travelled extensively around Galilee, going from village to village and town to town. Everywhere he went things happened: people were healed of all manner of diseases and disabilities, demoniacs were freed from evil spirits, and people gathered in considerable numbers to listen to his teaching. He was not just a teacher; he was a phenomenon.

For this reason, his significance must have been discussed in many a home in Galilee. He had also been in Jerusalem and other parts of Judaea, and there had been missions also beyond the bounds of Israel proper. His fame had spread so widely that his name and his works were known at least as far north as Sidon and as far south as Idumaea, and that from a comparatively early stage of his ministry (3:8). Soon, in a somewhat remote spot in northern Galilee (as we will see in the next chapter), he would raise with his immediate disciples in a most explicit manner the question of his identity.

In some ways the whole Gospel has been moving towards this crisis point when his identity and also the nature of his work would come into sharp focus. In the section of the Gospel that is before us now, Mark appears to be drawing some threads together and to be preparing his readers for his account of that important event. He does this by directing attention in turn on the common people, the Pharisees and the disciples, showing

143

us something of the attitudes each of these groups were exhibiting at this time.

1. The healing of the deaf mute (7:32-37)

This story is peculiar to the Gospel of Mark, and we can be glad that he was led to record it, for it is most instructive and it teaches us important lessons about communication. Once the New Testament books had been written, it was possible to gain knowledge of the gospel of Christ through reading, but, of course, during the New Testament period itself the normal way to encounter it was through preaching. Paul tells us that faith comes from hearing the word of God (Rom. 10:17), and he will have seen that happen countless times during his ministry. It is true that what is especially in view in this story is the man's physical healing rather than his spiritual salvation, but Jesus wanted to encourage the man to trust him. How could he have faith when he had no hearing?

Our Lord's approach on this occasion shows us that we should be concerned to overcome communication problems. He was asked by the friends of this man to place his hand on him. We can be sure that Jesus could easily have healed him even without such an action, for he was sovereign over his own actions, but on this occasion he did not less but more than he had been asked to do. This was in order to make faith possible, despite the man's disabilities.

When barriers to communication are physical, love expressed through special skills will often find a way. Helen Keller became blind, deaf and dumb when she was a year and a half old, but a gifted and loving teacher found ways of communicating with her and eventually Helen actually learned to speak. If communication is possible even in such extreme circumstances, the gospel itself can be made known to those with serious physical disabilities. Many with mental handicaps, too, have been brought to a simple but real trust in the Lord Jesus as the Holy Spirit has used loving and resourceful Christian communicators. There are other barriers, too, problems raised

other factors, which are
ake the gospel known and
ed by them, as the matter is
rayerful thought to the best
esus clear to particular people
ntact. There is such a thing as

the crowd, perhaps to ensure
was important for him to be
cant things Jesus was doing.
hed both inoperative parts of
tongue – would convey his
d therefore they could have
courage faith.

however, for he reinforced
e of a particular word. The
ry quickly, for the doubled

pn, if pronounced properly, requires a very distinct articulation with the lips, as any reader of this book may discover by trying it. This would make for unambiguous lip-reading and the man's faith will have risen as he realized what it was Jesus was saying. Apparently, he had not been completely dumb, as Mark indicates to us by telling us that he 'could hardly talk' (v. 32). Now he was able to speak as plainly as the word Jesus had used in addressing him.

Jesus had been in the same general area at least once before (5:1-20). He had performed a notable exorcism there, but the present miracle was somewhat different and the instructions given by Jesus after he had performed it differed too. On that earlier occasion, he had told the man to tell his friends what had happened. This time he enjoined silence. Why was this?

It may have been due to the reaction Mark mentions in the final verse of this chapter. The exorcism performed by Jesus on his last recorded visit to the area, wonderful as it was, is not likely to have been viewed by the people as associated with a messianic vocation, as there is no Old Testament passage which mentions exorcism in connection with the future King or kingdom. The present miracle however could easily be understood messianically. In fact the words the people used to express their reaction remind us somewhat of the words of Isaiah 35:5,6, 'Then will the eyes of the blind be opened and the ears of the deaf unstopped. Then will the lame leap like a deer, and the mute tongue shout for joy.' Whether the observers of this miracle made an explicit connection of prophecy and event in their own minds we cannot say, but the very fact that this was possible probably determined the injunction given by Jesus. Their image of messiahship was almost certainly not free from the militaristic connotations which he wanted to avoid.

Incidentally, if their words do indicate that they had made the messianic connection, it may remind us of the fact that the area known as the Decapolis, although peopled by quite a lot of non-Jews, was not entirely Gentile. It is also possible, of course, that messianic expectation had spread to some extent among the Gentile population here, because the place was not far from Galilee.

Here then was an attitude both of amazement and of warm approval on the part of those who had observed the work of Jesus. Does this mean that they became his disciples? Mark does not say so. Certainly every true disciple shares that warmth towards Jesus, but discipleship is far more than this. It is characterised by trustful commitment to him and a recognition that life is now to find its centre in him, not in myself.

Jesus is still an attractive person to a great many people, and in some cases even to those whose religious adherence is to some other deity and not to the God of the Bible. Within Judaism at this time there were people who recognised him to be in the line of godly prophetic succession (8:28), but without identifying him as God's Messiah. It would not be appropriate to call them his disciples. Perhaps some of them did become disciples in the fullest sense later. Inadequate and yet positive views of Jesus may lead to something much fuller, as a study of a developing faith, recorded in John 9, will show us.

2. The feeding of the four thousand (8:1-10)

We have noted that Mark's book is the shortest of the four Gospels and that he is highly selective in his choice of material from the ministry of Jesus. Because of this, it is interesting that he records two feedings of a large company of people. Why did he take the time and space to do this?

He does not tell us, but good reasons may be advanced. Each Gospel writer records the feeding of the five thousand, so that in Christian circles this must have been regarded as important. As John shows us in his Gospel, it had in fact been followed by a major discourse on the significance of Jesus as the Bread of Life. Nothing of this is given by Mark, but he will probably have expected Christian readers of his Gospel to discern the spiritual significance of the fact that Jesus met people at the point of one of their most basic needs. To record a second miraculous feeding would be to underline this important truth.

If, as seems likely from a comparison of 8:1 with 7:31, this event took place in Decapolis, then Mark has recorded a feeding of Jews and one of a largely Gentile group. This is virtually confirmed by the words of Matthew's account, where his comment that the people praised 'the God of Israel' (Matt. 15:31) certainly seems to imply they were not themselves Israelites. The Roman Church for which Mark was writing included both Jews and Gentiles and they would be encouraged by the fact that Jesus showed compassion in this way both for Jews and Gentiles.

If these two stories had occurred in different Gospels, historical sceptics would have concluded that they were different records of the same event, with some confusion of detail. Actually, close study reveals quite a number of differences, which is exactly what we would expect in records of two separate events. It would be worth reading the two passages together, with the use of two Bibles and noting the various differences.

These two miraculous feeding events give us some idea of the great crowds that surrounded Jesus when he was teaching and healing. The figures given are by no means impossible. Galilee and the surrounding regions were well populated in our

147

Lord's day. We should not imagine most of the people living in small villages, for there were quite a number of sizeable towns there. The succession of towns along the lakeside must have made it seem almost like the continuous 'ribbon development' found in some seaside areas in our own country. It is likely that there was a sizeable population also in the Decapolis.

The fact that on both occasions loaves and fishes were employed should not surprise us. After all, this was a fishing area. These two items would have been the staple diet of those who lived on and near the lakeside, whether to the west or to the east. Loaves would have been found everywhere, but fish most frequently in this general area. This kind of detail may seem unimportant, but it serves to strengthen the reader's assurance of the authenticity of the account.

The location of Dalmanutha, to which Jesus went next, is not known. Immediately after his account of this event, Matthew refers to the vicinity of Magdalan (Matt. 15:39), which may have been a little further south than the other lakeside towns frequented by Jesus. The whole area was comparatively small and it would have been easy to move from one town to another.

3. The Pharisees call for a sign (8:11-12)

Mark inserts his brief record of this event between the feeding of the four thousand and the comment that Jesus made on the two miraculous feeding miracles. We have seen other examples of this kind of insertion in the course of our study of this Gospel. In each case, he must have had some purpose in mind and it is not difficult to discover this here. For one thing, we have an interesting parallel at an earlier point in the Gospel. In 3:20-30, Mark recorded the adverse but not necessarily malevolent comment made by the family of Jesus, and he followed this by showing the bitter antipathy of the Pharisees to him. Here he does something similar. The obtuseness of the disciples in verse 4 is followed by the rank unbelief of the Pharisees in verses 11 to 13. It is as if to say that lack of discernment is one thing but bitter antagonism quite another.

Also, of course, the call for a sign appears particularly incredible and unbelieving after such a miracle as this. What does 'a sign from heaven' mean? Is it simply another way of saying, 'a sign from God'. Possibly, but we should note that, in connection with the gift of manna to the people during the wilderness wanderings, 'the LORD said to Moses, "I will rain down bread from heaven for you" ' (Exod 16:4). Their demand may therefore suggest that they thought Jesus was claiming to be the new Moses, who would give the new manna. See John 6:30, where, after the feeding of the five thousand, the people ask Jesus for a sign and make reference to the Old Testament story of the provision of the manna.

There was plenty of evidence already that Jesus was a very special Person, and the Pharisees must have been very much aware of this. So the demand for a sign was itself a sign, a clear revelation of their unbelief. The demand for miracles before believing is itself unbelieving, for all faith needs is God's clear word. At the human level, the measure of our trust in a person is very much related to our confidence in what he or she says. On this occasion, of course, the demand was a test, and so, Mark is suggesting, was not really sincere. For a second time within the space of sixteen verses (see 7:34), the Gospel writer tells us that Jesus sighed. On both occasions this shows his true humanity. On this second occasion it probably reveals how profoundly troubled he was at the unbelief he was finding and which the Pharisees, among others, were expressing.

4. The obtuseness of the disciples (8:13-21)

Once more the lake was crossed. The detail that they had one loaf of bread with them in the boat (v. 14) is revealing, for, as something not absolutely essential to the story, it points to the presence of an eyewitness, presumably Peter. Again then this kind of thing assures us that although Mark's purpose in writing is to show us the message of the gospel from the story of Jesus, he has also been concerned for truth of fact.

Already, as recorded in verse 4, the disciples had shown that they had not really learned from the feeding of the five thousand the important lesson that Jesus was equal to any adverse situation. Now, while they were crossing the lake, their lack of understanding came to the fore again. Jesus challenged their failure to learn from the two miracles of feeding he had performed. They should have been convinced by now that God could be trusted to supply all their needs in his service. We are meant to learn general lessons about God and his ways from particular events in which his character and purposes are shown, because of course he is utterly consistent in character, although this does not mean, as we see in 2 Samuel 5:17-25, that he is always bound to act in the same way in similar circumstances.

Here again then Jesus encountered their gross literalism and their lack of spiritual discernment. The word 'still' in verse 17 emphasises his concern at the fact that they continued to be so lacking in true understanding. The Writer to the Hebrews later made the same point when referring to the immaturity of his readers, who had been Christians long enough to make their spiritual dullness culpable (Heb. 6:1ff).

The conversation between Jesus and the disciples at this time began when he told them to beware of the yeast of the Pharisees and that of Herod. Their literalism here appears particularly wooden, but we need to remember that preoccupation with physical things may divert our attention from spiritual issues. Yeast here appears to symbolise the permeating power of evil. The reference to Herod finds no explanation in the context. The Pharisees and Herod were very different indeed in their general outlook, for Herod was a Roman appointee whereas the Pharisees were prepared to cooperate with the occupying power only when this was strictly necessary. What united them, however, was their desire for a sign. In his account of the trials of Jesus, Luke tells us of Herod's desire to see a miracle (Luke 23:8). The words of Jesus here in Mark's Gospel may therefore show his prescience, or it may be that Herod had already shown such a desire.

Mark perhaps included this detail in his account as a reminder to us of the unholy coalition of the Pharisees and Herodians to which he refers in 3:6. Certainly this is very fitting in view of the fact that he soon shows us Jesus starting a course of instruction to his disciples to make them aware that he was to suffer and die (8:31).

Some questions for personal reflection

1. Can it ever be right to seek a sign from God?

2. God's repetitions are often his way of teaching us lessons. Can I think of examples of this in my own life?

Chapter 9

His Messianic Sufferings (8:22–9:1)

This is a very important part of Mark's Gospel, and the events recorded in it form a kind of watershed in the ministry of Jesus. All that has gone before in this Gospel has really been a preparation for these events, just as these in their turn prepare us for the final drama at the close of the ministry of Jesus.

1. A two-stage cure (8:22-26)

This miracle, peculiar to Mark, is most unusual, and so we need to give its significance special consideration. The Gospels record many healing miracles and of course they vary much in their details, but this is the only recorded example of a cure performed by our Lord in two stages. The nearest biblical parallel is found in what happened to the dry bones of Israel in Ezekiel 37:7-10, although that passage is somewhat different in that it is the record of a vision, not of an actual physical miracle.

This story illustrates the sovereignty of Jesus in his healing ministry. Sometimes he healed just by speaking a word of healing and sometimes by a word accompanied by a touch. Here he used touch but also applied spittle to the man's eyes. He had done something similar on an earlier occasion (7:32-37) when dealing with a man who was deaf and had a speech impediment. Then, as here, his actions clarified for the person exactly what he intended to do, because he touched the parts of the body that were disabled. Realising that there were barriers to normal communication in each of these cases, he found ways of crossing these barriers and of encouraging faith.

It is strange, however, that the blind man was not completely healed immediately. Mark has already told us that in his own area Jesus did few miracles and that the reason for this was the erection of a barrier of unbelief on the part of the people (6:4-6). There is however no evidence of the presence of unbelief on this occasion, and even if there was we would still have to account for the fact that there was complete healing before the story ends. Neither does this event show any inability on the part of Jesus to effect a healing without any delay. What the Gospel tells us about him makes this unthinkable, and in any case the range of the powers he exhibited, as shown in the Gospel, was enormous. There must then have been some other factor in operation. What can it have been?

There can be little doubt that the key to this passage's significance is its position in the ministry of Jesus and in the Gospel in which Mark records that ministry. There are several factors that suggest this: It precedes the important events in the Caesarea Philippi area, when Jesus raised with his disciples the question of his identity. It was not only the estimates given by other observers and relayed to Jesus by the disciples that were incomplete. Peter's confession certainly showed spiritual insight (which is highlighted in the parallel passage in Matthew 16), but this, although real, proved to be only partial. The two-stage healing prepares us for this, and may well show us how aware Jesus was of the limited nature of Peter's faith at this time, because of course he must have had some special purpose in doing what he did at this particular time.

The story here also follows 8:14-21, in which Jesus rebukes the disciples for their lack of spiritual perception. His words to them, 'Do you still not understand?' (v.21) are particularly striking when they are followed immediately by this miracle. So this two-stage healing becomes a kind of acted parable, with limited spiritual understanding as its theme.

As the earlier part of chapter 8 records the miracle of the feeding of the four thousand and verses 14 to 21 record the comment Jesus made on this miracle, we are probably meant to see the whole of 8:1-26 as serving a special function in the structure of the Gospel. It introduces the enormously important section which follows it, which focuses on the significance of his Person.

2. His Identity (8:27-30)

Caesarea Philippi is a beautiful place on the northern edge of the Galilean region. It is a place of running water where streams come down from Mount Hermon, which is just a few miles to the north, on their way to a meeting-point where they form the upper reaches of the River Jordan.

Beauty is not everything, however. Athens was undoubtedly a beautiful city in New Testament times, but when he was there Paul 'was greatly distressed to see that the city was full of idols' (Acts 17:16). At Caesarea Philippi today there is a shrine in the cliff-face with empty niches in it, and these would have been used for pagan images in New Testament times, for the Greek god Pan was worshipped there. Also there was a temple to the Roman Emperor Augustus. In the same area, too, was the old city of Dan, where there was a notorious idolatrous shrine in Old Testament times, to which the people of the northern kingdom came to offer sacrifices before a golden calf. So then in this area it was easy to become aware of the great spiritual needs of Jews, Greeks and Romans. What a place for the revelation of him who came to meet those needs and whose cross would bear a notice about him written in the languages of all three (John 19:19-22)!

In his Gospel, Mark has recorded for us various questions about Jesus asked by the disciples and by the people in general, for example in 1:27 and 4:41. Jesus was such an unusual Person; all that he did and all that he was provoked questions in the minds of people who watched him and heard him. He still raises questions in people's minds today. At this stage in his ministry he asked his disciples what people were saying.

Of course, there had been some adverse comments on him and Mark recorded these for us earlier in his Gospel. Members of his family said, 'He is out of his mind' (3:21); and at about the same time, the teachers of the law who had come down from Jerusalem bluntly declared, 'He is possessed by Beelzebub! By the prince of demons he is driving out demons' (3:22). The first of these, of course, was due to the fact that his family were bewildered by what was happening, and the latter by the bitter antagonism of the religious leaders to a Man who was challenging their whole approach so radically. The great bulk of the people, however, seem to have viewed him with considerable favour, as the answer of the disciples reveals to us.

People very often speculate about the significance of something or someone unusual and this must have been going on all the time in relation to Jesus. If the disciples mingled with the crowds when Jesus was surrounded with people hearing and watching him, they must have heard many a comment, many a theory as to who he was. The answers they quoted (and Matthew 16:14 indicates that Jeremiah also was mentioned by the people) were all wrong, and yet there was some truth in them, for they had at least recognized Jesus to be a great Man of God. It is certainly possible to see aspects of the character and work of Jesus that could remind people of the prophets in general and of John the Baptist, Elijah and Jeremiah in particular. Like each of these men, he was challenging the establishment, for John had spoken words of judgement to the Pharisees and also to Herod, at whose hands he met his death, Elijah had challenged an ungodly king and his wife, and Jeremiah had stood almost alone against ungodliness in the monarchy and against the false prophets in his day.

In truth, however, Jesus was far more than these, and Matthew shows us his pleasure at Peter's confession, which is recorded in his Gospel in a somewhat fuller form (Matt. 16:16ff). It surprises the reader who comes to Mark after Matthew to find that although the event is recorded, our Lord's commendation of Peter, which is a leading feature of the story in Matthew, is absent from Mark's account. Why should this be?

Probably this is because of Mark's special preoccupation with the sufferings and death of Jesus. It is these he wants to emphasize. To confess Jesus as Messiah, although good, was not enough. Others had sometimes been acknowledged mistakenly as Messiah, and this would be true of men who were still to come, but the even deeper question concerned the nature of his messiahship. What sort of Christ was he?

We are not surprised, in view of what we have seen already (see the comment on pages 109-10), to find Mark recording a warning from Jesus to his disciples to keep silent, for, as we have noted, messiahship was misconceived by most Jews. To them the Messiah, the Christ, was going to be a glorious figure, with a very visible kingly authority and a highly public commitment to military methods in ridding the nation of its Roman overlords. The teaching of Jesus about his destiny of suffering cut right across that image of the Christ. So, for him, the confession of his messiahship was only really acceptable when it was linked to this radically different concept. In fact, the messianic style, as Jesus conceived it, involving a vocation of suffering, had first to be lived in front of the people before the claim was made explicitly. It was in fact in the most improbable of situations, when he was a prisoner soon to be condemned and put to death, that Jesus confessed openly that he was the Christ (14:61,62).

3. His Work (8:31-33)

Jesus here uses his favourite self-designation, 'Son of Man'. In connection with it he says four things about his destiny:

He was to suffer. That was intensely surprising to those who had been taught the standard Pharisaic doctrine of messiahship, which stressed victory rather than suffering. Without doubt the teaching of Jesus here was quite unfamiliar to them, and quite shocking. It was a most startling reinterpretation of the current doctrine of the Messiah.

Also, he said that he was to be rejected by the religious leaders. How astonishing this was for those who had been brought up to give them great respect! The disciples had of course seen how Jesus had been in conflict with the Pharisees and teachers of the law over and over again, but they may well have hoped that some reconciliation between him and these religious leaders would take place eventually.

The words of Jesus about 'the elders, chief priests and

teachers of the law' must have seemed particularly ominous to the disciples. They may well have recalled the visiting deputation of teachers of the law from Jerusalem referred to earlier in Mark's account (3:22). Perhaps they had taken an adverse report back to Jerusalem. The religious leaders who were to reject him would also include the chief priests. These were Sadducees, a group of leading priests closely associated with the high priest, who were in charge of the temple. The inclusion of the elders, who were respected laymen, made the reference to those who would reject him an exact description of the membership of the Sanhedrin, the great Jewish council that had powers of trial under the Romans. So there was no question simply of opposition by particular groups among the leaders. The issue would involve confrontation with the great council itself, so that it was not simply rejection by individuals but, in a formal manner, by the nation's religious leaders meeting to transact official business for the nation. This was in fact what actually happened, as we shall see.

What then would be the result of such an encounter? He must be killed. This disclosure will have been absolutely devastating for those who heard it, with two dimensions to this devastation. At the personal level, the disciples loved Jesus so dearly. They had spent every day with him for many months and would be unable to contemplate separation from him. Not only so, however, but they now believed him to be the Messiah. How could this possibly be true, however, if he was to be killed? It would not make any kind of sense to them.

It is very important to notice that Jesus uses not simply the language of fact but of necessity here. He *must* be killed. Was this because of the power and authority of those forces which were gathering against him? It is quite clear that he was referring to something much deeper. Often, especially in the Gospel of John (e.g. John 2:4; 7:6; 13:1; cf. Mark 14:41), we find him expressing his conviction that there was a divine timetable and therefore a divine plan for his life. This means that the necessity to which he refers here must be a divine and not simply a human one. If this was so, he must have been aware that his death was to have some special meaning, and he was to explain this more fully later on, as we see in the great utterance recorded in 10:45.

The Messiah to suffer, to be rejected by the religious leaders, to be killed – how terrible were these disclosures! But there was to be something else. He was to rise again. It seems strange that, as later events reveal, they did not really take this in. This is however psychologically authentic. A person who is told that somebody he or she loves is to be killed, is in no fit state to take in anything else that is said, no matter how startling or how wonderful it may be. No doubt the glorious fact of his forth-coming resurrection was lost on them because the disclosure of it followed such terrible revelations. It could even be that they hardly heard the words at all because of a total preoccupation with the awful disclosure Jesus had just made to them.

We note that on each of three occasions when Mark gives the content of the course of teaching about his cross and resurrection the phrase 'after three days' occurs (cf. 9:31; 10:34) This makes us think of the interval between his death and resurrection. It was actually quite brief, but it must have seemed interminable to the disciples, for whom the bottom had dropped out of life. What assurance and joy the resurrection must have brought them when it took place!

Mark says that Jesus 'began' to teach them these things. This, plus evidence from the next few chapters (e.g. 9:12, 30-32; 10:32-34, 45), shows that he was really beginning a whole course of instruction about the fact and meaning of his death. This is not surprising, both in view of the central importance of his death for our salvation and also because the earlier teaching these men had received had conditioned them against it. So from this time onwards it was a central concern of Jesus to make sure the disciples faced these uncomfortable facts. Mark tells us that Jesus 'spoke plainly about this' (v.32). He did not clothe it in parabolic language or say something enigmatic the significance of which was not immediately evident. Crystal clear understanding was important. The modern preacher also needs to show the great importance and special significance of the cross.

As several commentators have pointed out, one reason for the special importance of verse 31 lies in its relationship to the words that immediately precede it, where Mark says, 'Jesus warned them not to tell anyone about him.' The fact that these two verses have been placed together and may be interpreted in terms of each other is really the nearest we get in the Gospel to an explanation of this kind of command from our Lord. There can be little doubt that Mark intended perceptive readers to see the significance of this.

We see from the story that Peter's spiritual sight was only partial, very much like the partial physical sight the blind man had at one stage in his experience with Jesus (8:24). He rejected the unfolding of a suffering destiny for Jesus and so, although a disciple, was an unwitting agent of the tempter. We are so familiar with the use of the word 'Satan' here that we may give it little thought. It is quite amazing that Jesus should see God's will to lie in suffering for him, but he saw this very clearly, and so the idea of avoiding this suffering was bound to come from the devil. Here Jesus turns normal human value-systems upside down (or perhaps we should say 'right side up'). Peter's thinking here is human and so, because this is a fallen world, it could be used by Satan for his purposes.

It was when he had turned and looked at his disciples that Jesus rebuked Peter. Sometimes it is appropriate to a situation to put right a spoken error by a word said in private, but it was very important that the disciples should realise how wrong it was for Peter to rebuke Jesus, and especially in connection with such a vitally important disclosure of truth. Notice too what the command, 'Get behind me!' implies. Jesus is not just saying, 'Get out of my sight!' At this point Peter was presuming to lead Jesus, and he was being plainly told that his place at this time was to be a follower, not a leader. It was the place of Jesus to give authoritative teaching; it was the place of Peter to listen and to receive this teaching.

4. His Challenge (8:34-9:1)

Jesus now takes the challenge to Peter's thinking to a deeper level still. Not only is the true disciple to accept the necessity for a cross for Jesus. He is to accept a cross for himself. Here, even in the region of Caesarea Philippi, which was twenty-five miles and more north of the familiar lakeside, there was still a crowd close at hand. Jesus gave this challenging teaching to them as well as to his disciples.

It is notable that Jesus did an unusual thing on this occasion. He invited the crowd to draw near to him. This meant of course that he was giving emphasis to the fact that the teaching he gave here was not meant simply for his closest disciples. There was an important lesson that needed to be heard and understood by all who were giving Jesus a hearing. This teaching was relevant to everybody, and it represents basic truth about Christian discipleship that applies in every place and in every age, for these conditions have never been amended or modified by the One who gave them.

The presence of the crowd in the story reminds us that, at a certain level, Jesus needed no recruiting drive for disciples. If all discipleship involved was following him from place to place, many were willing to do that. It might involve leaving one's familiar surroundings and the various comforts of a settled home-life, but there were many compensations. Drama was never far away, for people were constantly being healed, and this irrespective of the kind of ailments or disabilities they had, and demons were being cast out. In fact, you never really knew what might happen when Jesus was around. The travelling band of disciples were constantly being surprised by the things that happened. Moreover Jesus had such a gift for telling stories that gripped and fascinated all who heard, and people hung upon his words. No wonder his presence acted like a magnet everywhere he went! There had to be more to discipleship than this, and Jesus made this very clear on this occasion.

The same Greek word is used in two sayings of Jesus in this passage, those in verses 33 and 34. In the first of these, the NIV translates it 'behind' and in the second 'after'. The word was regularly used in a physical sense, but Jesus makes it very plain here that he is not simply referring to a physical following. What did he mean by denying self? He certainly did not mean the temporary loss of a few luxuries, the absence of which might even do us good, but rather a total revolution of outlook, a major readjustment of values and so of priorities. It involved a complete about-turn. It meant in fact embracing a way of thought that came from God (v. 33). For Jesus, this way of thinking God's thoughts after him meant accepting the cross, and this is what it would mean also for the disciples.

At that time a cross would be immediately understood as a place of death, and this it was, yet the word 'death' does not adequately sum up the full horror of crucifixion. Death can sometimes be sudden, even momentary, and sometimes it can even be relatively painless. Crucifixion however meant a lingering, dreadfully painful death. If it was comparable to anything, it was to being tortured to death. Crucifixion also meant a deeply shameful death. It was such for the Jews, for they would recall the words of Deuteronomy 21:23: 'anyone who is hung on a tree is under God's curse.' The Romans too regarded it as the most ignominious of deaths, and they reserved it for slaves and for the worst of criminals. So it meant social ostracism and utter loneliness at a time of the deepest suffering, when the slightest crumb of comfort would have been longed for. Here then are the conditions of discipleship given on the authority of the Christ of God.

Jesus then goes on to explore the implications of this call. The NIV translation fails to reveal to the reader that 'life' in verse 35 and 'soul' in verses 36 and 37 are translations of the same Greek word. This points up the paradoxical nature of this teaching. To be unconcerned about my life is in fact to show the greatest concern for it. Losing it, I will find it. This mystery, puzzling at the intellectual level and quite unacceptable to most non-Christian thinking, shows itself to be profoundly true in the actual experience of the Christian disciple. It is out of death that true life comes. Paul has much to say about this in his Second Letter to the Corinthians, especially in the later chapters of it, where he applies this principle particularly to Christian service.

The linking of Jesus and the gospel in verse 35 and of Jesus and his words in verse 38 are probably two different ways of saying virtually the same thing. At this stage, Jesus was the preacher of the gospel, and he had been proclaiming the good news of God ever since the beginning of his ministry (1:14,15). Through his death and resurrection, however, he was to become the very gospel itself.

It is interesting to find that he links loyalty to him with the fact that the generation is adulterous, for adultery was often used in the Old Testament as a figure for apostasy, for religious disloyalty. It was the Pharisees and Pharisaic ways of thinking that dominated the religious scene not only in the Holy Land but also everywhere in the Gentile world where Jews had gone. That this generation should be described as adulterous, with all the Old Testament associations with idolatry that this would bring, would have been enormously surprising and deeply shocking, and the use of a figure of speech with such a background means that there can be little doubt that Jesus had his own Jewish people in mind in saying them. The word suggests that there had been, despite their preoccupation with the Law, a departure from God. Perhaps he had in mind their concern with outward things to the neglect of the inward.

The words of Jesus here also suggest that loyalty to him is not in fact disloyalty to God, as if he were a rival, but an expression of it, for he is in fact the Son of God. We wonder if Peter reflected on the solemn words of verse 38 after his threefold denial of Jesus. If so the forgiveness that Jesus brought to him must have seemed almost beyond belief, wonderful fact as it was. This verse contains the first clear reference in this Gospel to the second advent and, along with the reference to the resurrection (v. 31), was a note of strong hope for the future of his cause. His death would certainly not be the end.

A great deal has been written on 9:1. The fact that not only

163

in this Gospel but also in the parallel passages, in Matthew 17:1 and Luke 9:28, a note of time is given that links this saying with the Transfiguration, indicates that the two events should be understood together. This event was a quite special revelation of the power of the kingdom in the glory of its King, but, as this saying of Jesus indicated, only some of the disciples would witness this. To this great event we must now turn.

Some questions for personal reflection

1. What are the main questions people today are asking about Jesus, and am I ready to answer them?

2. How convinced am I that the death of Jesus was an absolute necessity -for me?

3. Is the challenge of Jesus to deny self, take up the cross and follow him central to my conception of Christian discipleship? If not, what idol have I put in its place – personal soul culture, self-fulfilment, or what?

Chapter 10

His Messianic Glory (9:2-29)

This section of the Gospel story is most intimately related to the one that immediately precedes it, and the two really need to be interpreted in terms of each other. Here matters of central importance are in focus, and it is clear that the whole idea of what messiahship entailed which was current among the Jews at that time was being seriously challenged by Jesus.

The Jews had the Old Testament, of course, and it was in that inspired literature that the Messiah was promised and foreshadowed. Moreover many of them were most diligent students of it, and yet, as a review of the Jewish literature which records the ideas current at this time clearly shows, it had been widely misunderstood in contemporary Judaism. There is little doubt that our interpretation of Scripture can be adversely affected by our personal desires, and the Jews at this time had a very deep desire for political and religious freedom. Except for part of the second and first centuries BC, they had not had complete political freedom for over six hundred years, and there had been times too when their religious freedom had been under serious threat. How they longed for real liberty!

We can readily understand how these very natural feelings influenced the way they read the Old Testament, so that everything there that suggested that messiahship could be understood in terms of political and religious freedom would be emphasised, and everything that suggested that the Coming One would have to suffer and even die would be understood in some other way. We need to ask ourselves if we sometimes see in Scripture what we want to see rather than what is actually there! Some writers today are over-emphasising the role of the individual reader in the interpretation of Scripture, as if to suggest that it is inevitable that we find in Scripture what we

165

feel we need to find. It is true that none of us is completely free from personal prejudice in our reading of Scripture and that the same passage may minister to a variety of needs, but we need to insist that it has objective meaning and that the Holy Spirit can lead us into a proper understanding of this if we are responsive to him.

1. His Glory (9:2-8)

After the death of Jesus would come his resurrection. The apostles were being prepared for the great task of proclaiming both these great facts and their saving significance. It was therefore fitting that the revelation he had just made to them of his coming sufferings should be followed by an anticipation of his risen glory. In a sense this whole series of events that happened up there in northern Galilee, both in the region of Caesarea Philippi and on the Transfiguration mountain, pointed towards the final crisis events of the Gospel story.

The three disciples chosen to be with him on the mountain were with him, Mark tells his readers, on two other occasions. They were present when he raised a dead girl in the house of Jairus (5:37) and also when he faced in Gethsemane the fact of his own imminent death (14:33). Why three were selected and why this particular group is never explained, but the evidence of Acts shows them to be particularly prominent members of the apostolic group (e.g. Acts 1:15; 8:14; 12:2). Peter was to preach the gospel on the Day of Pentecost, James was to be the first of the apostles to suffer death for Jesus, and John was not only to be closely associated with Peter on several important occasions in the early story of the church, but he was to write a Gospel of great depth and yet in the simplest of language. Perhaps then they were being given supplementary training for leadership roles in the infant church of Christ. They were confronted first of all by the reality of death, both that of ordinary mortals and then that of the Son of God himself, before getting a foretaste of his triumph over death, a triumph that was to be both for himself and for others.

There have been attempts to identify the 'high mountain' where the transfiguration of Jesus took place. The traditional site is Mount Tabor, some miles southwest of the Sea of Galilee, but this is not particularly high. The most likely identification, especially in view of its proximity to Caesarea Philippi, is with mighty Mount Hermon, the highest mountain in the whole area.

Mark notes that on that mountain Jesus and the three disciples were all alone. So then this vision was not intended to be seen by all and sundry. Is this then another example of the 'Messianic Secret'? We can certainly understand that such a vision could well have fostered a strongly triumphalist view of the messiahship of Jesus. If he was indeed such a Person as this event revealed, then nothing would be impossible for him. The Roman oppressors would stand no chance against such a glorious Person. It was, however, safe for the disciples to see such a great sight at this stage of things, for they had already been told in no uncertain terms that he was going to suffer and die.

There could have been another reason. In the New Testament, only two people are recorded as seeing the risen Lord in all the outshining glory of his Person, and they were the apostles Paul and John. His other resurrection appearances seem to have been in the normally visible form that he had during the days of his flesh. It is true that others were present with Paul on the Damascus Road at the time when he saw the risen Christ, and they undoubtedly saw something, but a comparison of the three accounts of this in Acts 9, 22 and 26, seems to indicate that they saw a light and heard a sound but not the glorious vision and not the verbal revelation that came to Paul at this time. Perhaps then such a vision was for believing eyes only, as was the sight of his glory given to three men on the Transfiguration Mount.

White symbolised holiness and purity. Here, as on so many previous occasions, Mark's description bears all the marks of an eyewitness account, which would come from Peter. That Peter was deeply impressed by all that happened is shown in 2

Peter 1:16-18, where he refers to the 'power and coming of our Lord Jesus Christ' and stresses the aspect of divine majesty in the transfiguration. Incidentally his language there accords well with the reference to the coming of the kingdom with power in 9:1. There was a real coming of the kingdom with power in this revelation of the power and glory of the King.

The appearance with Jesus of the two figures from the past may well have had more than one purpose. The two main sections of the Old Testament were the Law and the Prophets, as the remainder, although important, had something of a miscellaneous character. These two men would represent the Law (Moses) and the prophets (Elijah) in their testimony to Jesus. They had several things in common. For one thing, important events in the lives of each of them were associated with mountains. Moses had spent a long time up Mount Sinai, receiving the Law from God, while Elijah had confronted the prophets of Baal on Mount Carmel, and the Lord had indicated so clearly that he was the true God and that Baal was no god at all. Also they had something in common as there had been an unusual end to the ministry of each, for Moses had been buried by the Lord (Deut 34:6) and Elijah had been taken up to heaven in a chariot (2 Kings 2:11).

A number of figures from the past were associated in the minds of the Jews with events connected with the coming of the Messiah, and this was the case with both Moses and Elijah, although Elijah was the more prominent figure in this aspect of Jewish eschatology at the time of Jesus.

Perhaps the words of Peter, 'It is good for us to be here', intend a contrast, as if he was saying, 'It is good to be here on the mountain with you, Lord; here, where we can see you in the glory that you truly deserve, not there on the road that you tell us will lead to crucifixion.' If this is the case, he was still not fully willing to face what Jesus had disclosed to him and his fellow-disciples. His suggestion about the three shelters, as Mark's comment in verse 6 perhaps suggests, did not take sufficient account of the uniqueness of Jesus, which he had already confessed (8:29) and which was shown by his Transfiguration to be quite special. Moses and Elijah were most highly regarded by the Jews at that time, so that to suggest he occupy a shelter next to Moses and Elijah recognises something of his greatness but without in any way acknowledging his utter uniqueness.

Already, prior to the divine voice which spoke from heaven, they were frightened. How would they have felt after they had heard it? The voice echoed the valuation of Jesus that was given from heaven at his baptism (see the comments on 1:11). So the Son of God is to be recognised as unique, and it follows from this that his teaching must be thoroughly accepted and not questioned. It has the divine imprimatur on it.

The command, 'Listen to him!' was in effect a rebuke to Peter for his words in 8:32 and 9:5, and its wording was probably influenced by Deuteronomy 18:15,18. This passage promises the coming of a prophet like Moses, and in it the seriousness of not obeying the promised prophet is underlined. Messiahship involved the combination of a number of roles, normally separate in the Old Testament, and it is clear that the apostolic church believed Jesus to be the fulfilment of this promise (Acts 3:22, 23; 7:37).

Perhaps, too, this sudden disappearance would prepare Christ's men for such occurrences during the forty days between his resurrection and his ascension, although in that case the person to appear and disappear was Jesus himself (e.g. Luke 24:31). In this and in other ways the transfiguration was a kind of foretaste of his resurrection.

As we have already noted, the two events of Peter's confession and the Transfiguration together provide a kind of watershed in the ministry of Jesus and in Mark's record of that ministry. The Transfiguration event also symbolised the watershed between the Old Covenant and the New.

Here were two men of the past, great representatives of the Old Covenant. As the Writer to the Hebrews, says, that covenant was destined to fade away (Heb. 8:13; cf. 2 Cor. 3:10,11). This fact is here symbolized by the disappearance of these two men. Having done their work of testimony to the Christ, they could withdraw, leaving him centre stage. This implies that a great purpose of the Old Testament is to point to Christ. Here too were three men of the future, leaders of the church that should be, the church that would be based on the New Covenant to be established through the sacrifice of Jesus. Here most of all was 'the Man for all ages', the Son of God, to whom the Old Covenant pointed and on whose work the New Covenant would be based.

2. His Programme (9:9-13)

Once again the command of silence is given (see the comment on pages 109-10). Mark notes their obedience to this command (v.10). Here was the first recorded command of Jesus since the heavenly injunction to listen to what he said, and they were evidently taking it seriously.

An outstanding experience makes us think hard, and for the three disciples this stimulus to think was intensified by what Jesus said to them on the way down the mount. They were perplexed by what they had seen and heard. Jesus had already spoken to them about his resurrection (8:31), but they had probably not taken it in because at the same time he had made the shocking disclosure of the fact that he was going to die. Now perhaps they were more open to instruction in this. Whatever though could 'rising from the dead' mean in reference to such a glorious Figure as they had just seen? This majestic revelation would have seemed quite incompatible with what Jesus had told them about his death. No wonder they were puzzled! Not only so, but how did this event fit into the prophetic scheme they had been taught in the synagogues and which they would never have questioned before they met Jesus?

The preoccupation of Jesus, however, was with his sufferings. He was prepared to say something about Elijah, for Elijah had his place in God's plans, and this was not unimportant, but far more central to God's purpose was Jesus and the sufferings he was to endure. Most of us have encounters from time to time with people who want to interest us in some 'off-beat' form of the Christian faith. So often they show more interest in some 'Elijah', some side-issue, than in Jesus himself. That in itself is good enough reason for questioning the truth of their message. The Transfiguration event shows that it is Jesus himself who must always be at the heart of everything for us.

In his account of the aftermath of the Transfiguration, Matthew shows how the disciples understood the words of Jesus recorded by Mark in verse 13, 'Elijah has come, and they have done to him everything they wished, just as it is written about him.' They understood this to be a reference to John the Baptist (Matt. 17:13). He also records an earlier occasion when Jesus himself had made this link between the two men (Matt. 11:13,14), and his teaching on that occasion would have been the basis of this understanding.

John's Elijah-like ministry had itself ended in death (6:27). A study of the Old Testament as well as the experience of John shows that those who prepared the way for the Christ often participated to some extent in his experience of suffering and so foreshadowed him, just as Christians are now called to take up the cross as they represent him in the world. So, under the Old Covenant, words pointing forward to Christ were illustrated in the lives and characters of those who proclaimed his coming, and this combination of word and character must also be true of Christians today. We need to remember that death and resurrection are the centre of the Christian life as well as of the gospel. Romans 6, which may be viewed virtually as a profound interpretation of the challenge of Jesus to deny self and take up the cross in following him, shows us this.

3. His Power (9:14-29)

Lowry, the artist, once painted an urban scene with a street just crammed with people, dozens of them. They are all walking in a somewhat leisurely fashion, with one exception. One man is very evidently in a great hurry. This is conveyed very simply but clearly, the artist having such skill that he could indicate this simply by a few strokes of his brush. Mark had that kind of gift, but with words rather than paint. We can hardly help but visualize the scene that he has presented so vividly here.

Why were the people 'overwhelmed with wonder' (v. 15)? It could be that there was some comparison with one particular aspect of the story of Moses on Mount Sinai, an aspect that struck the apostle Paul as particularly significant, for he makes considerable theological comment on it in 2 Corinthians 3. Moses had been up alone on the mountain communing with God. When he emerged from God's presence and came down that mountain, his face bore something of the divine radiance, and the people were afraid (Exod. 34:29-35). The radiance of Jesus came from within, of course, rather than from without as in the case of Moses, and moreover it shone from his entire being, not just his face. Could it be though that his person still showed some of the marks of that divine glory which was properly his and which the three disciples had been so privileged to see?

The story of the boy with the evil spirit shows the great power of Jesus. The description of the effects of demon-possession are outlined more fully here than in any other reference to this phenomenon in the New Testament. It looks like a severe epileptic attack, but we certainly should not assume from this that this is usually or even often a result of demon-possession. This would be to make an enormous blunder. In the New Testament, all kinds of physical phenomena are associated with such possession, while there are also accounts of similar phenomena without a hint of demonic possession. This makes us aware of the fact that mere examination of such physical phenomena cannot be an infallible guide to demon-possession. There must be some other factor indicating clearly an antipathy to the purposes of God, for this is the nature of the activity of Satan and his minions.

We keep on meeting details in which particular miracles differ from each other. Human beings differ and we need to learn, from the example of Jesus, that we must recognise this as we seek to minister to others in his name. His enquiry about the length of time the boy had had this condition, which is a detail found in Mark's account alone, seems strange. By far the most likely explanation of it is that it was a demonstration of his sympathy with the lad's suffering.

The appeal of the man to Jesus in verse 22 was expressed in terms suggesting a mixture of faith and doubt, and Jesus makes him face this fact. The reason for it was probably the inability of the disciples to deal with the boy. He may well have wondered whether the leader of this group really had special power when his followers had shown such impotence. The behaviour and actions of disciples of Jesus can, unhappily, make faith in him seem less rather than more credible.

Honesty is of great importance and especially honesty about ourselves. Unless in the presence of God we face facts about ourselves, we cannot make spiritual progress. The man declared the weakness of his faith very honestly. He did the right thing, for he looked to the object of faith for its increase. Faith is a gift of God (Eph. 6:23) and we can never work it up within ourselves. Subjectively it is due to the work of the Holy Spirit within us, who directs us to look at Christ, the great faithful object of faith. This by no means excuses lack of faith, for it hardly needs arguing that failure to trust the God who made us and loves us is always sinful. It is in fact because one of the effects of sin is to make us helpless and unable to mend our faults, that we need the inner working of the Spirit of God.

Others were coming quickly to join the crowd, drawn perhaps simply by the commotion or possibly because Jesus was now on the scene, with all his reputation for the healing of diseases and the casting out of demons. Jesus too acted swiftly, presumably not wishing to create an even greater stir that might hinder the progress of his preaching work.

The expulsion of the demon was immediate and explosive. It is not surprising therefore that the boy experienced an extreme of physical exhaustion. It was the touch of Jesus that revived him. So many people in Mark's record of the ministry of Jesus experienced the loving and powerful touch of his hand!

The disciples were perplexed about their inability to expel the demon. This perplexity is understandable, for they had been given authority over the demons by Jesus (3:15). Perhaps their experience in this realm had made them somewhat presumptuous and they had fallen into the error of thinking that Christ's commission had made them sources of power. They were in danger of forgetting that any effectiveness their ministry had was because they were God-appointed channels of divine power. Real work for God can never be done effectively simply by going through particular rituals or reciting stock formulae, as though right procedure is its key. Nor dare we imagine that gifts of ministry bestowed on us by him remove the necessity for our total dependence on him.

The reference to prayer (coupled with fasting in some manuscripts of the gospel) was a reminder of this need for total dependence on God. In fact even prayer can be ineffective unless it is an expression of our dependence on him. The glory must be his, never ours.

Some questions for personal reflection

1. How Christ-centred am I? Am I in danger of giving some idea or experience or even some secondary truth too central a place in my Christian life?

2. What experiences of powerlessness have I had as a Christian and what have I learned from them?

Chapter 11

His Journey (9:30–10:52)

The Galilean ministry, which Mark began to record in 1:14, is now practically at its end. What has been happening?

Jesus has been constantly on the move. The busy fishing town of Capernaum, so convenient for tours around Galilee and across the lake to Decapolis, appears to have been his Galilean base (see comments on 1:21; 2:1), but his mission tours have taken him farther afield, as far as Sidon (7:31), fifty miles away. Preaching and teaching were his primary activities, and we notice that there was an increasing concentration on the instruction of his disciples, something which was to continue on the last journey he was to make with them to Jerusalem. There was also a great deal of healing and exorcism.

Chapter 1 of the Gospel presented Jesus as a Man of great authority and power, compassion and grace, and at every point in his Galilean ministry these qualities were seen. People were challenged to think about his significance and to commit themselves to him. He told his disciples very frankly (from 8:31 onwards) that his destiny was death and resurrection and, long before this, we see the human forces of opposition that were intent on his death beginning to gather (from 3:6 onwards).

Remember that the disciples had lived very close to him. They had heard the sound of his voice, felt the touch of his hand and lived in the shadow of his cross, and some of them had been privileged to see his glory (9:2-8). Now, as he goes on towards Jerusalem, he is still concerned to give them teaching that will prepare them for the future.

1. The need for realism (9:30-50)

If the high mountain of the Transfiguration was Mount Hermon, as we have suggested, the journey southwards towards Jerusalem started at this point. In fact a survey of the next few chapters shows that Mark gives us even more indications of the movements of Jesus than he has done before, and that these form a series which starts at the mountain and ends in Jerusalem (9:30, 33; 10:1, 17, 32, 46; 11:1, 11). In this way he shows us that the teaching Jesus gave his disciples about the necessity for his death was followed by a journey to the place where that death would take place. In this way, he shows us that Jesus took the initiative in the final encounter with his enemies.

They went through Galilee (v. 30), but this appears to have been simply because the road to Jerusalem lay that way and not for purposes of public ministry. Mark stresses that the main occupation of Jesus at this time was disciple-teaching (v. 31). In 8:31 he had made it clear that Jesus was beginning a sustained course of teaching about his death and resurrection, and he again underlines this fact here by his double use of the past continuous tense, so that we might render the opening of verse 31, 'because he was teaching his disciples and was saying to them....' In fact, we find him occupied in this right to the end of the chapter. He was concerned to concentrate on it uninterrupted, and Mark indicates that this was why he felt the need of some secrecy at this particular time. This may serve as a warning to us that the secrecy factor in the Gospel of Mark should not always be interpreted as concealment of the messiahship of Jesus because of possible misunderstanding.

It was vital, both theologically and spiritually, that the disciples should understand and accept the fact of his coming death. The only detail added to what he had already said was the fact that he was to be 'delivered up', which is the literal meaning of the verb translated 'betrayed' in verse 31. The NIV translation seems to suggest that this refers to the human act of betrayal by Judas. If, on the other hand, we simply translate 'deliver up', which does not in itself suggest malice or treachery, it could designate God's sovereign act. In this case it would teach the same message as the word 'must' in 8:31. As Peter was to put it on the Day of Pentecost, 'this man was handed over to you by God's set purpose and foreknowledge' (Acts 2:23). We will never understand the cross if we think of it simply as an act of murder by evil men, even though, at one level, that is undoubtedly what it was. God had an amazing purpose of grace in it, as Jesus was himself to make clear to his disciples before long (10:45).

Why were the disciples afraid to ask Jesus what he meant? This is quite understandable. After all, he had rebuked Peter sternly when that disciple had reacted against his teaching about the cross (8:32,33). Not only so, but God had said, 'Listen to him!' to three of them, speaking the words in most awesome circumstances just a few days later (9:7), a command which had obvious reference to Peter's adverse reaction.

They had now arrived in Capernaum, so that they were back on familiar terrain once more. Perhaps they imagined the Galilean ministry would be resumed and that their own association with Jesus in this work would feature once again. Whether that is so or not, Mark tells us that on the journey there the proud self-seeking that was in their hearts showed itself in bickering. Our Lord's question to them, 'What were you arguing about on the road?' produced a reaction of shame. They had not come to terms with the teaching he had given them about his death. Because of this, they probably had not embraced wholeheartedly the need for self-denial and cross-carrying on which he had insisted prior to the Transfiguration (8:34ff). Certainly this passage shows that they were very much concerned with their status, a concern not normally associated with deep spirituality.

Jesus sat down, perhaps adopting the position which in those days was often associated with an intention to teach, so that by his body-language he might underline that they had an important lesson to learn. Their argument had revealed how far apart he and they were in thought and attitude. Jesus taught them the

177

nature of true greatness, and he reinforced his teaching with a visible object lesson. How do the verbal and visible lessons relate to each other? Jesus is saying that true greatness reveals itself in two qualities, willingness to be last in status and therefore to serve instead of being served, and also concern for others, especially those who cannot fend for themselves. Anyone serving in this way actually does this service for him and therefore for his Father. How different is this teaching about the greatness of loving service from the outlook of the world, and not only his world but ours! He was to emphasize the servant theme again later (10:35-45).

We notice that Jesus caused the child first of all to stand among the disciples. This would draw their attention to him and also might even suggest that a young child could be viewed as a disciple, despite his youth. Then Jesus took him into his arms, showing how warmly he welcomed children.

Now the issue of true discipleship is driven home (vv. 38-41). Unhappily, his disciples were not only self-seeking but partizan in spirit. It is remarkable that they should rebuke a man for doing, in the name of Jesus, what they had themselves recently been so unable to do (9:18). The First Epistle of John, with its emphasis on the gentle virtue of love, shows how much John was to change in his attitudes.

Jesus, by reiterating 'in my name' (see also v. 37), showed them that it was allegiance to him, not membership of the travelling party, that constituted real discipleship. Judas was to provide a sombre lesson in this by his actions later on. It is always this personal commitment to Jesus, not simply involvement with his people, that matters. For the modern church there is here a rebuke of every form of entrenched denominationalism or sectarianism. We may have our special convictions, but this should not cause us to unchurch those who, like us, have believing allegiance to Christ.

The word 'Christ' in verse 41 lacks the definite article. When it has this, as it has almost everywhere in the Gospels, it really means 'the Messiah'. Later, as we see especially in Paul's epistles, it was to become a virtual name, not simply a title. A passage like this suggests to us that Jesus himself may have occasionally anticipated this somewhat by using it this way himself.

Verses 42-50 give the solemn teaching of Jesus about judgement, stressing the awfulness of causing others to sin and of sinning oneself. The phrase, 'who believe in me', is interesting in view of the fact that this incident probably took place in the home where Jesus was staying (9:33). Notice too the word, 'these', which probably implies either the presence of children, or at least a child, when Jesus was speaking. We know from 1 Corinthians 9:5 that Cephas, which is the Aramaic equivalent of the Greek *Petros*, 'Peter', had a believing wife. This makes us wonder whether the child of verse 36 could have been Peter's son, brought to faith in Jesus because reared in a believing home.

Gehenna ('hell') gained its name from the valley of Hinnom, which was associated in the past with the pagan fires of child sacrifice (2 Chron. 28:3; 33:6) and so, not only with idolatry but with flagrant abuse of God's gift of children. Later, as we learn from extra-Biblical sources, it was the place where rubbish was destroyed. Fires burned there perpetually. It came to symbolize eternal punishment.

When Jesus speaks of the voluntary loss of limbs, his language may seem to be extreme, and we may well react in horror. If so, this is surely what he intended, because the justification for such language lies in the awfulness of the prospect of eternal punishment. The Biblical writers and speakers often use very concrete language, and we may rationalize these words of Jesus by saying that it is the actions of those bodily parts that are really in view rather than the organs themselves, but we must be careful not to take the severity from his language and so tone it down. Such language sometimes awakens unconcerned people in a way that milder expressions may not, and this may well be its intended function.

Note the way Jesus parallels life (shorthand for 'eternal life') in verse 43 and 'the kingdom of God' in verse 47. This shows

179

that if eternal life is to be conceived spiritually, so also is the kingdom of God. As Paul says, 'the kingdom of God is not a matter of eating and drinking, but of righteousness, peace and joy in the Holy Spirit' (Rom. 14:17).

Verses 44 and 46 do not appear in the NIV. In some manuscripts the words of verse 48 are anticipated at these two points, so that there is repetition, but the textual authority for their omission at these points is stronger. They are solemn enough in the verse where they certainly do occur, with their suggestion of a punishment whose source is both from within ('their worm', within the body) and from without ('the fire').

Verse 49, one of the Bible's shortest verses, is particularly difficult and has been variously understood. The most likely interpretation, because it does justice to the context, is that this is a sacrificial reference. We are to be prepared to lose hands, feet and eyes if they cause us to sin, but in fact the whole body, like a whole burnt-offering, is to be offered to God, a theme which Paul takes up in Romans 12:1. Old Testament offerings were accompanied by salt (Lev. 2:13). In our offering of ourselves to God as a living sacrifice, the fires of persecution may take the place of the sacrificial salt. If this interpretation is correct, then the references to fire in verses 48 and 49 are in strong contrast with each other.

Now Jesus goes on to illustrate a further truth from salt, and it is one that occurs also in the Sermon on the Mount (Matt. 5:13). Salt has a distinctive flavour and considerably influences food by its power to preserve it. The disciples were not to lose their distinctive flavour nor their power to influence society, including their own little community of disciples ('be at peace with each other'). Their argumentativeness and self-seeking (verses 33 and 34) were in danger of destroying peace in their midst and so of rendering their discipleship insipid.

If this teaching was given in Capernaum, Jesus was using something very familiar to illustrate his teaching, for this was a Galilean fishing port and there were on the shores of the lake facilities for salting the fish. In our own communication of the gospel, it is always helpful to seek illustrations from what is near at hand and familiar to our listeners.

2. The need for standards (10:1-12)

The journey, which probably started at Mount Hermon (see comments on 9:2) and proceeded through Galilee (9:30), including Capernaum (9:33), now continues in the direction of Jerusalem (10:1), for the reference to Judea shows that they were going farther south, and the crossing of Jordan may have been due to the refusal of passage to him by a Samaritan village (Luke 9:51-53), for Samaria lay on the direct route from Galilee to Judea.

Luke gives a very full account of this journey, and Luke 9:51 to 19:44 is often called Luke's 'Travel Document'. He is the most biographical of the Gospel writers, giving more detail about the course of the life of Christ than any of the others. It is notable, for instance, that he alone gives us a story from the boyhood of Jesus. Mark though is brief, and the events and teaching of this chapter show clearly how the Gospel he wrote centres on the gospel, for every item in it relates to the good news.

Jesus went down the east bank of the Jordan for part of the journey to Jerusalem (v. 1). Much of the Transjordanian country was always regarded as part of Israel, even though it was quite vulnerable to foreign invasions, for two and a half of Israel's tribes had been settled there in the days of Joshua (Jos. 1). It is not surprising that once again the crowds are much in evidence. Jesus may not have been along this route before (although we cannot be sure of this), but he was so well-known in Galilee by now that rumours about him must have spread southwards and eastwards quite extensively. After all, as early in the story as 3:8, we find people coming to see and hear him from as far away as Tyre and Sidon and even distant Idumea. Every miracle in fact would result in the spreading of the news about his onward progress; hence the crowds.

There were Pharisees everywhere, for every town had its synagogues, which were central to their work, and so he was liable to meet them at any time. Some of them now test him on an important practical matter, that of divorce. We know from contemporary Jewish literature that at that time the Pharisees were divided between two schools. This division affected their outlook on all kinds of practical issues. The law about divorce in Deuteronomy 24:1 refers to a man's wife becoming 'displeasing to him because he finds something indecent about her'. The school of Shammai reckoned that meant that divorce was permissible only for a sexual offence, whereas that of Hillel held that other causes of offence to the husband, even quite trivial ones, could form grounds for the ending of the marriage.

Significantly, Jesus made no reference to these discussions, but took his hearers back to the Scriptures. This is consistent with his earlier insistence that the written Word of God is not to be set aside nor devalued by the traditions of men (7:1ff). The Pharisees with whom he was conversing quoted the permission of divorce given in the Mosaic Law. Jesus however went back still further in the history and in the canonical Scriptures and referred them to Genesis 2 and the first marriage, the union of Adam and Eve. Here clearly was the original intention of God; and it certainly implied that marriage was meant by him to be permanent. This shows that Christ and his gospel are associated not with lower but if anything with higher standards than the Mosaic Law.

We should notice that the passage from Genesis relates marriage to two facts. The first of these involves a man in leaving his father and mother. A new family is to be set up. There is much to be said for an extended family situation, and this is much more part of the eastern social scene than it is now in the west, but we should balance this with the assumption here that a marriage means the setting up of a new home. Then there is the actual union itself. The physical nature of the language here ('making one flesh') seems to imply that the sexual relationship is an essential element in the making of the marriage. National laws normally recognise this by an annulment where a marriage has not been consummated. 'No longer two, but one' has, of course, other implications, for it suggests that there is to be a sharing together in a very full way, two streams of life now joined in one.

As marriage is a divinely-constituted relationship, it is a serious thing to drive a wedge between husband and wife. The words of verse 9 were probably aimed chiefly at the adulterous intervention of a third party, but of course they can have wider implications. The malicious or irresponsible behaviour of others, such as deliberately playing off one marriage partner against the other, is also ruled right out by what Jesus says here, for it can lead to marriage breakdown.

In view of the fact that the disciples had been reared under Pharisaic teaching, it is no surprise to find them asking him further about this when they went indoors again. He now went beyond what he had said in answer to the question of the Pharisees. He recognized something that was unknown among the Jews, a woman's right to divorce her husband as well as his to divorce her. This was quite revolutionary and is one of the ways in which the teaching of Jesus has raised the status of women in those parts of the world where Christianity is the dominant faith.

The precise significance of the prohibition of remarriage has been much debated in recent years, largely prompted by the marital chaos prevailing in many western countries. Some hold that the passage is to be understood as prohibiting the remarriage of divorced persons in any circumstances. This seems on the surface to be the most natural way to take it and there is little doubt that few would dispute this if we had a record of this event only in Mark's Gospel.

The incident is, however, recorded also by Matthew, and his account (Matt. 19:3-12) adds an important detail to what is said in verse 2 of Mark's account. There the question of the Pharisees has the extra words, 'for any and every reason'. It was normally taken for granted by the Jews that sexual sin severed the marriage bond, and so, when divorce issues were discussed among them, it was not this but other suggested causes which were in view.

Another addition, in Matthew 19:9, is a word which normally means 'fornication' but was sometimes employed more broadly to cover other sexual sins. If it is right to understand it, as in the NIV translation, to refer here to 'marital unfaithfulness', then, it is often argued, this makes it clear that the whole discussion was simply about divorce and remarriage for causes other than adultery. The reference to 'one flesh' in the quotation from Genesis in Mark 10:8 itself stresses physical union in marriage, and might suggest to us, it is argued, that the sexual intervention of another person raises questions as to whether the marriage bond is still binding as far as the innocent party is concerned.

As can be seen, the issue is not an easy one, and is one where both faithfulness to Scripture as conscientiously understood and also pastoral wisdom and sensitivity are needed. It is well for us to emphasize what is perfectly plain in the passage, and that is that God intended marriage to be permanent, and that if the marriage-bond has been broken, its cause is sin.

3. The need for faith (10:13-16)

It is appropriate that instruction about marriage should be followed here by teaching about children, and this shows too that Mark has had structural considerations in view in the way he sets out his material. We have already seen in 9:36 something of the gentleness of Jesus with a child, and this is reinforced here. It is not only the status of women, then, that concerned him (10:11,12) but also the value of children.

Those who brought the children to Jesus wanted them to feel his touch. Mark has already given us many examples of the powerful and compassionate touch of Jesus (1:31, 41; 5:23,41; 7:32,33; 8:23; 9:27,36). In this respect, his book is a very physical Gospel. There is no suggestion here that the children concerned were sick and in need of his touch for their healing. The parents must have felt that their little ones would benefit from contact with such a loving Person. Jesus responded by taking them into his arms and blessing them.

This is in line with modern psychological findings. More

and more we are being told that it is important for parents to cuddle their children to give them security. In this way, the sense of physical safety given by the womb is extended into life beyond it. It is perhaps significant too that in western societies where marriage breakdowns have become more and more frequent and where people, especially children, often suffer deep hurts because of this, the hug has become almost as common as the kiss as a form of greeting among relatives and friends.

Jesus had already spoken about the preciousness of children who believed in him (9:42). Mark now tells of his indignation at the attitude of the disciples, once again showing him to be a Person capable of strong emotion and therefore to be truly human. He loved these men and had borne with many of their failings with great patience, so that this shows clearly how deeply he felt about the matter.

He never lost an opportunity of teaching. What did he mean when he said, 'the kingdom of God belongs to such as these'? Children were coming to him, and, of course, the kingdom of God consists of people who have come to Jesus, drawn in faith to him as by a spiritual magnet. Children gladly receive gifts in a trustful spirit. This is the way to gain the kingdom, not, the word 'receive' seems to imply, by giving but by receiving, not by making an offer but by accepting a gift. We always begin in the life of grace by receiving. When proclaiming the kingdom at the start of his ministry (1:14,15), Jesus had called for faith. Here then was an illustration and, based on the example of the children, a virtual definition of it.

4. The need for repentance (10:17-31)

As we have already noted, there is plenty of evidence that the Gospel of Mark has been most carefully constructed. It therefore would seem most significant that teaching on the subject of faith should be immediately followed by an underlining of the need to turn from sin, which is what repentance is. The gospel as preached by Jesus had included such a call right from the beginning (1:14,15).

The way Mark presents the story certainly gives us the impression that this man was both serious and sincere. This comes out in his own actions and words and possibly also in the fact that Mark says Jesus loved him, suggesting perhaps that although not yet in the kingdom of God, he saw how earnestly he desired eternal life. The response of Jesus to him, 'Why do you call me good?' was a challenge to him to think about the words he used. They were the expression of a conventional politeness, in some ways similar to the use of the word 'sir' by children in our society when addressing a teacher. Socrates tried to encourage people to think about the words they used and to make sure they were aware of their implications. Here Jesus does this too, and in his case the point at issue was of the very greatest importance.

Is Jesus suggesting that reflection on the words he was using and on the character of the Man who stood before him might lead him to discern the divine nature of this Person? This would certainly accord with the implications of the title 'Son of God' (or sometimes simply 'Son') used of Jesus a number of times in this Gospel, and spoken as recently as 9:7 by none other than the very voice of God himself on the Mount of Transfiguration.

The form of the Greek verb in the young man's question, 'What must I do to inherit eternal life?' strongly suggests that he was asking what one thing he could do to clinch his inheritance of eternal life. He apparently thought that some action by him would clear up the whole matter once and for all, and this suggests a high measure of self-righteousness. His claim to have kept the commandments was, of course, made in ignorance of the searching teaching Jesus had given about the importance of the heart and of its motives (Matt. 5:21, 22, 27, 28). That Jesus is here said to have looked at him and loved him is a strong reminder of the amazing fact that we are the objects of God's love even when we are least aware of the depth of our need.

Jesus makes reference to six of the ten commandments, and it is instructive to note that these all relate to human relationships.

The teaching of the First Epistle of John provides us with a clue as to why this is. John tells us, for example in 1 John 2:9-11 and in 1 John 3:11-18, that how we treat others shows whether or not we truly love God. The one unexpected feature is that Jesus spoke of defrauding instead of coveting, so that he put emphasis on a practical manifestation of an attitude rather than on the attitude itself. Also, in Matthew 15:4-6, Jesus makes it clear that honouring parents was a very practical matter and that it revealed itself in giving to them. This practical concept of honouring also finds expression in Proverbs 3:9, 'Honour the LORD with your wealth, with the firstfruits of all your crops.'

So, this man probably thought of all these commandments as concerned chiefly with a person's actions and so declared that he had always kept them. The response of Jesus was also in terms of practical actions. He makes no reference to the heart, but without doubt his words showed that he knew the man's riches had found their way into his inner being. He needed to give his heart to Jesus, and he could not do so when that heart had been given to his wealth. So, as in the case of Paul (Rom. 7:7,8), it was in principle the tenth commandment (the most inward of them) that showed what was in his heart. Despite his earnestness, he loved money more than God's kingdom.

Why were the disciples so amazed by our Lord's teaching on this occasion? Because the Pharisees, making a broad generalisation from such examples as Abraham and Job, believed that riches were evidence of God's blessing, and they would have heard them teach this in the synagogues. Verse 25 needs to be understood in the light of verse 27. Riches are necessarily a hindrance if they become the main things in life, and their power to captivate us can only be overcome by God himself. In becoming Christians we begin to embrace new standards of value which are quite different from those which so often operate in worldly society.

Sometimes it has been suggested that Peter's words in verse 28 show little awareness of the great difference between what he had given up and what this man was being asked to surrender for Christ's sake. The gap, although probably considerable, may however have been less than we think, for fishing on the Lake of Galilee was a lucrative business at this time. Moreover, if I am being asked to give up all I have, does it really matter greatly how much that actually is? The widow's two small coins were not necessarily easy to surrender (12: 41-44).

Christ's words about recompense in verses 29-31 are striking for several reasons. One is that they make little reference to material possessions. In actual fact, life consists more of relationships than of things, and some of the former may be even greater causes of stumbling to us than the latter. The word translated 'home' is usually rendered 'house', but the NIV translation, which is more suggestive of family relationships than of property and which is quite permissible, seems more likely in this context to reflect the sense intended, because it introduces a series of relationship terms.

Again, we notice that this is no mere 'Prosperity Theology', encouraging us to give up things in order to get more things. How could this be when the disciples had been told by Jesus that they needed to embrace self-denial if they were to be true followers of him (8:34)? The chief fulfilment is, of course, within the church, the family of the Christ (cf. 3:31-35), into which his true disciples are welcomed. Remember too that to the list of promised blessings Jesus realistically added 'and with them, persecutions', so that there is a continuing cost for the disciple.

Again we see here the close connection between the kingdom of God and eternal life (vv. 23-25,30; cf. 9:43-47). We tend to think of the former in more corporate and the latter in more personal terms, but this suggests that both of them possess both these dimensions. Salvation is wonderfully personal, but it is also coming, with others, into acknowledgement of God's right to rule over us.

In the teaching of Jesus there is a reversal of many human values, and the words of verse 31 warn the disciples to expect surprises.

5. The need for Christ's death (10:32-45)

Faith and repentance, necessary as they are, are not the basis of salvation, for this is the death of Jesus Christ. The course of instruction on this theme that Jesus is giving his disciples becomes even more explicit, certainly in Mark's record of it, and presumably this reflects the gradual revealing of more detail as Jesus talked to these men about his destiny. He now mentions Jerusalem as the place where he is to die. There has been no reference to this so far in this Gospel, although the disciples may have picked it up from the obvious reference to the Sanhedrin, the Great Council of the Jews, in 8:31 (see comment there), for it was in Jerusalem that they normally met.

The reference to the Gentiles is the first clear indication that they would be involved at all, although this too could perhaps have been inferred from the references to his death, if this was in fact to be by execution, for, although the Sanhedrin possessed delegated authority from the Romans, this did not include the power to implement such a sentence themselves.

The wording of verse 34 makes this verse both solemn and staccato. Here four verbs follow each other in quick succession and yet each is a long word in the Greek text, three being compounded with prepositions. This use of language serves to give the whole disclosure great solemnity without robbing the account of any of its vividness. This sequence of words shows us that the sufferings of Christ, apparently following swiftly on each other, were steadily to intensify. In fact they involved successive acts of humiliation as well as the infliction of pain.

The first three of them bear a striking similarity to the destiny of the Servant of the Lord as outlined in Isaiah 50:6 and of course the final one to Isaiah 53. Perhaps Jesus had these Old Testament passages in his mind when speaking in this way, for we know he believed that his sufferings fulfilled Old Testament Scripture (9:12). It is ironic that when the Roman soldiers mocked Jesus, this was probably intended largely as an insult to the Jews, whose religious leaders had in fact handed him over to the Roman authorities.

A study of 8:31, 9:31 and this passage shows that, although the description of his sufferings is not always expressed in the same way, this is not true of his resurrection. He never amplifies it and never details it apart from the reference to a three-day interval between his death and resurrection. They were not ready for fuller disclosure and, of course, whereas his sufferings went on over a period, his resurrection was instantaneous.

The understanding gulf strongly suggested in verse 32 is starkly presented in the shocking request of the sons of Zebedee, prompted perhaps by the answer of Jesus to Peter (vv. 28-31). We should remember that James and John and Simon Peter had worked together in the fishing business and that Zebedee, the father of James and John, had presumably been the head of the firm. Perhaps they imagined they should have been preferred to their father's employee.

Jesus teaches them that willingness to suffer and to take the lowly place make for spiritual greatness, which has no connection with pride in status. Little did they know it, but there certainly would be men on either side of Jesus, when he hung on the cross (15:32), but they would not have wished for such places!

The cup and the baptism were standard terms for the wrath of God and for suffering, and they have a background in the Old Testament (Pss. 75:8 and 69:1,2). Jesus was in fact to endure penal suffering as a substitute for sinners, as he would soon teach his disciples (10:45). That they too would receive a cup and undergo a baptism meant that they would themselves be called on to suffer for his sake, as he had already indicated to them (8:34f), although not, of course, with an atoning purpose, for that could be his alone. 'There was no other good enough to pay the price of sin; he only could unlock the gate of heaven and let us in.'

The other ten disciples were actually no better than these two brothers, for they too were motivated by the same desire for places of authority and privilege. Jesus therefore calls them all together to teach them. No doubt they will have seen something of the pomp and ceremony surrounding those reckoned important among their Gentile rulers. They were to be completely different, says Jesus. In this, as in so many other ways, the values of the kingdom of God are quite different from those of the world. The use of the term 'minister' by churches, and its meaning, 'servant', should be a constant reminder of this. Luke also records for us a saying of Jesus spoken at the Last Supper, 'I am among you as one who serves' (Luke 22:27). He suited his actions to his words, for he is himself as ever the supreme example of his own teaching as the story of the washing of the disciples' feet in John 13 shows us.

The great saying of 10:45, which many have regarded as the central declaration of Jesus in this Gospel, is remarkable for the clarity with which it interprets his death in terms of substitutionary atonement. The preposition translated 'for' in verse 45, has the force, 'in place of'. The use of the word 'many' in this connection is probably an echo of Isaiah 53:11,12 and the picture there of the Servant of God bearing sin and its penalty as a Substitute for sinners.

6. The need for faith (10:46-52)

The story of Blind Bartimaeus here strongly suggests that it came from an eyewitness, presumably Peter, who carried in his memory how large the crowd was, the fact that many called on the blind man to stop shouting, the fact that Jesus stopped, and that the blind man threw aside his cloak. After all, not one of these details was essential to the story, but all give it extra vividness. He was a hearer as well as an onlooker, for he recalled what a noise the man made to secure attention from Jesus.

Bartimaeus addressed Jesus as 'Son of David'. This was a standard title for the Messiah among the Jews, and had its basis in the Old Testament (e.g. in Jer. 23:5,6), although our Lord taught later (12:35-37) that it was not fully adequate because he was God's Son, not simply David's. Probably the crowds of pilgrims were already beginning to use this kind of language in connection with Jesus, if not in communal shouts (as in 11:9,10), at least in comments that Bartimaeus overheard.

This story again teaches that Christ mediates the blessings of God and also that it is faith that appropriates these blessings, two lessons of paramount importance for the New Testament gospel. So the chapter comes to an appropriate close.

Some questions for personal reflection

1. Are there ways in which my discipleship is unrealistic, in expecting service to be rewarded in this life, in expecting that prayer will bring deliverance from suffering rather than grace to bear it – or in some other way?

2. Christ's Kingdom has been called, 'the upside-down kingdom', because it reverses so many of the values we hold. What examples of this can I recall?

Chapter 12

His Arrival (11:1-26)

We have now reached a most important point in the ministry of Jesus. How differently the Gospel writers tell the story of their Lord! Each presents a true account and yet each is different, for each has his own particular selection of material and his own emphasis. This becomes particularly evident in their accounts of the final events.

Take Mark and Luke, for example. Both had a strong sense of drama, and the Spirit of God used this in their presentation of the life and ministry of Jesus, but they expressed that dramatic sense in quite different ways. One striking example of this is the way the two writers deal with the disclosure that it was at Jerusalem Jesus would die.

Luke uses the word 'Jerusalem' over thirty times in his Gospel, and this is about the same as the number of its occurrences in the other three Gospels put together. In contrast to both Mark and Matthew, he tells us what Jesus and Moses and Elijah were talking about on the Mount of Transfiguration. 'They spoke about his departure, which he was about to bring to fulfilment at Jerusalem' (Luke 9:31). It is clear from all that he says about Jerusalem in that Gospel that it was to be a place of destiny both for Jesus himself and for the Jews. Its name came to have a somewhat ominous sound. In this way, Luke builds up the expectation of his readers.

Mark does it quite differently. He delays this revelation about Jerusalem. The discerning reader with some knowledge of the Jewish background to the story would perhaps pick up something. He would note the references to visiting parties of Pharisees from Jerusalem (3:22; 7:1) and indications that the death of Jesus would take place at the hands of the Sanhedrin, the Great Council of the Jews which met in Jerusalem (as was noted in the comment on 8:31). Many readers though would not know where these things were to take place, and would be left wondering. Most of the story so far had taken place in Galilee. Was this then to be the place of destiny?

At last, in 10:32-34, the disclosure is made to the disciples: 'They were on their way up to Jerusalem.... Again he took the Twelve aside and told them what was going to happen to him. "We are going up to Jerusalem and the Son of Man will be betrayed...." ' At the start of chapter 11, our anticipation increases still more with the words, 'As they approached Jerusalem...' (v. 1).

1. The people's praise (11:1-10)

Like so many others in Mark's Gospel, this event is vividly presented by the author, with many a detail likely to have come from an eye-witness, and so probably from Peter. The references to Bethany and to the Mount of Olives make it clear that Jesus and his disciples were travelling the normal route from Jericho. This road has a place in the parable of the Good Samaritan as told by Luke (Luke 10:25-37). It was a steeply sloping road from the deep depression of the lower Jordan valley to the mountain height that overlooked the Holy City. It was always thronged with pilgrims at Passover time. The village to which Jesus sent the two disciples is not specified in the record, but may have been the otherwise unknown Bethphage, the name of which means 'house of figs'.

The mission of the two disciples raises questions which cannot be answered with full confidence because of the limitations of the information given. Did Jesus know about the animal by normal human sources of knowledge, or is Mark suggesting special divine knowledge? If the former, had he made a definite arrangement with the owner at some earlier time? It is a good principle, in handling Scripture, not to assume a miracle when a purely natural interpretation of an event can be given in such a way as to do full justice to the details recorded by the

Biblical writer. On the other hand, we have to be open to the possibility of a miracle and not close our minds to it.

What does 'the Lord needs it' (v. 3) mean? The word translated 'Lord', which implies superior authority, was used with many shades of meaning, ranging from a polite acknowledgement of another person's slightly higher status, rather like our own 'sir', to an awed submission to the Creator of the universe. Was the owner of the animal a disciple and were the two men simply to ask for it in the name of Jesus so that it might be loaned to him? Surely not, for we would have expected Mark to tell us this clearly.

Does 'the Lord' simply mean 'God'? This is certainly possible, but the assertion that he would send the animal back shortly makes it seem more likely that it is a reference to Jesus. Certainly it is not Mark's custom to describe Jesus as 'Lord' in his narrative before the resurrection, but there are at least two thought-provoking uses of the term in earlier chapters. There is the reference to him as 'Lord of the Sabbath' (2:28), which certainly has transcendent implications because of the fact that the Sabbath was divinely ordained. There is also the very significant change of wording that we noticed between 5:19 and 5:20 (See the reference to this at that point in the commentary). These facts strengthen the probability that the reference at this point is to Jesus.

Why are we making a point of this? For the simple reason that if the disciples understood the term to refer to Jesus, the people standing by would see it as a reference to God, for to a Jew 'the Lord' normally simply meant 'God', the true God, their God. Jesus himself would know this. It gives us therefore a glimpse into his divine self-consciousness. He was going into Jerusalem and to death in full awareness as to who he was, a point made quite explicitly in the Gospel of John: 'Jesus knew that the Father had put all things under his power, and that he had come from God and was returning to God' (John 13:3).

Luke tells us that the ass's colt was unbroken ('a colt tied there, which no-one has ever ridden', Luke 19:30). This means that it would be very difficult to ride, prompting an experienced horseman's comment, 'What hands he must have had!' Of course God has all power, but we need not attribute this strength to the deity of Jesus rather than to his humanity. In human terms he must have been a strong Man, used to manual work and to handling heavy material.

Why did Jesus choose this way of entering Jerusalem? It was, after all, a moment of high drama, one of the most dramatic in his whole ministry, and we might have expected some other animal than a humble ass. There were good reasons for his choice. To ride in on a horse would have been disastrous. The horse was a military animal. To enter the city in that fashion would have fostered the notion that he was to be the conventional warrior Messiah expected by the Jews at this time, and, perhaps, that his immediate purpose was to free the people from Roman rule and to take over the reins of government in the capital city. This could have provoked all kinds of violent scenes with much bloodshed. Nothing could have been more remote from the purpose of God.

An ass, on the other hand, strongly suggested peace rather than war. Solomon, the original kingly son of David, had accumulated many horses in the land (1 Kings 10:26), contrary in fact to Deuteronomy 17:16, which occurs in the divine constitution for the kings of Israel. David, his father, although himself a man of war, had a much simpler lifestyle than Solomon, and was, in any case, the specially named forerunner of the Messiah, who was to be the Son of David (10:47; cf. 11:10). Jesus would not emulate the ostentatious pomp of Solomon but rather the simplicity of Solomon's father.

There was also a special prophetic reason for the choice of an ass's colt. Zechariah 9:1-8 gives a dramatic account of the victorious march of the Lord from northern Syria to Jerusalem, coming to its climax in the assertion, 'I will defend my house against marauding forces. Never again will an oppressor overrun my people, for now I am keeping watch.' The same kind of martial theme recurs in the latter part of that chapter, but in between there is a verse in which the language of warfare and of victory disappears and is replaced by the language of peace and the very surprising picture of a victorious entry to Jerusalem on an ass (Zech. 9:9).

The people who witnessed the entry of Jesus were very excited and they shouted words from Psalm 118:25,26: 'Hosanna! Blessed is he who comes in the name of the LORD!' 'Hosanna' means 'save', and so is itself a quotation from the psalm, where, in verse 25, the cry goes up, 'O LORD, save us; O LORD, grant us success!' This is a psalm of praise and joy. The psalmist's references to the gates, to the building of an edifice, to the house of the Lord and to a 'festal procession' provide evidence that this was a processional song to be sung by the people on the way to the temple to worship.

There is another feature of it that made it most appropriate at this particular Passover Feast. Much of the psalm is written in the first person singular and it is often thought that the person who speaks is the king. Eventually however this gives way to the first person plural, and the words the people quoted on Palm Sunday come soon after this. Here then, the people of Israel who had been bereft of a king of David's dynasty for centuries at last have a king amongst them again, going up with them to the temple. He was in fact the ultimate Davidic monarch, the very Messiah himself.

What was in the minds of the people when they used the words of this psalm? It is true that it was always used at the Passover and that these were folk anticipating this annual event which would take place just a few days later. In fact the imminence of the Passover would have been the very reason for the presence in the city of a great many of them. Yet to follow it with a reference to 'the coming kingdom of our father David' indicates that they must have recognized the Messianic role of Jesus, for this phrase has very evident Messianic implications.

The whole event was, of course, initiated by Jesus. As we have seen, he had not broadcast the fact during his Galilean

197

ministry or on the road to Jerusalem, just the reverse, but he must have believed the time had come for an open assertion of his messiahship. We should bear in mind that this Palm Sunday entrance into Jerusalem occurred only a few days before his death, as this will provide a perspective from which to view what happened in the days between the two events. Many of the things that happened furnished a kind of teaching programme, instructing the observer in the meaning of messiahship as Jesus understood it. As we read Mark's account, we see more and more clearly how differently Jesus viewed the messianic role from the way it was presented in the teaching given in the synagogues.

2. The temple's cleansing (11:11, 15-18)

We have already noted Mark's dramatic gift. Drama frequently surprises us, with several twists and turns as the story runs its course. At this point, Mark records an event that must have caused amazement to those who had witnessed the Triumphal Entry, simply because it seems the very opposite of dramatic. Paradoxically (and we will meet a good deal of paradox in Mark's story from this point onwards), it is at the same time highly dramatic, simply because of its unexpected nature. We recognise that a 'dramatic pause' has a real function in the acting of a play, and an audible whisper may command more attention than the loudest of shouts.

We will explore this a little further. The story of the Triumphal Entry induces in the reader a sense that everything is building up to a great denouement. Then comes verse 11, with its seeming anti-climax. It was rather like going up a very long and wide drive to find nothing but a tiny house at the end of it. Not only did Jesus do hardly anything, he did not even stay overnight in the city which he had entered to such acclaim. No doubt Mark had a purpose in writing verse 11. He probably intended his readers to go back a few chapters to re-read the teaching Jesus gave to his disciples on the way south from Galilee. In this teaching, of course, we find the clue we need to enable us to understand. It was not military victory but rejection and suffering that were to be the portion of Jesus very soon.

Instead of taking kingly power, Jesus went into the temple and 'looked around at everything'. How significant is that simple statement! The abuses against which he would act in judgement the next day would be evident around him. What hidden abuses too would be seen by One whose eye could penetrate beyond outward shows of piety, of which there were probably plenty in evidence, to discern inner motives!

It was too late in the day to follow the course of action which must inevitably result from what he had seen. Probably by then the temple courts were almost deserted and what he intended to do was of such a character that it was important for it to be seen by many people. The next day however he took action. The delay may have served another purpose. To enter the temple and cleanse it immediately on entering Jerusalem might well have fostered the expectation that this was the beginning of a violent programme that would culminate in the military overthrow of the Romans. Instead there was an interval, during which perceptive onlookers could have noted the fact that a comparatively unimpressive entry was followed by an even more unimpressive first act in 'the city of the great king'.

A scandalous trade was carried on by men employed by the chief priests. The Old Testament Law made the priests responsible for examining all animals brought by the people for sacrifice, to make sure they had no blemishes that would make them unsuitable for this purpose (cf. Lev. 4:28; 6:6). The chief priests, consisting largely of the high priest's family, flagrantly abused the real purpose of this regulation, which was of course to emphasise that God should have nothing but the best from his people. They saw in it a possible avenue for much financial gain. They instructed their fellow-priests to reject, on some pretext, the animals brought for sacrificial purposes by the people and to offer 'suitable' animals at extortionate prices. Many of the people would feel they had no choice but to settle for this.

As John tells us (John 2:13-17), Jesus had apparently acted against this trade early in his ministry. We do not need to regard the two passages as accounts of the same event, with the Johannine placed early in the Gospel for a symbolic purpose. This is not impossible, but it is not necessary to take such a view. Our knowledge of human nature will make us aware that such a trade was most likely to have re-established itself. The chief priests would certainly not accept the great loss of face they would suffer if they accepted what Jesus had done. They could probably, in their imagination, hear regular visitors to the temple asking, 'Whatever happened to the animals?' They could not risk that.

Here was Messianic authority indeed, but directed not, as the people would have expected, against the Romans, but against fellow-Jews, and the religious leaders of the people at that! In this respect it was not unlike the fact that John the Baptist had called Jews to recognise their sinfulness and to be baptized (1:4,5).

The chief priests now join those who had been plotting the death of Jesus ever since the early days of his Galilean ministry (3:6). If these plots were to issue in a judicial decision to put him to death, this could not be done without their involvement and particularly that of the high priest, for he was the president of the Sanhedrin, the only Jewish body in the country that could pass sentence of death, although of course it was the Romans who carried it out. The forces of evil were now marshalling for their final onslaught on God's great Servant-King, and it is important for us to remember that they were predominantly religious. It is a sobering fact that religion can be an enemy of God.

3. The nation's judgement (11: 12-14, 19-26)

The character of Jesus is widely admired, and not only by Christians but also by people of quite different religious persuasion. Few events in his life have been criticised adversely, but the cursing of the fig tree is probably the chief one among those that have. A number of commentators frankly deny that it happened, not because there is any real evidence against its authenticity, but simply because they find the whole thing incredible and out of character with the other actions of Jesus.

But is it really incredible? It is said that it is the only miracle of destruction recorded in the Gospels, but even this is not completely true. We must not forget the destruction of the swine which followed the exorcising of the Gerasene demoniac (5:11-13), although of course this was a negative aspect of an act which had wonderfully positive results for the man concerned. Certainly we cannot conceive of Jesus cursing this tree simply out of annoyance because he was expecting to be able to eat figs from it and found there were none. This would certainly be completely out of character.

Some have suggested that it is really fiction and that it was based on knowledge that Jesus had told a parable about a fig-tree, the parable found in Luke 13:6-9. Why though should we accept the parable and deny the miracle? Certainly they both have the same basic message, although in the parable the fig-tree is reprieved for a while! There are quite a number of Old Testament passages where we see the prophets acting out their messages. Isaiah 20 and Ezekiel 4 give us two examples among many. If Jesus was a prophet, should we not think rather in terms both of a spoken and an acted prophecy, but with slightly different applications?

The explanation of this act of Jesus is to be found in the way Mark has positioned it in his Gospel. As we have already seen in chapter 5 in the stories of the woman subject to bleeding and that of the raising of the daughter of Jairus, he has a tendency to interweave stories. This interweaving is nowhere more significant nor more deserving of notice than it is here.

There was plenty of precedent for the portraying of judgement on the nation by the use of a symbol from the plant kingdom, as we see, for instance, in Isaiah's powerful song of the judgement on the vineyard (Isa. 5:1-7), which incidentally our Lord was to adapt to his own message, as we will see in Mark 12. In Jeremiah

24, the people of Israel are represented by two baskets of figs, one bad and the other good. So the cursing of the fig tree here seems to be symbolic of God's judgement on those who carried on the 'bad fig' tradition in Israel. The cleansing of the temple pointed to the evil trade in the temple as a cause of this judgement, and the action of Jesus on that occasion was a foretaste of it.

Mark says it was not the season for figs. This seems at first sight to pose a major difficulty, as it would appear to make the judgement quite inappropriate, even irrational. A little knowledge of the development of fig-trees in the Holy Land throughout the year, however, helps us to understand. Two months or so before the fig harvest the leaves appear on the trees. At the same time, little 'pages' (the word appears, incidentally, as part of the name 'Bethphage', v. 1), small green fruit, normally appear with the leaves. They are edible although not particularly pleasant to taste.

This tree, possibly unlike the others around it, had leaves, and therefore it might be expected to have these small green fruit on it. This means therefore that, to the observer from a distance, it promised what it could not fulfil, rather like a mirage which suggests the presence of an oasis in the desert. Could anything be a better symbol for the showy but barren religious leaders of his day?

Mark certainly seems to suggest, by recording Peter's comment on seeing the withered tree, that this act of judgement on the tree was performed in order to teach the disciples. He does not spell out for us what the lessons actually were. Perhaps he thought it so obvious, especially because the cursing and the withering occurred before and after the cleansing of the temple. This should suggest to his readers, as it was presumably meant also to suggest to the disciples, what the meaning was. The life of the people of Israel had a religious sham at its core, and it could not avoid the curse of divine judgement.

Often God may teach his people more than one lesson through a particular event. Not only were the disciples meant to see the symbolism but they were also to learn the power of faith in God. This made the event a vehicle for teaching two lessons.

No doubt the reference to the removal of a mountain (v. 23) was determined by the greatness of the miracle entailed. In the following verse, Jesus says, 'whatever you ask for in prayer, believe that you have received it, and it will be yours.' Does this mean that God gives us 'carte blanche' to make any request, no matter how unreasonable or how obviously out of harmony with his holy will, in the confidence that it will be answered with a miracle? Surely not! That would make nonsense of all the teaching of Scripture that implies that God's will and ours are often at variance. How incredible that we should now be taught that God is actually prepared to pander to our wants, whatever they are!

The truth is that this passage is not about the content of our prayers but rather about our attitude in praying. So it does not teach us what to pray for – there are plenty of other passages that instruct us in that – but rather, on the assumption that we know what to pray for, it tells us what should be our frame of mind as we bring our requests to God. We are to believe and not to doubt. We can, of course, only do this if we are in harmony with God's will as we understand it from his Word, and not simply trying to use prayer to fulfil our own selfish desires.

Jesus goes on, in verse 25, to stress also the importance of being right with God and with others when we pray. Is there a connection with the previous verse and if so what is it? It may well lie in the fact that faith needs soil in which to grow, and that an unforgiving heart contains poisons that cause faith to shrivel up. Experience certainly confirms this sobering fact. Matthew and Luke both record the Lord's Prayer, which also makes reference to this (Matt. 6:12-15; Luke 11:4), and Matthew also recounts a story Jesus told about the importance of a forgiving spirit (Matt. 18:21-35).

Some questions for personal reflection

1. What can I learn from the Palm Sunday story as to the nature of true greatness?

2. Why should a miracle of judgement seem out of place when the Gospels contain dozens of miracles of blessing? If this is my reaction, what does this tell me about my view of God?

Chapter 13

His Answers (11:27–12:44)

The Gospel account of the life of Jesus is full of surprises. We see here that he spent much of 'Holy Week' teaching in the temple. Is this really what we would have expected? I think most of us would answer 'No!' After all, we have the evidence of his own words that he knew he was going to die, that Jerusalem would be the place of his death, and that it would take place as a result of a judicial decision of the religious leaders (10:33,34). In view of all this we might have expected him to be self-absorbed. Instead here he is showing concern for others and spending time in the last week of his life answering their questions. How extraordinary too that he should choose the temple as his main teaching place at this time! Here the religious leaders who hated him would have such easy access to him.

So his presence in the temple, teaching the people, tells us a great deal about his character, about his concern for others, about his commitment to the will of his Father. Of course, we should not really be surprised, as his conduct now was in perfect accord with what he had done throughout his ministry, where these concerns had always been his priorities.

As in chapters 2 and 3 and on a number of other occasions (as we see, for example in John 7 and 8), we find Jesus deeply involved in controversy. Just as the godly and the ungodly co-exist in the same world, so the truth of God never exists in a vacuum. It is present in the same world as error, and of necessity comes into conflict with it. We need to realise too that false teaching is not just negative, the mere absence of truth. There is something about error that is aggressive. Often those who are gripped by it mount an assault against the truth.

The questions raised here each highlighted issues important

in connection with the Person and work of our Lord, as we shall see. This fits in with Mark's purpose to show the great significance of Jesus. So our interest in the questioners should not overshadow our interest in Jesus himself as he is presented here. Constantly we need to keep in mind the perspective indicated in 1:1, with the focus of our attention always on him.

1. The question about authority (11:27-12:12)

In speaking about his coming death, Jesus has already made reference to the chief priests, the teachers of the law and the elders (v. 27, cf. 8:31), the three groups who together made up the Sanhedrin, the Great Council of the Jews, presided over by the High Priest of the day. The Romans had delegated some authority to this particular body and from time to time they constituted a judicial court, so that Jesus clearly implied that he would be put to death after a formal trial.

It is not surprising that the first question that day was addressed to him by a group that included the chief priests. After all, it was they who were responsible for the temple and also for the trade in sacrificial animals. How incensed they must have been by his actions when he cleansed the temple (11:18)! These actions had raised the issue of authority most sharply. The others too, because of their involvement in the Sanhedrin, would have an authority concern.

Instead of giving a direct answer, Jesus put a counter-question to them. This too was related to the authority issue. John the Baptist had been quite a phenomenon in the land. Since great crowds of people went out to hear him preach and to be baptised by him (1:4-8), his significance must have been the subject of a good deal of debate both by the common people and also by the religious authorities. Who was he? Why had he appeared at this time? After all, he professed to be a prophet, and this would make him the first authentic one for several hundreds of years. Not only so, but he had voiced strong criticism of the religious leaders, as we see, for example, in Matthew 3:7-12. There was plenty of precedent for this kind of thing, for the Old Testament prophets had often criticised the religious leaders of their day, as we see, for instance, in Jeremiah 2:8 and in Ezekiel 22:23-29, but it was hardly calculated to make him friends in the religious hierarchy.

Jesus referred not to the teaching of John but rather to his baptism. What is the significance of this? It was because it is one thing to accept teaching in theory and quite another to demonstrate commitment to it. John had called for personal repentance and for baptism as outward evidence of it. Today it is often the case that a person of a non-Christian faith may express much interest in the gospel of Christ without encountering too much antagonism but that this begins to come strongly once he or she has been baptised.

John's call to the people to be baptized must have been highly offensive to the religious leaders. Until then, nobody had called Jews to baptism. We have clear evidence, outside the New Testament, that the practice of baptism existed in Judaism around AD 70 (and it was probably practised before this), yet it was not for Jews but for Gentiles who had repented of their former paganism and were seeking to become proselytes, which meant their official entry to the Jewish faith.

The religious leaders and the common people probably thought quite differently about John the Baptist. If the crowds of ordinary folk heard Jesus with delight, as Mark tells us in 12:37, it is more than likely that they listened with rapt attention to John. We certainly get the impression that large numbers of them came to be baptized by him, for Mark says that 'the whole Judaean countryside and all the people of Jerusalem went out to him' (1:5). For the leaders, at that moment, however, it was convenience, not truth, that was important, and this is always a wrong way of assessing relative values.

Jesus would not give a direct answer to their hypocrisy. Is there any point in answering people who have no concern for truth? Such folk have no openness, no willingness to be convinced. When, a few days later, as Luke tells us (Luke 23:8-12), Jesus stood before Herod, who put many questions to him,

Jesus did not say anything in reply. On the present occasion, however, he does give them an answer, but an indirect one, and he does this by using his favourite medium, the parable.

They knew the Old Testament well and so the description of the vineyard would immediately remind them of Isaiah 5:1-7. In that passage, instead of speaking, the prophet sang God's word to the people of Israel. He pictured them as a vineyard, loved and carefully tended by its master, and this description is given in very soft and gentle Hebrew, with an avoidance of strong consonants such as gutturals. Then the thought, the language in which it is expressed, and even the poetic rhythm, changes, for most unexpectedly the vineyard produced only wild grapes and so it became subject to the master's judgement. Israel itself was the vineyard. At two points in the unfolding of the story, the prophet had asked the opinion of the listeners and they began to realise they were actually inside the parable. It was about them, and the message God had for them was anything but comfortable.

Just the same happened now. Jesus adapted this parable to a new use, taking the vineyard analogy further and making application of it to the present situation. In this version, the vineyard was let out to tenants. The master sent servants to them to gain the fruit that was his rightful due, and the presumption is that this had been agreed with them as a condition of their tenancy. Who then were these servants? Without doubt, Jesus intended the prophets and there can be little doubt that the people would have seen this. It is not likely, however, that our Lord intended us to identify particular individuals from what he said, although, of course, John the Baptist was clearly in his mind as one of these because of the context in which he gave this parable.

It is always very serious to reject God's message, and it was a most solemn matter that the nation had so often refused God's word, whether through the Old Testament prophets or through John the Baptist. What though was the ultimate in rebellion against God's authority? It was to reject his Son. It is clear here that Jesus appears to assume his enemies had some realisation that he was a special person, for in the parables the tenants say, 'This is the heir. Come, let's kill him, and the inheritance will be ours.' This has fearful implications, for it means that they were sinning against the light.

The parable describes the prophets as servants, while the last to be sent is the master's son. This not only shows the uniqueness of Jesus, but at the same time asserts his continuity with the prophets, for in the story the servants and the son were all sent by the master. The distinction of Jesus as God's Son plus the phrase, 'last of all,' make links between this parable and the Epistle to the Hebrews. In that great Epistle, Jesus is presented in all kinds of ways as the fulfilment of the Old Testament. He is also shown to be better than its particular persons, such as Moses and Joshua, better too than its offices, such as that of the Levitical priests, and even better than institutions such as the sacrifices. A study of the Old Testament, of course, reveals that all of these people were sent by God, and all these offices and institutions were divinely ordained. This superiority and yet continuity included the prophets, as is clear to us from Hebrews 1:1-2, 3:1-6. So then the Son of God brings the lengthy history of God's special revelation to Israel to its conclusion in a blaze of light.

Again, as in 11:9, Psalm 118 is quoted, but this time by Jesus himself. Perhaps he quoted it now because the people had used it during his entry to Jerusalem and also it would be in their minds because of its invariable use at times of Passover. It looks like an implicit recognition that the people were right in acknowledging him as Messiah, even though their image of messiahship was very much out of focus.

The capstone (v. 10) was the final stone inserted in a building. If it fitted perfectly, this vindicated the architects in their planning as well as the builders in their construction work. In the psalm this capstone appears to have been Israel. How then could Jesus apply it to himself? For exactly the same reason that Matthew was able to apply an Old Testament passage about

Israel to him (Matt. 2:15; cf. Hosea 11:1). Jesus was the incarnation of all God intended Israel to be: humble, obedient, trustful, doing God's will from the heart, truly representing him in the world. Even more fully and perfectly than Nathanael, it could be said of him that he was 'a true Israelite, in whom there is nothing false' (John 1:47), and the true Servant of God called 'Israel' while also distinguished from that nation (Isa. 49:3, 5,6).

In the psalm itself, the builders who rejected the stone appear to have been the pagan nations that surrounded Israel. In the application these builders are now the religious leaders of the nation itself. What a shock for these men to realise that Jesus was saying that their rejection of his messianic claims was an evidence of ungodliness that was on a par with paganism's antagonism against Israel!

2. The question about taxes (12:13-17)

The words, 'they sent', in verse 13 seem to suggest that the next group of interlocutors came on the initiative of the Sanhedrin rather than their own. If so this is extraordinary, for the Herodians would hardly have been regarded as *persona grata* by that body. Matthew 22:15-17 however sheds some light on this, for it is apparent there that at first the group consisted simply of the Pharisees, who then made contact with their new allies, the Herodians. So we see that the unholy and unnatural alliance between these two parties, noted earlier in 3:6, was still very much in place. How badly they must have wanted to get rid of Jesus!

The approaches of these two parties to the payment of taxes would have been quite different. The Herodians, supporting Herod, Rome's puppet, would have been in favour of the payment, while the Pharisees would pay only with the greatest reluctance. A flat refusal to pay was the stance of the Zealots, whose antipathy to the Roman occupation took a very active form. Either a positive or a negative answer would have played into the hands of the questioners, for a positive answer would alienate support from many of the people who anticipated that their Messiah would be emphatically anti-Roman. To ally himself with the Zealots, on the other hand, would probably have meant immediate arrest when his answer became known to the Roman officials.

Their flattering, hypocritical words in verse 14 were meant to suggest they were treating him as an independent arbiter. In this they were trading on the fact that he would anticipate they would be at variance with each other over the matter they were raising with him together. Of course it is possible that their words were said with a sarcastic sneer, and so were more cynical than hypocritical. In either case, they reveal what kind of spirit they had.

Tertullian, the early Christian writer, made a comment on this incident and on the reply of Jesus, and what he said is justly famous. He said that we are to give the coin of political tribute to Caesar because his image is on it, but that we are to give God ourselves because his image is on us. Here then Jesus mediates the radical demand of God, a demand which in fact finds a place also for a proper relationship to those in authority in the world of men. Our membership of the kingdom of God does not release us from our earthly citizenship. Rather it means we are to be good citizens as part of God's vocation for us. To call this a 'dual citizenship' concept, as some have done, although accurate up to a point, is also somewhat misleading, for the two citizenships are not equal. Our earthly citizenship is always to be viewed within the context of our heavenly one and never *vice versa.*

Our Lord's treatment of this question was typical of many of his utterances, which so often encapsulated in concrete form a great principle very widely applicable. We all have to come to terms with the principle underlined here, but for some Christians this is not at all easy. When the decrees of God and of 'Caesar' are flatly contradictory, it is evident that we must obey God rather than man, as the apostles said to the Sanhedrin when it commanded them not to speak or teach at all in the name of Jesus, so going against what he had expressly commanded them to do (Acts 4:18-20; cf. Acts 1:8).

There is a close relationship between the ethical teaching of the New Testament epistles and the ethical principles established in our Lord's teaching. Often the former amplify the latter and apply them to a variety of situations. Consider, for instance, the way that in Romans 13:1-7 Paul applies the principle found here in our Lord's teaching. There once again it is the payment of taxes which is most in view. Peter applies the same principle in 1 Peter 2:13-17, where various structures of authority are in view. The Christian is to be a good citizen and to be so as one aspect of his or her submission to God's will.

3. The question about resurrection (12:18-27)

Another planned group question is asked by the Sadducees, the party of the chief priests. We know less about them than we do about the Pharisees. They have left us little literature, and much of the information we gain about them from early sources comes to us in literature written by Pharisees. Because there was some antagonism between the two groups, we cannot be sure how much of this is free from bias, so that we cannot put too much reliance on it. Another source of information, of course, is the New Testament itself, and there is a an important reference to their beliefs in Acts 23:8, where Luke alludes to their rejection of resurrection and of the existence of angels and spirits.

It is clear that their interest in religion was shallower than that of the Pharisees. 'Professionalism' in a bad sense has so often been the enemy of true faith and it was so in their case. They were priests and they officiated in Jerusalem at the national shrine. They had a legal right to receive tithes from the people and also parts of many of the sacrificial animals. These had some financial value and so they were tempted to greed. When they yielded to it, they really became the spiritual descendants of Hophni and Phinehas, the sons of Eli the priest (1 Sam. 2:12-17), anything but a good precedent.

We do know that they believed all doctrines must be established from the Pentateuch, the Five Books of Moses. It is not quite clear how they viewed the rest of the Old Testament. Probably they treated this too as the Word of God but as less fundamental for belief than the primary Scriptures, the Pentateuch. Their special concern with the Five Books of Moses is not surprising. They were priests and so, by the nature of their vocation, they had to spend time in the study of the ritual law, which has a place of importance in four out of the five books of the Pentateuch.

Theologically, the Pharisees were much closer to our Lord. It was of course on the vital issues of the person and work of the Messiah and the attitude of God to the penitent sinner that Jesus and the Pharisees parted company, but on other matters their outlook was similar. Luke tells us of a time when Paul, himself a Pharisee who had been converted to Christ, was brought before the Sanhedrin, which was composed of Pharisees and Sadducees. In this mixed company, he referred to the resurrection of the dead. This had the effect of dividing the council, as his fellow-Pharisees accepted the doctrine of the resurrection while the Sadducees did not (Acts 23:6-10).

Two groups who are sharply divided and yet who often meet, tend to employ stock questions and stock arguments with which to confront members of the opposite party, especially if they find that such questions prove very difficult to answer. The story the Sadducees tell our Lord here looks like a stock question of this sort that they would often put to Pharisees. It was based on the 'levirate marriage' prescriptions of Deuteronomy 25:5-10, and it was calculated to make the doctrine of the resurrection seem absurd.

It is very important for understanding our Lord's answer to see that in it he was basing his teaching on the Pentateuch, so that it should carry conviction to his Sadducean hearers. There is a lesson here for us. We can begin from any convictions we share with others. For instance, there is common ground we share with Jewish people, because of our common acceptance of the Old Testament, and even the simple belief in the existence of God can be a starting-point with many other people.

What is the point Jesus is making? He draws attention to a

grammatical detail, laying emphasis on the use of the present tense in the passage from which he quotes. The great 'I AM', the one true and living God, takes the redeemed people of the Old Testament into living and eternal fellowship with himself, and because of who he is, it is clear that this fellowship must survive death, for he is himself eternal. In this way, Jesus drew out implications from the passage that had probably never been seen before.

4. The question about the commandments (12:28-34)

Matthew 22:34-36 suggests that this question came as an initiative from the Pharisees and that it was a 'test'. It does seem, however, from the passage that the man who was actually put up to ask the question was sincere. He raised an issue that we know was much debated among the Pharisees, who, although accepting all the Old Testament Scriptures, were very Law-centred in their approach to the Old Testament. It is interesting to read especially the words of the great Rabbi Hillel (who taught Gamaliel the Pharisaic mentor of Saul of Tarsus), because of their similarity to part of the answer of Jesus here, except for the fact that the teaching of Jesus was positive instead of negative in form. In answer to a question, Hillel said, 'What you hate for yourself, do not do to your neighbour: this is the whole Law, the rest is commentary.'

The first of the two Old Testament quotations Jesus uses comes from the Shema. This is the name given to Deuteronomy 6:4-9, and it is taken from its opening Hebrew word, translated 'Hear!' This passage was regarded as of great theological and practical importance by the Jews, and it was the first Old Testament passage a Jewish mother taught her child. No doubt Mary would have taught it to her divine Son at a very early stage of his infant life. Its words were also worn by the scribes on their garments.

The terms 'heart', 'soul', 'mind' and 'strength' are not intended to be understood analytically, as if, taken together, they give a complete summary of human nature in its different parts, with the word 'strength' perhaps representing the body. Certainly 'heart' suggests the motivating centre of the personality and so is appropriately placed first, 'soul' a person's living quality, especially in relation to the inner life, 'mind' the intellect, and 'strength' the forces of bodily action, but the accumulation of such words really simply emphasises the fact that we are to love God with our whole being. The two commandments Jesus quotes both emphasize motive, and between them they sum up the two tables of the Law.

The man's answer showed that, unlike so many of his kind, he understood the priority of attitudes over the letter of the Law. This itself was made clear in the Old Testament, not only in the references to love in connection with these commandments, but also in passages like Deuteronomy 5:29, so close to the great Shema passage, where God said of his people Israel, 'Oh, that their hearts would be inclined to fear me and keep all my commands always, so that it might go well with them and their children for ever!' It is just not true that the Old Testament was concerned mostly with outward deeds, although there were tendencies in this direction in the Judaism of our Lord's day.

This passage is of great importance in that it makes it clear that Jesus accepted the oneness of God. We must remember this in connection with the New Testament doctrine of the Trinity. This doctrine does not mean a plurality of gods, as in many pagan systems of belief, but rather it points to an unique fact, that there is a distinction of Persons within the unity of the one true God, and that both the unity and the distinctions are eternal. This is something the Christian accepts by faith, although inevitably, as it is an unique fact, it is not possible to find adequate analogies of it.

5. The question about the Messiah (12:35-37a)

Up until now Jesus has been responding to the initiative of others and dealing with their questions. Now he asks his own question. In the nature of the case, a question put by him is bound to be more important than even the most pressing ones asked by others. We must therefore pay special attention to it.

In this question, Jesus raises an issue which impinges on the nature of his own Person. It is quite impossible that he was questioning the Davidic lineage of the Messiah. After all, he had responded to blind Bartimaeus when he called out, 'Jesus, Son of David, have mercy on me!' (10:47-49). Rather he was denying that this is all there is to be said about him, for he is much more. That he is the Son of David is, in other words, a true but inadequate statement.

Already in the parable of the vineyard he had asserted his divine Sonship (12:6). Now on the basis of Old Testament Scripture he declares the Messiah to be Lord. 'Son of God' and 'Lord' are the two expressions most often employed in the New Testament with reference to the deity of Jesus. John tends to use the former more frequently and Paul the latter. These two great terms are not, however, identical in what they imply. The first stresses the special relationship of Jesus to the Father and the second his special relationship to the universe, and, of course, especially to people. So then he is God's Son and he is our Lord.

Psalm 110 is more often quoted in the New Testament than any other Old Testament passage despite the fact that it is not very long. It is evident then that the New Testament writers must have been in agreement that it was very important and a major Scripture passage for interpreting who Jesus was. We can see here where they got this idea; without doubt they got it from Jesus himself.

The point here is of course the significance of the words used in the psalm. The Messiah is seen not just to be David's son, but to be his Lord. This ought, in fact, to have been plain already to the teachers of the Law when they read the passage itself, especially if they were familiar with the Septuagint, the Greek version of the Old Testament, which is quoted here. In that version, both occurrences of the word 'Lord' are in fact *kurios*, so often used where God himself is called 'Lord' in that translation.

Incidentally, note how verse 36 underlines the inspiration of this Davidic Psalm, and in so doing gives great added weight to the significance of David's language there. It was by the Holy Spirit that David wrote. As we have seen, Jesus did not accept the authority of the oral law, which was so important for the scribes and Pharisees (7:1-13), but he did take with great seriousness the authority of the Old Testament itself. Here we can see the reason for this: it was because God's Spirit had inspired it. Modern Christians should follow their Lord in this.

6. Contrasting pictures (12:37b-44)

This section forms a kind of appendix to the series of questions recorded by Mark. There in the temple Jesus was teaching in a fully public way and he had the ear of the people. He therefore took the opportunity of saying something to them about the teachers of the law, whom they were so used to hearing in the synagogues that were to be found throughout the land. Other English translations often use the word 'scribe' of them and this accurately renders the Greek word employed, although the NIV translation spells out what their main task was in relation to the people.

So much about these men spoke of ostentation. They were treated by the people as men of considerable status. In the synagogues they had seats at the front, close to the place where the Biblical scrolls were kept. Disciples of Christ should not be concerned about their status in a church or Christian organisation. No form of Christian service we undertake should ever be thought of in terms of status. It is a privilege and is just as much due to the grace of God as is our salvation itself (Eph. 3:8,9).

Jesus had already told his disciples to 'watch out' for the yeast of the Pharisees (8:15). This warning was necessary because of the great influence these men had, and so the disciples needed to be aware of their failings. They loved people to show deference to them (cf. John 5:44; 12:43). This was all of a piece with their stress on outward things with reference to God's Law. In Matthew 23:1-4 Jesus said both to the crowds and to his disciples that the Pharisees should be obeyed but that they should not be treated as role models. He said that they did not practise what they preached.

It was common for widows to give rabbis financial support. Mark tells us later (15:41) that there were women who followed Jesus and cared for his needs, so that there was nothing wrong with this in itself. It could, however, be very easily abused. Apparently many of the rabbis were presuming on this support and, with greedy insensitivity, taking what the widows could ill afford to give them.

Their long prayers were in reality addressed not to God but to men. A report an American newspaper gave of a Christian service described the minister's prayer as 'perhaps the finest prayer ever delivered to a New York congregation'. Prayers should be addressed to God and to him alone. In fact, in the Sermon on the Mount, Jesus told his disciples, 'when you pray, go into your room, close the door and pray to your Father' (Matt. 6:6).

The words of verse 40b are most solemn and remind us of James 3:1: 'Not many of you should presume to be teachers, my brothers, because you know that we who teach will be judged more strictly.' Of course, if there is a God-given teaching gift, that gift should be used, as Paul makes clear in Romans 12:7, but this has to be done with a deep sense of responsibility to God. The teaching office, whether exercised in the Judaism of our Lord's day or within the Christian church, is not something to be undertaken lightly.

The reference to the poor widow in the final story of this chapter is particularly interesting in view of the mention of widows in verse 40. Once again Mark has shown his narrative gift by placing these two stories so close together in his Gospel. This incident must have taken place in the Court of the Women in the Temple. The Talmud, which is a major source of information about Jewish practices during this historical period, says that within the Court of the Women were thirteen large trumpet-shaped receptacles into which the people put their monetary gifts. Earlier that week, just after his entry to Jerusalem, Jesus had watched what was going on in the temple (11:11). Here he demonstrates also his ability to see beyond outward show and to look right into the human heart. John 2:23-25 also highlights this and John then goes on, in his third chapter, to illustrate it from the story of Nicodemus the Pharisee and his encounter with Jesus.

On this occasion recorded by Mark, the all-seeing eye of Jesus saw not only the people and their money but also the attitude of their hearts. He was also aware of the proportion of their available cash which they were committing to God in this way. The coins referred to were the smallest currently in circulation among the Jews, but they were all the woman had. We need also to realise that her action must have been an act of faith as well as of generosity, for she would need now to trust God for the supply of her needs. Here again then Jesus places emphasis on motive rather than outward appearance.

Some questions for personal reflection

1. Am I guilty sometimes of placing knowledge above wisdom? What is the use of knowledge if I do not know how to use it?

2. What can I learn from the record of the Day of Questions about the way to answer people who ask me questions about the Bible and about Christ?

3. Jesus commended the apparently tiny and yet actually very full gift of the widow at the temple. What story in Mark shows how Christ can take something small and make something very big out of it?

Chapter 14

His Return (13:1-37)

The title, 'Day of Questions', which describes the cut and thrust of question and answer between various interlocutors and Jesus in the previous section of the Gospel, could well be extended to cover this chapter. The various Jewish parties have asked their questions; but now it is the turn of the disciples. These questions from the crowd and from his immediate followers may all have been put to Jesus on the same day, although we do not have enough notes of time in these chapters to be certain.

Notice the important link indicated by the opening words of the chapter. In verse 2 Jesus speaks strong words of judgement in relation to the temple. The opening words of the chapter, 'As he was leaving the temple', with its reminder of what had recently gone before, may be Mark's way of indicating that it was the attitudes of so many referred to in the previous section of his Gospel that was the moral cause of that judgement. They had really condemned themselves out of their own mouths.

1. The occasion of this teaching

The chapter begins as Jesus is leaving the temple with his disciples and then, in verse 3, the scene shifts to the Mount of Olives. Probably they were on their way out to Bethany for the night, and the fine view they would gain of the Temple as they passed over the Mount of Olives prompted some of the disciples to ask Jesus questions arising from the sombre comment he had made earlier.

Notice that Jesus gave this teaching when he 'was sitting on the Mount of Olives opposite the temple' (v.3). Of course the characteristic posture of a teacher in Israel was a seated one, but the specific nature of Mark's words strongly suggests that he saw some special significance in this action of Jesus on this occasion. What could it be? Earlier that week, Luke tells us, he had wept over the city (Luke 19:41). This was because, despite the fact that he had to pronounce its judgement, he loved its people. Mark's words remind us that Jesus gave this teaching while Jerusalem was in full view, not in some place remote from it. It may well have been a deeply emotional experience for him and it is possible that Mark is suggesting that he could see what it was really like.

Religious buildings that are expected to last for a long time often go through periods when parts of them are reconstructed, as we can see from the history of many of Europe's great Gothic cathedrals. Herod the Great had spent many years reconstructing the temple in cream stone and clothing it in gold. From what is known of his character, this was probably much more for his own glory than for the glory of God. The work commenced in 19 BC and continued for many years beyond his death. Ironically, it was completed only a few years before the Romans totally destroyed it in AD 70.

The question in verse 4 was not asked by all the disciples but by four of them, and asked privately. Three of this group had already received special revelation privileges (for instance, they were the ones Jesus had taken up the Mount of Transfiguration) and, of course, Andrew had been closely associated with them even prior to their call by Jesus. Were they perhaps wanting the privilege of a disclosure that would not be made to the others, another manifestation of the 'one-upmanship' shown by James and John on the way to Jerusalem (10:35-45)? Possibly, although if this was the case we might have expected Jesus to rebuke them.

It would be worth comparing 13:4 with Luke 21:7 and Matthew 24:3. The Lucan passage, like Mark's account, shows that the question of the disciples was chiefly about the temple, while Matthew adds the important information that they asked also about his coming and the end of the age. Because of this, we might expect Jesus to begin with events associated with the temple's destruction, but also to go on to his second advent and the close of the present age. We should bear this in mind as we approach his teaching here. In fact, verses 24-27 are clearly eschatological (dealing with the Last Things) and the second coming of Jesus is specifically mentioned.

The Second Advent may be viewed both as a great manifestation of God's salvation and also as a revelation of his judgement. It is of course the final judgement of the present age. There is in Scripture a principle of typology, and when this principle is in operation, we find a series of events anticipating a final event, which is the great climax of all that went before it. In the New Testament, which often interprets Old Testament events typologically, that great climax is always related to Jesus. He is the great Antitype to whom all the Old Testament types point. So we should not be surprised to find here that the Fall of Jerusalem anticipates the second advent in important respects, making the one a sort of type of the other. The fact that there is a link between the two would account for the fact that Mark spends so much space in telling us about the teaching Jesus gave on this occasion.

2. The beginning of birth pains (13:5-13)

The Jews used to speak of 'the birth pains of the Messiah'. This phrase referred to a period of trial and tribulation which they believed would precede the coming of the Messiah. The Old Testament uses this metaphor, quite extensively, usually in a context of judgement, in passages like Isaiah 13:8; Jeremiah 6:24, Hosea 13:13 and Micah 4:9,10, so that it really became a technical term with particular connotations for the Jews.

Jesus predicts the coming of deceivers (vv. 5,6). The deviousness of Satan is revealed right from the beginning of his activity on the human scene (Gen. 3) and, of course, his human agents make use of deception too, and we can trace this theme through much of the Bible. A century or so after the close of our Lord's earthly ministry, Simon bar-Kockba, a high-profile messianic pretender, came on the scene in Jerusalem.

223

His activity there caused the Romans to act against the Jews once more. In fact in AD 132 the Roman authorities banned all Jews from Jerusalem on pain of death. Even the Babylonians had never done that.

What does Jesus mean when he says, 'Many will come in my name'? It suggests not so much that there will be people claiming to be the Christ in opposition to the claim of Jesus in this regard, but rather claiming to be Jesus himself in his second advent. This phenomenon is not restricted to one period, for there have been instances of it in modern times, often associated with mass suicides and murders.

Jesus also warned the disciples of the coming of wars and rumours of wars and also of the conflict of states against each other. He came as the Prince of Peace, but a world that in large part rejects his claims cannot expect to have peace without him. There was, of course, to be a terrible war within the lifetime of most of his disciples, when a revolt by the Jews in AD 66 brought a Roman army against the holy city. It was this that became the human cause of the destruction of Jerusalem and its temple four years later. Such things would come and, without doubt, they would point to the end, although that end would still lie in the future.

Jesus spoke also of calamities in the world of nature (v. 8). The Old Testament writers relate the spiritual and the physical in such a way that even the physical environment is affected by the judgement or the blessing of God. We see this in the physical repercussions of the Fall as outlined in Genesis 3, but it is also true of the gracious purpose of God as outlined in passages like Isaiah 35, where the whole habitat of God's people blossoms under the blessing of God. The environment in which human life is lived may reflect what is happening in the realm of God's purposes. So we are not surprised when we are told, in connection with God's ultimate purpose for human beings, that there is to be both a new heaven and a new earth (Isa. 65:17; 66:22; Rev. 21,22).

This kind of thing on its negative side was manifest in the

period that led up to the Jewish War against the Romans in AD 66–70 to which we have already referred. In Acts 11:28, for instance, we learn that Agabus, a Christian prophet, predicted the coming of a severe famine on the whole Roman world, and Luke tells us that this prophecy was fulfilled during the reign of Claudius, who reigned from AD 41 to 54. There can be little doubt that, when this happened, those Christians who knew of the prophecy would think not only of what Agabus had said but also of the prior prophecy given by their Lord himself.

False Christs, wars and rumours of wars, earthquakes and famines, have in fact all characterized much of the whole age since the time of Christ. This suggests to us, therefore, that Jesus was speaking not simply of a number of special events associated with the period of Jerusalem's fall, but that these events would point to general characteristics of the world order between the two advents of Christ. They would all act therefore as signposts pointing to his return.

It is notable that all these events are manifestations of instability in the world. This instability is, of course, of different kinds, for the passage refers to it as being seen in the religious, political and physical spheres. In all these areas the unstable element may be seen as a cry for the coming of the stable order of Christ's kingdom, the general longing of a marred creation for the coming of perfection at Christ's return (cf. Rom. 8:18-25). The universe was originally made perfect and it longs for that perfection again. Every such event is meant then to deepen our awareness of the fragility of this world-order and to cause us to long for Christ's return.

How would all this affect the disciples themselves? Jesus was very frank with them, making clear that they would feel the effects of taking a stand for him and so of moving against the tide, which was certainly not running in his favour (vv. 9-13). He had already told them what his destiny was to be and that the Jewish leaders would play a prominent part in it through their rejection of his claims. He had also warned them that true discipleship meant taking up the cross and following him (8:31-38).

Here we see that the disciples were to suffer at the same hands as Jesus himself. 'Local councils' were committees of leaders set up at local level, and this, with the reference to synagogues, suggests that the disciples could not assume they would be free from persecution in any place where there were Jews. They were themselves Jews, who had been nurtured in the Jewish faith by the synagogue teachers, and so this must have hurt them deeply and made them very sad. We can see in the Acts of the Apostles how often the gospel was rejected in the synagogues (e.g. Acts 6:9; 13:44,45), and this certainly confirms the truth of the predictions of Jesus.

The reference to governors and kings might have seemed to be possible of fulfilment within an Israelite context, for Pilate was a governor and Herod a king, but it raised the possibility of a wider mission and therefore of a more extensive persecution. We are not surprised, therefore, to find Jesus going on to say that the gospel must first be preached to all nations. This anticipates of course, his command to them after the resurrection to declare the gospel everywhere (16:15).

So then, along with the many sombre signs of his coming again, such as the manifestations of religious deception, political strife and physical instability, Jesus the true Christ gave this positive sign which, at the human level, required the co-operation of the disciples themselves. In a world showing so much evidence of its need for Christ, they were to declare the glorious gospel which would centre in his person and work. The activities of human agents can often be seen in the fulfilment of what is predicted in Scripture and here is evidence of God's sovereignty over history.

The counsel Jesus gave in verse 11 should not be misinterpreted. It has, of course, nothing to do with preparation for preaching, for such an interpretation is alien to the context. Biblical preaching should be prayerfully undertaken and based on diligent study of the Biblical text. What Jesus promises here is rather that God will give appropriate words to speak in answer to the accusations of persecutors. Luke, who also records teaching from Jesus along these lines (Luke 21:14,15), gives us examples of this promise being fulfilled in his recording of events such as those found in Acts 5:29-32; 6:9,10; 7:51,54,55. Extensive examples could also be given from the pages of church history, both ancient and modern.

According to Matthew 10:34-39, Jesus had already said that his coming would divide families. Modern times have witnessed many cases of the betrayal of people by members of their own families. This has happened under totalitarian regimes of more than one political or religious colour which are often antagonistic to each other but united in having an anti-Christian bias. Christ is a disturber, and his claims are absolute. Totalitarianism, by definition, cannot tolerate rival claims, and so it is not therefore surprising that allegiance to him sets up movements of opposition directed against his loyal disciples.

Trial is never welcome, but it can test and purify, and in the future it certainly was to do this for the Christian church, so that those of true faith might be revealed by their positive reaction to it (v. 13). This reminds us of the Parable of the Sower, as there the seed sown on rocky places stands for those who quickly fall away through trouble or persecution, whereas seed sown on good soil represents those who accept the word and produce fruit (4:8, 20). We might also note that Jesus was soon to say to his disciples, 'You did not choose me, but I chose you and appointed you to go and bear fruit – fruit that will last' (John 15:16).

3. The destruction of Jerusalem and the time of tribulation (13:14-23)

So far, the teaching of this chapter in the Gospel has been straightforward and relatively simple to understand. We can see that it relates to what lies ahead for the disciples, but also that much of it embraces later times too. At this point, however, Jesus introduces a somewhat enigmatic expression taken from the Book of Daniel, where it occurs three times (Dan. 9:27; 11:31; 12:11). It is 'the abomination that causes desolation'.

What does it mean? 'Abomination' certainly suggests something deeply repugnant to God, and 'desolation', followed by the words, 'standing where it does not belong', appears to be a reference to something alien and illegitimate that would cause worshippers to leave the temple of God. A study of the Danielic passages tends to confirm this. The words of Jesus too clearly imply that this temple would become devoid of worshippers.

This raises the question as to the time of the fulfilment of this prophecy. In considering this, we need to remember that the phrase started life within the Old Testament period, in the Book of Daniel. In fact, Daniel is expressly mentioned in the parallel passage in Matthew (Matt. 24:15). It is widely agreed that there was some fulfilment of these Daniel prophecies during the Maccabean period, when a representative of the pagan Syrian monarch, the political overlord of the Jews, profaned the altar in the Jerusalem temple.

The use of this prophecy by Jesus and with a future reference, however, certainly indicates that this does not exhaust its meaning, and so bears witness to the fact that he himself accepted the principle of typology. When, then, was it to be more completely fulfilled? A case can certainly be made out for the events of the Jewish War of AD 66-70, which culminated in Jerusalem's destruction. The Roman soldiers who besieged Jerusalem and destroyed its temple carried standards with images on them and these were considered idolatrous by the Jews. The parallel passage in Luke mentions that Jerusalem would be surrounded by armies (cf. Luke 21:20). Certainly the teaching of Jesus could apply to something like this.

It is interesting though that Mark's account of his words here uses a masculine form for the Greek participle translated 'standing' (see the NIV margin), and that Paul does the same sort of thing in 2 Thessalonians 2:3-10 when he is writing of the man of lawlessness. This certainly suggests that the ultimate abomination is to be a human object of worship, and the fact that in Matthew's account this abomination is mentioned in a passage dealing with questions of the disciples that included

228

explicit reference to the coming of Jesus (24:3,15,27,30) strongly suggests that Jesus has the end-time in view.

Probably therefore Daniel's prophecy is a germinal one, related to a repeated sequence of events, culminating in a happening just prior to the return of Christ. This would in fact make it parallel to the references to religious, political and physical disturbances of God's order to be found earlier in this chapter, except for the fact that, unlike them, it appears to culminate in a single event. The words, 'let the reader understand,' may have been spoken by Jesus himself or they may be Mark's own comment at this point. A further question is that of the identity of the book to be read. Is it the Book of Daniel or the Gospel of Mark? Either is possible. On the whole it seems most likely that the words were spoken by Jesus and that they were meant to apply to the Book of Daniel. The exhortation contained in the following verse could hardly apply to readers of the Gospel who were situated in Rome, but it would have great relevance to Christians in Judea at the time when the Roman armies were approaching Jerusalem.

This then raises a further question: to what should we apply the words of verses 14b to 23? This is not an easy matter. These verses certainly look as if they apply to the events associated with the Fall of Jerusalem. They are very specific and detailed. They assume that there is a dreadful threat to Judea and so, by implication, to Jerusalem, its capital. Just as the people of Israel had to leave Egypt with all speed after they had kept the first Passover, so now there was to be no thought of anything else when the warning signs were seen. Eusebius, the first great Church historian after Luke's account of the early church in the Acts of the Apostles, tells his readers that when the Christians in Jerusalem saw the Roman legions approaching, they thought of this prophecy and left the city for Pella, amongst the mountains of Peraea, east of the Jordan.

The problem of interpretation becomes acute when we come to verse 19. This verse seems definitely eschatological, and should be compared with Daniel 12:1; Jeremiah 30:7; and

Revelation 7:14. Yet, despite this, it occurs in a context appearing to relate to AD 70. In fact, the question of the disciples in verse 4, referring as it does to our Lord's affirmation in verse 2, certainly appears to apply to the destruction of the temple, which we know to have happened in AD 70. This provides one of the two historical foci of the chapter. The other is provided by verse 26, the coming of the Son of Man in glory. Whereabouts in the chapter, then, does Jesus move in his teaching from events associated with the first advent to those associated with the second?

There have been four approaches to it by those who accept this chapter as authoritative teaching given by a Teacher with divine authority. Two of these see the chapter as referring only to one great event, whereas the other two see it as referring to two great events.

First of all, some have interpreted everything in the chapter in relation to the Fall of Jerusalem. Everything then applies to the first century AD. Even the coming of the Son of Man here referred to is not the Second Advent, but is a coming like the coming of God in judgement to Israel in so many passages in the Old Testament. We might then compare 9:1, if, as we have suggested, this applies to the Transfiguration of Jesus rather than to his second advent. If this is what it means, however, it is not easy then to understand the reference to the gathering of the elect in verse 27.

Secondly, there are those who apply everything to the Second Advent. This would be simple were it not for verses 1 to 4. If this is the meaning, how can the teaching of Jesus be reckoned in any sense an answer to the question asked by the disciples?

Thirdly, there is the view that the change from the Fall of Jerusalem to the events associated with the Second Advent comes at or around verse 19. This is in fact very difficult, for there is no indication whatever there of a change of subject. The tribulation seems, on this view, to be related first of all to the Fall of Jerusalem but then, because it is depicted in such extreme language, to the events preceding the Second Advent. This interpretation, popular as it is, bristles with problems.

Lastly, there are those who hold that all applies to the Fall of Jerusalem except verses 24 to 27, which relate to the Second Advent. Everything before this applies to the first century (although some of the events form a series which goes on beyond this). Verses 29 and 30 require very careful interpretation. According to this way of understanding the chapter, the phrase, 'these things', in verse 30 refers to the same events as 'all these things' in verse 29, which, the careful reader will note, do not and cannot include the coming of the Son of Man. To notice this is of great importance for understanding the chapter. So then all the signs will take place, not only before the Second Advent, but even before the Fall of Jerusalem, so that the latter is truly an anticipation of the former. This means that it is important to keep abreast of world news.

There is one further problem for this interpretation, and it stems from the words that introduce verse 24, 'But in those days, following that distress.' Do they rule out the possibility of a very long time gap between verses 23 and 24? No! The problem is resolved if we take it that the phrase, 'that distress' refers to the whole period of trouble outlined by Jesus in verses 5 to 23 and not simply to the 'days of distress unequalled from the beginning' associated with the Fall of Jerusalem, and which are referred to in verse 19.

I recognize the difficulties of the passage, but see less problems in the last interpretation than in the other three.

4. The Second Advent (13:24-27)

Are the dramatic events of verse 24 to be taken literally or could they symbolize world-shaking events in human history? This is a question of the same order as the one that faces the interpreter of the Book of the Revelation, especially in chapters like 6 and 7. It is probably best to allow for either possibility, although a comparison with 2 Peter 3:5-13 would incline us towards the literal interpretation.

The events that are of crucial importance for human beings are, of course, those taking place on the stage of human history itself, including most if not all the events associated with the first advent of Christ. If however the fall of mankind into sin had repercussions in the physical environment of human life, why should this not be true of the restorative events connected with the Last Advent? If restoration is to be truly radical, it would not seem inappropriate for the existing order to be thoroughly disturbed prior to this radical re-creation. After all, Jesus had already made reference to physical events, to earthquakes and famines, earlier in the chapter (13:8), and heavenly bodies, great as they are, nevertheless form part of the same physical universe. If the Second Advent is the greatest event to take place in the future, it would not be surprising if it had far-reaching effects at every level of being in the universe, the physical as well as the spiritual.

There can be little doubt that verse 27 is the basis in our Lord's teaching for what Paul says in 1 Thessalonians 4:15-18. What Paul does is to spell out the fact that this gathering of the Lord's people will include both the living and the dead. Wherever they are in God's domain they will be united as they are gathered to the Son of Man. This will entail resurrection for those who are dead (1 Thess. 4:16) and glorification for all (2 Thess. 1:10). What an encouragement this is as we think of the trials and sufferings referred to elsewhere in the chapter!

5. The time of the Second Advent (13:28-37)

We have come across a fig-tree already in Mark's account of the life of Jesus. It had been a symbol of judgement as he approached Jerusalem only a few days prior to his delivery of the prophecies recorded here (11:12-14, 20,21). Now he teaches his disciples another lesson from the same kind of tree. Successive periods in the life of a fruit tree are signs that there is a programme at work. Everything has to follow in ordered succession, and we can deduce certain facts about the seasons from watching such a tree.

So it is with the Second Advent. There are signs to be watched for, and Jesus has of course indicated these in his teaching in this chapter. In verse 29, we should probably read 'he is near' rather than 'it is near'. Either is a possible rendering of the Greek. James uses a somewhat similar phrase, 'standing at the door' in James 5:9 immediately after a reference to the nearness of Christ's coming which he makes in the previous verse.

What then did our Lord mean when he said, 'this generation will certainly not pass away until all these things have happened' (v. 30)? The Fall of Jerusalem and events associated with it would of course take place within about forty years of the teaching Jesus was giving at this time, and the general signs given by him are, of course, common to every age in the history of the church, for always there have been indications of the instability of this world order at the same time as good news of Christ and the coming of his stable order through his second advent are being proclaimed. So, as they are common to every generation during this age, this would clearly be true of the generation to which Jesus was then speaking. So every generation from the beginning to the present day has had to face the challenge of the coming of the Lord, and this has been good for the Christian church at every stage of its history.

At verse 31, Jesus declares the eternity of his teaching in words of great power, and he then follows this with a statement that his Father alone knows the day and hour of his coming. This second statement has often caused problems for Christians, and this is itself very strong evidence for its genuineness. A writer belonging to the Christian church could not conceivably have invented such a saying. Also the contiguity of these two statements is most significant. The eternal nature of his teaching makes it absolutely infallible, and it follows from this that we cannot infer, from his human ignorance of the time of his coming, that his teaching was ever fallible. There is a profound difference between giving erroneous teaching and not giving teaching at all. Clearly the first is inconsistent with infallibility, while it is equally clear that the second is consistent with it.

Here Jesus places himself not only above the whole human race but also above all the angels, so that he is greater than all

233

created beings. There is only One who, he says, has superior knowledge. He came to earth to do the will of his Father and it seems that it was not his Father's will that he, at the level of his human intellect, should have this knowledge or impart it. Here we encounter the sublime mystery of the Incarnation and the conditions of its expression, the mystery, that is, of his divine greatness and his human limitations, the mystery of the two natures, one fully divine and therefore omniscient, and the other fully human, and therefore learning truth progressively, in one undivided Person. We may seek to plumb some of the depths of this mystery but its ultimate resolution is beyond the powers of the human intellect. Therefore wonderment brings us to our knees in worship.

We must watch then for the signs and also engage in spreading the gospel (v. 10). What we should not do is specify or speculate as to the date of his return. We cannot presume to know more than the Man Christ Jesus. Jesus concludes his teaching here with a warning reinforced by a parable. He says, 'Be on guard! Be alert! ...keep watch ...keep watch ...What I say to you, I say to everyone, Watch!' He had already said, 'Watch out ...!' at the beginning of this discourse (v. 5). Could any command be stated more emphatically? The disciples are to watch for the coming of the Lord. That coming has not yet taken place and so the command comes still to us, as the current representatives of his church. We are to keep watch.

These urgent words come in the context of a parable. The NIV paragraphing here is difficult to understand for it seems clear that verses 34 to 36 all belong to the one parable. It is probable that the twofold reference to the servants with varied tasks and to the doorkeeper in fact apply to the same people, the disciples of Jesus. Our tasks are different and yet we are all called to watch. We should busy ourselves in the varied tasks he has given us and yet always be watching for his return. Until that return this command is ours to hear and obey.

Some questions for personal reflection

1. Which really interests me more, what I may learn about the sequence of events connected with the return of Christ, or what Scripture teaches about the right attitude to that return?

2. How much that is prophesied in this chapter can I see in the actual world in which I live today?

Chapter 15

His Sufferings – Among His Friends (14:1-42)

Go to the biography section of your local library. Browse among the books that are there. There you will find the life-stories of many fascinating people – politicians, musicians, scientists, actors, explorers and many others. Check the contents pages. How much space is given to the childhood, the adolescence, the adult life and work and finally the death of the person concerned? It will vary, of course, but the last days and the death of the person are not likely to occupy a strongly disproportionate amount of space. Usually they will occupy only a few pages, perhaps only a paragraph, even a single sentence.

There are some partial exceptions, of course. The circumstances of the death of Socrates, or of Captain Oates, Scott's Antarctic companion, might well rate a whole chapter. There will however be nothing approaching the concentration on the death of Christ and its circumstances that we find in the Gospels. Here is something on which all four of them agree. They may not select the same details to highlight in their presentation of Holy Week, but the high degree of concentration on these few days is evident in each of them.

Mark is in fact typical in this respect, for about a third of his Gospel is occupied by the final week in the life of our Lord. This is, of course, because this book is in fact a declaration of the good news (Mark 1:1) and that good news, throughout the whole New Testament, finds its centre in the death – and resurrection – of Jesus.

In the last few chapters, we have seen Jesus coming to Jerusalem and teaching in the temple and on the Mount of Olives. Now, at the beginning of chapter 14, the Passion Narrative proper begins. It is a narrative of the starkest simplicity and yet of the profoundest meaning.

1. Hatred and Love (14:1-11)

We have already seen a number of times, for instance in 12:38-44, how fond Mark is of juxtaposing contrasting events, and especially where they show greatly diverse characters. It has been evident almost from the beginning of Mark's book that Jesus divides people. What matters most of all is our attitude to him, and some who come into the Gospel story were definitely for him while others just as firmly against him. These varying attitudes are very much in view in chapters 14 and 15. Sadly we see not only how deep and lethal was the antipathy of his enemies, but also how frail and failing were his friends. Modern Christians need to remind themselves of this. We cannot throw stones at the disciples, for we all live in glass houses.

The Sanhedrin's members had been worsted in debate with Jesus (11:27-12:27), as Mark showed in his second and third chapters that the Galilean Pharisees and teachers of the law had been. No doubt they were smarting. Perhaps it would not have been quite so disconcerting for them if it had all happened in private, if they had taken a leaf out of the book of Nicodemus and visited Jesus by night with their questions (John 3:2). As it was, it had all happened in the temple, in an area set aside for public teaching and so within the hearing of many ordinary folk. They had undoubtedly lost face very badly – and they did not like it.

They now planned an imminent arrest. It is noticeable that the chief priests (who were Sadducees) as well as the teachers of the Law (who would be Pharisees) were now involved, and this is not at all unexpected. After all, the cleansing of the temple (11:15-18) had been carried out within their domain and the abuses Jesus attacked at that time were being tolerated or even fostered by them.

The Passover and Feast of Unleavened Bread were closely associated, for the Feast began on Passover day. The circumstances of the institution of both are recorded in Exodus 12. The Feasts of Unleavened Bread, of Pentecost (also called the Feast of Weeks) and of Tabernacles were known as the

Pilgrim Feasts, and they were a major feature of the religious life of Israel's people. God had commanded all male Jews to celebrate them each year at the place he would choose (Deut. 16:16). So men travelled to Jerusalem with their families from many parts of the land. In New Testament times, in fact, many came even from Jewish settlements overseas.

This means then that Jerusalem was just crammed with people at the time of the Passover Feast. It was at this time that the Exodus from Egypt was celebrated. God had often intervened savingly in the history of his people, but this was undoubtedly the greatest act of redemptive deliverance he had effected for them. Little did they know that it was to be exceeded, and indeed even outclassed, by another amazing act of redemption – through a Man hanging on a cross.

While in the vicinity of Jerusalem, Jesus appears to have made Bethany his centre rather in the way he appears to have treated Capernaum for much of his Galilean ministry. It is quite possible that he stayed with Mary, Martha and Lazarus. In the Gospel of John the incident recorded here in 14:3-9 is placed a little earlier, just before Passion Week (John 12:1-8). We note that Mark simply says, 'While he was in Bethany,' a time-reference vague enough to cover an occurrence slightly earlier. Mark has probably put it here in close connection with the act of betrayal by Judas in order to show a contrast in attitudes.

If we put John's account and Mark's together, we may well conclude that Simon the Leper was a friend of Mary, Martha and Lazarus. Perhaps he had been healed by Jesus and so was drawn close to this family, which also owed so much to the love and power of Jesus. Incidentally, it seems that the incident described in Luke 7:36-50 is not the same as this. It is true that some commentators identify them as the same event, fastening on the similarity of the anointing and the name of the host (incidentally, a very common one), but there are many differences as a detailed study of the passages concerned shows.

John tells us that the woman was Mary of Bethany. The jar may well have been one with a long neck which was broken to release the perfume. The expensive nature of the nard was due, at least in part, to the fact that it had to be brought from India, a very long and arduous journey in those days. It was probably the most valuable thing she had. What matters most in our giving to Jesus is that we give him ourselves, but this self-giving can sometimes find an expression in a physical offering that is sacrificial. Mary's nard and the widow's two very small copper coins (12:42) were very different in their monetary value, but they are united in this – they were sacrificially given.

Mark mentions the adverse reaction of some who were present, identified by Matthew (26:8) as the disciples. John specifically refers to Judas Iscariot. This reaction by the disciples was understandable but undiscerning, and is an example of the fact that they often failed to see the implications of the fact that Jesus was the Son of God. There was an unique quality about Jesus that made a special expression of love and devotion not only fitting but desirable.

Were the words of Jesus about the poor insensitive? No, for he did not by any means set aside doing good to them. In fact, in his sermon at Nazareth, he referred specifically to Isaiah's prophecy that he would 'preach good news to the poor' (Luke 4:18) and in this Gospel Mark tells us that Jesus commanded a rich man to sell everything he had and give to the poor (10:21). He had also been moved by the sacrificial giving of a poor widow. He did however acknowledge the special appropriateness of the woman's act at this particular time. In fact, poor people beyond numbering have found salvation through that death for which the woman's act was preparing him.

Jesus recognized a divine purpose in all this. Verse 8 certainly means that this act of love was divinely intended to have reference to his burial. Can we go further than this and say that Mary herself understood it thus? Luke (10:39) shows us that Mary loved nothing better than to listen to Jesus. Had she therefore understood and accepted what the twelve had failed either to understand or to receive – that he was going to die as a ransom for many? We cannot be certain, but it is not impossible.

Is there anything more discerning than love?

The comment of Jesus recorded in verse 9 is a very interesting and significant one. It shows an awareness on his part, not only of the fact that the good news about him would go out everywhere (cf. 13:10 and 16:15, 20), but also that its preaching would be based on the historical facts concerning him. We might even say that his words show the appropriateness of describing a book like Mark's historical account of the ministry of Jesus as a Gospel. The points of similarity between this verse and 16:15 will be commented on when we consider this later verse.

The fact that Jesus was in Jerusalem for the Passover gave the plotters their opportunity, but also their problem. The place would be thronged with people, and there must have been a goodly contingent from Galilee. Many of the latter would undoubtedly respect him greatly even if they did not regard him as more than a great prophet, and they would not take kindly to any move against him on the part of the authorities. The situation was difficult and delicate, but they decided it was a nettle that had to be grasped; so verses 1 and 2 imply.

The gaining of an unexpected ally through the defection of Judas Iscariot gave them an opportunity second to none. No wonder they were delighted and immediately offered him money!

References to Judas Iscariot in the Gospels are almost always accompanied by some indication of his betrayal of Jesus. Mark himself does this in 3:19. He does not do this here, but Mark's words, 'one of the Twelve' are just as damning. To be one of the Twelve, to spend many months on the road with him, to hear his words, to watch his works of love and power, and, most of all, to contemplate his character, to be so close to Jesus physically and yet to be so very far from him spiritually, what a horror is this! It is still possible to spend much time in the company of the disciples of Jesus and yet to be a million miles away from Jesus himself in our hearts.

Was the money he was offered the motive for this act? The fact that it was offered to him after his own offer of betrayal does not settle the question, for he might well have expected they would pay him. It is even possible that he made this a condition of the betrayal. Certainly, as John tells us, he held the common purse but was in fact a thief (John 12:6). It is not easy though to think that the kind of money Judas was given would be sufficient inducement for such a dastardly act – or was it?

It has been suggested that he may have had a political motive, that he expected Jesus would be a politico-military Messiah who would cast out the Romans and establish Israel in freedom once again. If this was the case, the incident of the anointing by Mary, coming on top of the fact that the entry of Jesus into the city had been such a peaceful one and that his chief preoccupation during the past few days seems to have been teaching, not gathering a military following, must have made him realize once and for all that this was a forlorn hope. It has been suggested that the betrayal was an attempt by Judas to force the hand of Jesus so that he would immediately spring into violent action when his would-be captors arrived in Gethsemane. Of course, none of the Gospels actually spells this out and it can remain only a theory. Not only so, but the way the Gospels describe Judas as a betrayer should warn us against attempting a mitigation of the seriousness of his act.

All the teaching Jesus had given about his death was now confirmed by that most final word of all, 'burial' (v.8). Remember that Paul says the heart of the gospel is the death, burial and resurrection of Jesus (1 Cor. 15:3,4). Burial testifies to death and psychologically often emphasises its finality for those have been bereaved. If the burial of Jesus testified to the reality of his death, so also the appearances of Jesus to which Paul refers in that passage bear witness to the reality of his resurrection life (1 Cor. 15:5-8).

2. Fellowship and Sacrifice (14:12-31)

The Jews were not altogether consistent in the way they referred to the Feast of Unleavened Bread. Sometimes they thought of it as starting the day after the Passover, so that the two might be distinguished, but sometimes as coinciding in its beginning with the Passover itself. This is what Mark has in mind in verse 12, for it was on the Passover Day itself (the 14th day of the month Nisan) that the lambs were killed.

That Jesus and his disciples were staying at Bethany and not in Jerusalem itself certainly seems to be implied by the instruction he gave, 'Go into the city...' (v. 13). Peter and John were the two chosen, as we learn from Luke 22:8. In the story of the early church, they would be much involved together in service for the Lord (Acts 3:1ff; 8:14). Perhaps they had had a long-standing friendship in their fishing days, for they had certainly known each other then (1:16-20). It is possible that they worked together when the disciples were sent out by Jesus two by two (6:7), although of course we cannot be at all sure of this.

They were told that they would meet a man carrying a jar of water (v. 13). Normally it was women who did this, so that a man doing it would stand out. Was this prescience on the part of Jesus or pre-arrangement? The same question arises in connection with the ass's colt in 11:1-6. The latter seems the more likely. The supernatural dimension in the life of Jesus is wonderful, but we probably should not assume it in relation to a particular incident if there is an adequate natural explanation, for he was truly human as well as truly divine.

The 'guest room', otherwise described here as 'a large upper room', shows the man to have been quite well-to-do. Most homes in the land consisted simply of one room which did duty for all domestic purposes. There were however two-storey houses, in which case the upper room was used to accommodate guests. There they would be relatively free from the hustle and bustle downstairs and from the noise and smell of the domestic animals.

We should note the word 'you' in the question of the disciples in verse 12 and that they were instructed to say to the owner of the house that Jesus had said, 'Where is my guest room, where I may eat the Passover with my disciples?' The Passover was normally a family meal, presided over by the head of the family. This language here places emphasis on Jesus himself, seeming to indicate that he saw himself here as the head of a kind of family, the spiritual family to which he had already referred in 3:31-35.

The Passover meal was always held in the evening, which was, according to the way the Jews conceived of a day, the beginning of the 15th day of the month Nisan. The table would be spread with the usual Passover fare, which had great symbolic meaning. The lamb was central, for this was a commemoration of the event just prior to the Exodus when lambs were slain to provide blood to put on the door-frames of the Israelite houses (Exod. 12), but there were other elements there too, some of which Jesus was to use in the establishment of the Lord's Supper.

It is significant that it was while they were reclining at table that he made reference to a betrayer, and described him as one who is 'eating with me'. Eating together, in most cultures, is an expression of a bond of friendship, and it was certainly this among the Jews. Treachery at the meal-table would be an unthinkable thing for them. John records that Jesus said, 'He who shares my bread has lifted up his heel against me' (John 13:18), which he saw as a fulfilment of Psalm 41:9. One by one the disciples said, 'Surely not I?' This showed a degree of healthy self-doubt, although very soon Peter was to demonstrate his lack of self-understanding (14:29-31). It is evident that the identity of the betrayer was clear to Jesus but not to the disciples.

Jesus makes his language even more specific. 'One of you .... – one who is eating with me' goes much further than if he had simply said, 'a disciple', for the latter could also include followers who were not present. The betrayer was from the inner circle itself, one of those who at that moment were expressing their fellowship as members of a redeemed race and, on this occasion, also as disciples of one Master. This must have been an appalling thought to all the disciples except Judas himself.

Verse 21 expresses the two poles between which the meaning of the death of Jesus must move. It is important to recall its divine significance, in fact its necessity ('must', 8:31) and therefore its certainty. It had been foretold long ago. In an utterance of quite special importance, he had said that he was to give his life as a ransom for many (10:45), and the language he used on that earlier occasion was highly reminiscent of Isaiah 53:10-12. Yet at the same time his death was a grievous expression of human sin, and nobody was to play a more dishonourable part in the series of events which led to it than Judas Iscariot.

We must always keep these two facts together. Here is the mystery of divine sovereignty and human responsibility. They often meet in the Bible story, and, of course, in the life of the Christian believer today, but they have never had a more significant meeting than in the story of the crucifixion of Jesus. Here indeed some of the deepest principles of God's activity in history find expression. Paul was to address this issue in an extended way in connection with the history of the Jews and of their reaction to the gospel of Christ in his Epistle to the Romans, chapters 9 to 11.

Jesus now takes two of the subsidiary elements of the Passover Feast and gives them new significance. The lambs which were the central items in the Old Testament Passover would of course be needed no more, for he was himself the Lamb of God (John 1:29), making the final Passover sacrifice (1 Cor. 5:6-8). So now the type was done away with, for the great Antitype had come!

The record of the institution of the Lord's Supper is quite brief in each of the three Gospels that tell us about it. For all his brevity at this point, however, Mark clearly shows how specifically it referred to the death of Jesus. Most expensive perfume had been poured over his head and probably most of those present will never have smelled such perfume before. Now however Jesus takes very simple elements, inexpensive every day items, and gives them symbolic meaning. The bread represented his broken body, the wine his outpoured blood. How amazing that before offering each to his disciples Jesus gave

245

thanks, for he knew what the elements stood for and the terrible agony of the cross was so near now!

He uses the word 'many' again (v. 24), a word almost certainly suggesting its use in the great 'Golden Passionale' of the Old Testament, in Isaiah 53:10-12, which depicts the atoning sufferings of the great Servant of God. This word forms a link between the two passages in Mark's Gospel where Jesus expounds the meaning of his cross, this and 10:45. On that earlier occasion, he had employed it when, on the road to Jerusalem, he had talked about service and about the giving of his own life as a ministry for others. There he had employed the figure of the ransom; now he spoke of a covenant.

A covenant is a relationship, and moreover a formal or structured relationship rather than a purely informal one like friendship. In fact the normal term for a covenant in the Old Testament was also used of treaties, which were, of course, formal agreements. In the Old Testament the covenants that mattered most were always initiated by God and were expressions of his grace-relationship with his people. Old Testament covenants were sealed with sacrifice, and the great covenant at Sinai is typical in this respect, for Moses offered sacrifices at the time of its establishment (Exod. 24:5-8).

For the second time in this chapter, Jesus uses the emphatic words, 'I tell you the truth' (v. 25; cf. v.9), this time about the consummation of the kingdom of God. This clearly shows that he believed the present phase of the kingdom would be succeeded by another. His words, 'I will drink it anew' need not mean that he thought in materialistic terms of the future, consummating phase of the kingdom. It is more likely that here the material is used as a symbol of the spiritual.

The hymn referred to here would of course be one of the psalms regularly employed at the Passover. We know, for instance, from Rabbinic sources that Psalms 113 to 118, known as the Egyptian Hallel because of their use in connection with the people's redemption from Egypt, were always used, and we have already seen how much the last of these was in the minds both of the people (11:9,10) and of Jesus himself (12:10,11). He had given thanks for elements that symbolized his death that was so soon to take place. Now, just before going out to a place where he would be taken by his enemies, he sang a hymn of praise with the disciples. Everything that happened in those hours showed his deep desire to honour the Father who had sent him before he honoured him finally in the most demanding submission of death. This was probably the last passage of Old Testament Scripture which Jesus read prior to the cross. It is worth reading it to see how its words may have ministered to him at that time.

The Mount of Olives had been the scene of his teaching about the destruction of Jerusalem and about his Second Advent recorded in Mark 13. It was on the way out to it again that Jesus continued to teach his disciples what was soon to happen. He now confronted them with a realistic fact that should have made them realize their sinfulness and frailty. 'You will all fall away,' he said (v. 27). Their presence at the Passover table with their Lord was certainly no evidence of their merit. Only one of their number was to betray him, only one to deny him quite explicitly, but they would all fail him.

In support of this statement, Jesus quoted from Zechariah 13:7. This prophet had portrayed the Messiah as a shepherd. In fact, the shepherd illustration is used in a number of different ways in the Book of Zechariah. In Chapter 11, there is the presentation of a good shepherd who would be rejected by the flock and who would then be succeeded by an evil shepherd who cared nothing for them. In John 10, Jesus refers to himself as the Good Shepherd in a passage which has some links of idea with Zechariah (John 10:11-14). Also, however, in Zechariah 13 there is another shepherd reference, where the shepherd is described by God as 'my shepherd ... the man who is close to me', who would be smitten and his flock would be scattered (Zech. 13:7), and this is what is referred to by Jesus here.

Both the smiting and the scattering would soon take place.

This was a picture of what was to happen to Jesus and his disciples. In view of the fact that the smitten shepherd in Zechariah is good, the reader of that book may be somewhat perplexed by the fact that it is God who calls for the sword to smite him. It is God himself who takes the initiative. In terms of the fulfilment of the passage in Jesus, this shows that there was a sovereign purpose of God at work through the whole story of his passion and death. The fact that history is 'his story' (i.e. God's story) has never been more clearly shown.

Verse 28 is a reminder of the resurrection of Jesus which, according to Mark (8:31; 9:9, 10, 31; 10:34), always accompanied the teaching Jesus gave the disciples about his death. Now he is not so much seeking to make the fact of it clear to them, but rather to go on from there. His resurrection would lead to a new period of activity. Not only so, but the way he puts this continues the shepherd/sheep analogy, for he said he would 'go ahead' of them into Galilee. In that part of the world the shepherd always went ahead of his sheep. After his resurrection, he would be their shepherd still.

Mark does not hesitate to feature an incident which reflects both well and badly on Simon Peter. His intention of loyalty, repeatedly and vehemently expressed (vv. 29-31), is commendable, but he did not have the self-knowledge to recognize his frailty and proneness to fail. The words of Jesus in verse 30 are most explicit and moreover emphatic, and these features are well brought out in the NIV. Peter's response too was most emphatic.

Mark has already indicated to us how self-seeking all the disciples were (10:35-45). He now shows that it was not only Simon Peter but all of them who lacked this self-knowledge, for 'all the others said the same' (v. 31). They did not deny him, for there is no evidence that they were put into a situation where they were challenged as to their allegiance, but Mark tells us that when Jesus' enemies came into the Garden of Gethsemane 'everyone deserted him and fled' (v. 50).

3. Sorrow and Slumber (14:32-42)

The Garden of Gethsemane appears to have been on the slopes of the Mount of Olives, a place to which Jesus and his disciples often went when they were in the vicinity of Jerusalem (Luke 22:39; John 18:2). The human figures in that garden were situated in different parts of it. There were eight of the disciples together, then three removed from them a little distance, and finally, after a while, Jesus on his own. He had selected Peter, James and John to share certain experiences with him which the others did not share (e.g. cf. 9:2). We have suggested that perhaps this was because they were to have some leadership role within the apostolic band.

It is possible that Mark has some intention of drawing a parallel between this and the previous incident. On that occasion, we see Peter's determination to stand by his beloved Master at any personal cost. His initiative in affirming this was then followed by the other disciples. As the story unfolds, of course, it was only one who died. Now, in the Gethsemane story, Peter and his two friends move with Jesus away from the rest of the disciples, but then Jesus leaves them and moves to a spot where he is alone with his Father and the subject of his prayer is the awful cup which he, and he alone, would drink.

The fact that the New Testament writers viewed the cross as the fulfilment of Old Testament prophecy, and that they saw the sovereign purpose of God being worked out in the events which led up to it, should not make us think that some kind of passionless 'acting' has now come into play in the life of Jesus. Nothing could be farther from the truth. The language of Mark in verse 33 and that of Jesus in verse 34 is very strong. It is evident that his sorrow was very deep indeed. In fact it was so intense that, as the words, 'to the point of death', indicate, he could have died of it there in the garden. The agony was so great as almost to extinguish the body's life, and it anticipated in some measure the sufferings of the cross. This is eloquent testimony to his true humanity and to the fact that he shared human emotions.

Three times he prayed. It may be that Paul followed his example when he prayed for the removal of his thorn in the flesh (2 Cor. 12:8), and that this was why he did not go beyond a third time of asking. He would not ask more frequently than his Lord for something that was being withheld from him.

Jesus recognized both the power and the purpose of God. Removing the cup was within his power but not, as we see, his purpose. The threefold request again shows the reality of his humanity, while the acceptance of his Father's will reveals the perfection of his loving obedience The three requests were made at intervals, and between them he returned briefly to the place where the disciples were. This shows most strikingly how human he was. When we face suffering we want to have human companionship and support. This was a very dark hour and he apparently longed for human fellowship at such a time.

It is perhaps significant that it is to Peter Jesus speaks when he finds the disciples asleep (v. 37). Peter had so recently protested that he was prepared to die with Jesus. Now he could not even keep awake to provide some comfort for his Master in his hour of deep distress! Mark reveals something of the embarrassment of the disciples on this occasion. Nevertheless Jesus did recognize that these men had really intended to watch with him, but that their weakness of body had been too much for them, and so sleep had taken over.

Entering temptation (v. 38) means, of course, not simply experiencing it but yielding to it. Was Jesus indicating that he was being tempted there in the garden himself? The temptation to retreat from his steadfast commitment to the will of his Father, whatever the cost, was overcome and he rose with a deep sense of predestination, and then moved forward into the hands of his enemies, among whom he had spied Judas Iscariot.

The die was cast. Events would now move with swiftness. Soon he would be hanging on a cross between heaven and earth to reconcile sinners to God.

Some questions for personal reflection

1. Despite knowing what Jesus said when the perfume was poured on his head, do I still have a little sympathy with the view that it was a waste? If so, for what reason am I wrong?

2. Can I think of events in my life when I have been aware both of God's sovereignty and also of my own responsibility. By the grace of God, did I rise to that responsibility?

Chapter 16

His Sufferings – Among His Enemies
(14:43–15:32)

Jesus did not shrink from his enemies. Verses 41 and 42 convey an unmistakable impression of decisiveness. The urgent staccato of the NIV is true to the Greek. In full awareness of God's purpose and timing and in equally full consciousness of the malignity of his enemies, the treachery of one disciple and the frailty of them all, Jesus walked forward determinedly to meet those who were coming to take him. Gethsemane shows us that he knew a cup of dreadful suffering awaited him and that, as it was his Father's will, he was completely willing to drink it.

1. Betrayal and Denial (14:43-72)

Mark's sense of drama is shown again when he writes, 'Just as he was speaking Judas, one of the Twelve, appeared.' Was Judas leading the way, so that he was the first Jesus and the others saw? The words of the text may suggest this, and it is what we might expect, for Judas would know where Jesus was likely to be and so could lead the others to him. Again, as in 14:20, he is damningly described by Mark as 'one of the twelve'.

Who were these people armed with swords and clubs who came with Judas into the garden? Mark says they were sent by the Sanhedrin, the Jewish Council, so they will have been the temple guard, as Luke makes clear, indicating as he does so that members of the Sanhedrin were also with them (Luke 22:52). The swords were the weapons of an official guard, but what about the clubs? The club is not a normal military weapon. They probably belonged to other people who joined on the way, picking up rough and heavy pieces of wood to use, so that what probably started as an orderly expedition eventually became much more like a vicious mob.

Verses 44 and 45 are strange. They seem at first to suggest that the members of the temple guard did not know what Jesus looked like. How could this be if he had in fact been teaching in the temple only a day or two earlier? Probably he was known very well, but those who sent this band of soldiers would want to make absolutely certain no mistake was made. Was it perhaps a condition of payment to Judas that he should personally indicate which was Jesus?

Betrayal, because it is a resolve before an act, started in the heart of Judas, but the moment when, in action, it reached the point of no return was the moment of the kiss, so horrifying since it is the universally recognised expression of love. To make matters worse, Judas addressed Jesus by a title used among the Jews in respectful address to a teacher, so adding studied insult to grave injury.

We know from John (John 18:10) that the man who drew his sword and cut off the ear of the High Priest's servant was Simon Peter. Mark has shown us many a glimpse of Peter's human failings and presumably it was Peter who provided him with the information about this incident. Why then no mention of his name in Mark's account on this occasion?

There can really only be one answer. Peter's action at this time may have been mistaken, as Jesus himself made clear to him (Matt. 26:52-54), but even so it was the act of a brave man, motivated by loyalty to his Master. If the arresting party had not been concentrating on the need to take Jesus, they might well have apprehended Peter or mauled him seriously after such an act. Also, of course, it occurred not long before a denial of which Peter was deeply ashamed. He evidently did not want anything to be told which would put him in a better light. He knew that he had failed badly, and he felt that nothing, not even an act such as this, should be placed on the credit side.

The words of Jesus in verse 48 are somewhat reminiscent of those of his ancestor David, when Saul, with an army of three thousand chosen men, came looking for him. 'Why is my lord pursuing his servant? What have I done, and what wrong am I guilty of?' (1 Sam. 26:18). The reason why they had left it until now, of course, was that they did not want all the disturbance that an arrest in a public place would have entailed, with the possibility of a demonstration of force by a crowd sympathetic to Jesus. Their evil deed would have to be done away from the public gaze, so that the relative seclusion of this garden would be good for the purpose.

The words, 'every day' (verse 49), may serve to remind us that even the record of Holy Week, which is obviously more detailed than the rest of the Gospel, is still only partial. There was so much that Jesus did and said of which we have no record, but the Holy Spirit has seen to it that we have all we need for our faith and obedience.

The reference to the need for fulfilment of the Old Testament Scriptures is very general. Perhaps it was Isaiah 53, with its prophecy of a Suffering Servant who would be violently taken, judged and killed that Jesus had in mind, or possibly the passage from Zechariah quoted in verse 27 or perhaps both of these and others too. The plural, 'Scriptures', suggests to us that this final possibility is most likely to be correct. The words of Jesus here emphasize his strong sense of a predestined path, as well as being an affirmation of the authority of the Old Testament.

The quaint incident referred to in verses 51 and 52 is strange. Why should this young man be mentioned? On the face of it, there seems little point in Mark's reference to this incident, especially in a comparatively brief book where details of little consequence would hardly be included. Some commentators, however, have suggested a possible reason. It used to be the custom at one time for an artist to draw or paint a small vignette of himself in some corner of his painting as a kind of trademark. Alfred Hitchcock, the film director, had his trademark too; for his unmistakable portly figure appeared fleetingly, usually in some very minor non-speaking role, in each of his films. Perhaps what we have here is the literary equivalent, so that the young man is John Mark himself. This could well be true, as otherwise the point of recording this detail would be quite unclear.

Matthew tells us that 'all the disciples deserted him and fled' (Matt. 26:56). Despite this initial desertion, Peter seems soon to have taken his courage in both hands. He followed the crowd, with Jesus in the midst, to the house of the high priest. This was evidently a large one, with a hall big enough for a meeting of the Sanhedrin, and with its rooms surrounding a courtyard.

It was only necessary under Jewish Law to find two witnesses in order to make out a watertight legal case, but everything turned on their full agreement. Lacking this, the case against a person was certain to fail. Apparently the plotters had found people prepared to act as witnesses and tell untruths to secure a conviction, but it looks as though they had been insufficiently primed for this evil task.

Verse 58 is interesting, because it is a point of contact with the Gospel of John. There Jesus is recorded as saying, 'Destroy this temple, and I will raise it again in three days' (John 2:19). As John points out, this was an enigmatic reference by Jesus to his body. Asian speech often makes much use of gesture and it seems likely he would have indicated his body in some way. Mark's record of the event incorporates additional words ('man-made' and 'not made by man') that would make the saying quite impossible to understand figuratively. These must have been fabricated by the false witnesses for the purpose. Half-truths are often more effective, and so also more dangerous, than total lies. It seems from the way Mark phrases verse 55 that it was the chief priests who took the initiative in looking for witnesses and the reference to the temple certainly indicates that priestly interests were much to the fore at this time.

Silence can at times be a more telling answer than speech. Jesus would not reply to the contrived testimony of false witnesses, for to him there was nothing of substance to which a reply needed to be given and, moreover, those making the accusation knew this themselves. A time came in the life of King Saul when God did not speak to him any more (1 Sam. 28:6). For years he had failed to listen and at last God's voice was silent. Could anything be more terrible than that? If the speech of God may sometimes be terrifying, how much more his silence!

The High Priest now put a direct question to Jesus about his claims, and to this he gave a direct answer. The whole encounter had now moved from the realm of deception to that of truth and so it was right for Jesus to make reply. He openly confessed his messiahship. There are several remarkable things about this.

First of all, it is very important for us to notice that he made affirmative reply to the whole question of the high priest. In other words, he accepted the definition of messiahship in terms of divine sonship. This was, of course, true to the Old Testament in passages like Psalms 2:7 and 89:26,27, in both of which a Davidic King is in view. What however did it really mean?

Was 'Son of God', for him, a mere synonym for 'Messiah'? Not if we take the Gospel of John seriously. We can see there in passage after passage that to call himself the Son of God was to affirm an unique relationship with God. So, for instance, in John 8:17-19 he made an analogy between the testimony of two human witnesses and the testimony of himself and his Father. Such a comparison would have been impossibly daring, in a Jewish context, if he had not believed in his own deity. Then, in John 14:8-14, he says, 'Anyone who has seen me has seen the Father,' and he then spells out some of the implications of this. This is not out of character with the way the term, 'Son of God', is used in this Gospel. For instance, when the evil spirits declare him to be God's Son (3:11), those they possess fall down before him. No doubt the high priest would have heard something of his claim, so that he deliberately formulated his question to include it.

The reply of Jesus is most emphatic. Greek does not normally use a nominative pronoun to indicate the subject of a verb where English requires it, for the actual form of the verb indicates this clearly enough. An exception occurs, however, when there is the need for emphasis, and the pronoun is then expressed separately. This is what happens here. This then raises the question as to whether this was simply a straightforward

257

affirmative reply or whether Jesus was identifying himself with the 'I AM', the great God of the Old Testament who revealed himself in this way in Exodus 3:14.

Certainly the Gospel of John shows him doing this, especially in John 8:58, where he says, 'before Abraham was born, I am.' Not only so, but in John 18:4-8 we find soldiers and officials reacting most peculiarly. They tell him they are looking for Jesus of Nazareth, and he simply says 'I am' (not 'I am he', as in the NIV). At one level this could simply mean, 'Well, you have found him', but John tells us that at his words they fell to the ground. It seems they took more from what he had said than a simple declaration of his identity. He must have said these words with great majesty. It is not impossible that we should see our present passage as exhibiting a similar phenomenon. Certainly it would help to account for the accusation of blasphemy (v. 64).

Jesus describes himself once again as the Son of Man. This term is used fairly often by him in this Gospel, especially after Peter's confession (8:38; 9:9, 12, 31; 10:33; 13:26; 14:21, 41), although Mark does record two earlier occasions of his use of it (2:10,28), and in the passages where it occurs in Mark it has connotations of suffering and of glory. It has a varied Old Testament background, but the way Jesus uses it here makes it certain that he had in mind the figure described as 'one like a son of man' in Daniel 7:13, 14, who receives from God, described as 'the Ancient of Days', a kingdom that was both universal and eternal.

To whom was Daniel referring? The Jews were never quite sure. Some thought this figure to be the Messiah, while others did not, largely because in this passage he is presented as a heavenly rather than as a great earthly figure. There is, however, a link with messiahship in terms of the universal and eternal kingdom he is promised, which was, of course, true of the messianic King also, as a glance at a great messianic passage like Isaiah 9: 6 and 7 will reveal.

The term, on the lips of Jesus, has been described as 'a veiled designation of messiahship.' On this occasion, he lifts the veil, for he makes a really clear identification of himself as both Messiah (and divine Messiah at that) and Son of Man. This was surely because of the public nature of the occasion. Jesus had received the ascription of messiahship in a private conversation with his close disciples and had clearly accepted this (8:29), he performed messianic actions, such as riding into Jerusalem on an ass's colt (11:7-10; cf. Zech. 9:9), but he never makes an articulated messianic claim in public until this point.

What is so ironic – and surely the irony was intentional – is that he reserves his public claim to be the Messiah and asserts his ultimate vindication as such just at the time when these claims must have seemed utterly ridiculous to the point of being totally unbelievable – when he was apparently a helpless prisoner in the hands of his enemies! How some of them must have laughed and sneered when they heard what he said!

In what did the charge of blasphemy consist? It meant they were saying that what Jesus had said was an affront to God himself. It is important for us to note that the act of the high priest in tearing his clothes was not simply an expression of emotion, as, of course, in many circumstances it would have been. This however was a courtroom and the act was a judicial one, somewhat akin to the custom, formerly observed in Britain, when a judge donned a black cap before delivering the sentence of death.

Those present were unanimous in their verdict of death (v. 64). We know that Joseph of Arimathaea (Luke 23:51) did not concur and that this was probably true of Nicodemus also, as he appears as a disciple at the death of Jesus (John 19:39). There could have been others, unknown to us, who were sympathetic to Jesus and his claims. Perhaps they did not show up at the meeting. It is possible, of course, that they were not informed of it in order that the chief conspirators could be absolutely certain that the vote would go against Jesus.

One of the many ironies of the passion story, which is shot through with irony, is seen in the fact that those who levelled the charge of blasphemy against Jesus were really guilty of it themselves because of the treatment they meted out to the Son of God in their cruel mockery. Their call to him to prophesy was perhaps because of the trumped-up charge that he had said he would destroy and rebuild the temple, so that they were really asking him to produce further ridiculous predictions.

While all this was going on, Peter was 'below in the courtyard' (14:66). This suggests that the trial before the Sanhedrin was being conducted in an upper room. The account bears all the hallmarks of an eyewitness account. For instance, Mark gives us the detail that Peter went out into the entrance between the first two denials (v. 68), presumably to try to escape attention so that he would not have to repeat the denial. Such a small detail is just what we would expect if Mark wrote his Gospel on the basis of Peter's memories of Jesus. Every detail of this particular event would have been etched on his memory, just as the emotion of it would return to his heart at the thought of what he had done.

Other Gospels make it clear that Peter's Galilean origins were detected from his accent (e.g. Matt. 26:73). The Judaeans despised the Galileans with their provincial accent, and one can almost see the curl of the servant-girl's lip as she accused Peter of being both a rough north-country man and a disciple of the 'pretender', himself a Galilean from Nazareth.

The word of Jesus, so vehemently rejected by Peter (v. 30), had proved to be all too true. Peter had been fiercely loyal to him when the conditions were right. He was a man of action and the situation in the Garden of Gethsemane, when his beloved Master was clearly in danger, had suited his temperament; hence the swift drawing of his sword (v. 47). The high priest's house though was so very different. Here the ambience was highly aristocratic. Even though he was not in the 'Upstairs' area but among the 'Downstairs' people, he must have felt totally out of his element. There are occasions when it is not too difficult to witness for Christ, while at other times it is highly embarrassing, but we need always to remember that we are called to be faithful to him at all times. In recounting the events of that day to Mark, we notice that Peter hid his name in the act of loyalty (14:47; cf. John 18:10), but revealed it here in the act of denial.

2. King and Rebel (15:1-15)

Mark refers only briefly to the official trial before the Sanhedrin (15:1). The one recorded in 14:53-65 was evidently a preliminary examination conducted before members of the Sanhedrin who had been contacted hastily during the night. This would have been to make certain that all was in order before the official trial, so that this was really a kind of dress rehearsal in which the hypocritical use of false witnesses was acted out to see how their testimony stood up.

Now comes the trial before Pilate. This would particularly interest Mark's Roman readers, as Pilate was a Roman official. Much as they would dislike doing so, the Jews had no alternative but to hand Jesus over to Pilate, for it was he who had the necessary legal function of confirming the sentence of death.

Jesus had been silent before the high priest until asked a direct question about his Person. The same was true of his trial before Pilate, except that this time an answer preceded his silence instead of *vice versa*. We can easily see why this was. Was he King of the Jews (v. 2)? Yes, he could affirm this, although of course he was not king in any sense that would make him a threat to established authority, either that of Herod or of the Roman emperor, whose local representative Pilate was. How ironic that the one released, Barabbas, was truly guilty of insurrection! We wonder if Mark, who had recorded the words of Jesus, 'to give his life as a ransom for many' (10:45), with their substitutionary implications, had seen this substitution of Jesus for Barabbas as an illustration of the gospel.

Mark does not tell us what accusations the Jews brought against Jesus before Pilate, but he does say that there were many (vv. 3,4). His silence was not really in response to Pilate but rather to the accusations made by the chief priests. Luke tells us that they said, 'We have found this man subverting our nation.

He opposes payment of taxes to Caesar and claims to be Christ, a king' (Luke 23:2).

It was apparently the chief priests, those who formed the inner core of the priestly group, who were leading the accusations against Jesus. Several of them had in fact been high priest, for the Romans rang the changes on this office, which they had made partly political, not wishing any man to hold its power too long. Probably the familiarity of this inner circle of priests with the Roman officials would make them seem the best people to front the accusations. It is more than likely that the leading Pharisees would not be as well known to the Romans.

It is significant that Pilate asks Jesus if he is the King of the Jews. The Jews had translated the messianic claim into political and military terms, which a Roman like Pilate might be expected not only to understand but to take very seriously. This meant then that, on the face of it, Jesus and Barabbas and the other insurrectionists were all on trial for the same sort of offence, rebellion against the rule of the Romans over their country.

The custom of prisoner release by popular request is known from recorded information about what happened in other parts of the empire. Pilate was shrewd enough to see through the vehemence of the chief priests. He discerned that they were envious of the great popularity of Jesus with the people. Only a powerful motive such as envy could lead the members of a subject race, particularly those who had official leadership positions, to hand over a royal pretender to their hated overlords.

There is little doubt that Barabbas would be representative of a good number of insurrectionists at that time. In the first century AD the Romans had a lot of trouble with the Zealots, whose general theological outlook was similar to that of the Pharisees, but who advocated and practised rebellion and guerrilla tactics, and Barabbas may well have been one of these. Mark's language does not make it completely clear that Barabbas had personally committed murder, as 'who had committed murder' is in the plural. Luke 23:19, however, puts this beyond doubt.

We can only guess at the method the chief priests used to stir up the people. Their malign motivation was, of course, extremely strong. If it is true that love can always find a way, so too can hatred. In another touch of irony, they called out for the death of their rightful King when they were themselves under foreign dominion! In fact they addressed this request to their oppressors! Sin leads people into all kinds of illogical positions. The Passion story is in fact full of such ironies.

Verse 15b is very brief but how much suffering it suggests! A Roman flogging was a dreadful experience which left the body grievously torn. In fact it often happened that a man who was flogged never reached his execution at all, for he either died under the flogging itself or on the way from it to the place of crucifixion. Pilate committed a most grievous crime and sin in sending Jesus to flogging and to death when he apparently saw clearly that no charge against him had been proved. This shows how wrong it is to so accuse the Jews of the sin of crucifying Jesus as to give the impression it was a Jewish act only. Pilate the Roman was deeply involved in the sin too.

It has been suggested that the verb 'handed over' is used deliberately here because of its place in the Septuagint (the standard Greek version) of Isaiah 53:12, which we might translate, 'he will divide the spoil with the strong, because his life was delivered up to death: and he was numbered among the transgressors; and he carried the sins of many and was delivered up because of their iniquities.' We cannot however be sure that Mark does this with deliberate allusive intention.

3. Mocking and Majesty (15:16-32)

The Praetorium was the official Jerusalem residence of the Roman governor. Pilate's headquarters were in fact at Caesarea on the coast, but when he was in Jerusalem he used Herod's palace for this purpose, presumably because it was by far the most prestigious dwelling in the city. Luke tells us that Herod was also in Jerusalem at that time (Luke 23:7), and they may well have been using different parts of the same building.

The Roman soldiers subjected Jesus to mockery. They wanted some mock symbols of royalty. The emperor wore a gorgeous scarlet robe and a crown and was addressed with the words, 'Hail, Emperor Caesar!' accompanied by a bowing of the knee. Very well, then, they thought, this pathetic 'King' shall have his day. The purple robe (v. 17) may well have been an old military cloak. There are plenty of plants in the Holy Land with vicious thorns on them and they would have been easy to find. Matthew tells us that they first of all placed the staff in his hand, somewhat like a king's sceptre, before then taking it from him and smiting him with it again and again (Matt 27:29,30). In virtually every culture spitting at a person is a particularly vulgar and insulting act. This mockery was not really directed simply at Jesus himself. These soldiers would have despised the Jews and would have been glad of this opportunity to revile them in this mockery of the one, who they had heard, claimed to be their King. They would show them what the Romans did to those who dared to rebel against their authority.

It was normal for a man condemned to crucifixion to be made to carry the cross-beam to the place of execution. After the terrible agony of a scourging, this would itself have been a terrible ordeal, far beyond the limits of physical strength, especially as the man's back would now have many open wounds on it. Was transferring the carrying of the cross to somebody else an act of kindness on the part of the centurion or was it for purely practical reasons, that he wanted to get the whole business over quickly? We do not know. No doubt he recognized that to command one of his men to carry it would have been highly insulting, so he pressed a passer-by into service.

The reference to Simon of Cyrene and his sons (v. 21) suggests that the family was known at Rome, for a Rufus is mentioned in Romans 16:13, and he could be the same person. Obviously Roman readers would be greatly interested in this. Simon could have been a black proselyte or else a member of a Jewish minority in Cyrene, which is now part of Libya. He could have had no clue when the day began that he would find himself involved in such an event. Up for the Passover, he suddenly found himself participating in the drama at the heart of the world's history.

Two different sites have been identified as the scene of the crucifixion. The balance of archaeological probability now favours the traditional site of Calvary (this word is the Latin equivalent of 'Golgotha') rather than General Gordon's suggested site. This hill, which certainly has a skull-like appearance, was a serious rival to the traditional site for some time. The matter is still not completely settled, however, and will probably never be resolved.

Jerusalem's women customarily provided a drugged alcoholic drink to deaden the severe pain somewhat for those who were being crucified, and apparently the Romans allowed this to be offered to them. It was a mark of the courage of Jesus that he refused it. This was probably because he was determined to drink the cup of suffering for our sins to the dregs.

The cross is the very heart of the Christian faith and has been since the beginning. It is therefore most remarkable that all the Gospel writers state the fact of the crucifixion of Jesus without going into any detail. Mark says simply, 'they crucified him'. No briefer statement of the central event of human history could possibly be penned. There is no attempt to play on the emotions of the readers. The simple fact was eloquent and moving enough in itself.

Mark gives the superscription in brief form. When all four Gospel accounts are put together, it appears that the full wording was 'This is Jesus of Nazareth, the King of the Jews'. It was, of course, intended as a further insult both to Jesus and to the race to which he belonged. He had been given a mock robe, a mock crown and a mock sceptre, and the mock submission of the soldiers to him. Now he was to have a sarcastically motivated title placed there on instructions from Pilate (John 19:19-22). Perhaps the two robbers were associated with Barabbas. The centurion no doubt thought it cynically apt for a royal claimant to be put in the centre of the group.

Insults are now heaped on Jesus by onlookers. Mark records that these came from three sources, the casual passers-by, the religious leaders and the crucified robbers (vv. 29-32). The passers-by no doubt had heard something of the charges brought against him in the high priest's house (14:57-59), for it is more than likely that such information would have been leaked to the outside world.

The word translated 'so' is an interjection which, in the Greek, sounds almost like the barking of a dog. It brings to mind Psalm 22 which pictures the enemies of the sufferer around the cross as wild animals and dogs. Can you hear the scorn in the description 'this Christ, this King of Israel' employed by the religious leaders, especially their contemptuous repetition of the word, 'this' (v. 32)? Even the robbers joined in, perhaps to distract attention from themselves.

How ironic all this was! Both in deed and in word they designated him as King and Saviour. Despite their evil motives and despite the sarcastic form their words took, both titles represented the real truth about him. This shows that there was really a double irony at work here, that of the people being countered by God's own design to mark out his Son as truly their King and Saviour, despite the fact that they acknowledged this only in mockery.

Could he come down from the cross? From the standpoint of his power – yes, of course! From the standpoint of his sacrificial commitment to the Father's loving purpose of salvation for sinners – no, he could not! Remember that insistent 'must' that he used in instructing his disciples on the road to Jerusalem (Mark 8:31; 9:12). What is physically possible is sometimes morally or spiritually impossible. So it was with Jesus.

No doubt many of the men involved in the passion narrative had high positions in their own estimate and in that of others. Yet they all appear so little in the light of the kingship of Jesus. They had given him, in mockery, so many of the trappings of royalty, yet they could not see that in placing him on the execution tree they were giving him a throne which would anticipate that heavenly throne from which he would rule over all.

Some questions for personal reflection

1. Are there situations in my own life in which silence may be more appropriate than speech?

2. Sin leads people into all sorts of illogical positions. Can I think of other examples of this?

Chapter 17

His Sufferings – On The Cross (15:33-47)

All four Gospels writers give generous amounts of space to the story of the passion and death of Jesus, but none more so, in proportion to the length of his Gospel, than does Mark. He also finds other ways of laying exceptional emphasis on the cross. The scholars are agreed on that, and it is evident even to the ordinary reader.

This certainly accords with what we might expect when we bear in mind that Mark wrote his Gospel on the basis of Peter's testimony to Jesus and to the facts of his life and ministry. Peter and the other disciples were with Jesus on his journey to Jerusalem. As they moved along, he kept telling them what the future held for him, and he insisted over and over again that it was his destiny to suffer and to die (8:31; 9:12, 31; 10:32-34).

Simon Peter was there and he heard it all. It horrified him and, as we have seen, when Jesus first spelled it out plainly, he had refused to accept it (8:31-33). On this occasion, Jesus rebuked him most severely, declaring that he heard the voice of Satan in the words of his disciple. Peter would never forget that.

It must have been still very much in his mind when, a week after this, he was in the little group that witnessed the transfiguration of Jesus. In the circumstances, it was an amazing example of the Saviour's grace that he was allowed to be part of that privileged group. At this time, the awesome voice of God had commanded them to listen to Jesus (9:7). As a Jew, brought up in the synagogue, Peter would have taken the Ten Commandments very seriously. Had they not been uttered by the very voice of God himself (Exod. 20)? Now, over a thousand years later, the same great God had again spoken from a mountain top. He would have to take this too very seriously indeed.

This does not mean that he would accept the cross with full understanding of its significance. That would not have come until after the resurrection, perhaps not fully until after Pentecost. Even after that, he may well have been led by the Spirit of God to a deeper and deeper appreciation of it. The profound revolution in his outlook shows up in the large place given to the sufferings and subsequent glory of Christ in his first letter. The two are mentioned together in every chapter. It is very striking that Peter consistently uses the messianic title, 'Christ', in connection with this (1 Peter 1:11, 19; 2:21; 3:18; 4:1, 13; 5:1), for it was not simply the sufferings of Jesus as a beloved Master that he had rejected, but specifically his sufferings as the Messiah (8:29-33). In his first epistle, he embraces this fact as central to God's good news. What a change!

No doubt Peter would have asked Mark to make sure he showed fully enough how important the cross was. This Mark does in several different ways. He does it by recording anticipations of this in the early part of the ministry of Jesus, in the warning Jesus gave that he, the Bridegroom, would be snatched away from his disciples (2:20), and in his reference to the antipathy of leaders within the Jewish community (3:6). An alert reader would also have picked up something ominous from an early reference to the fact that Judas would betray his Master (3:19). Mark did so too by placing some emphasis on the teaching programme Jesus carried through on the Jerusalem road, for he makes reference to it a number of times, and then, of course, by giving much space to the events of the passion itself.

1. Darkness and Dereliction (15:33-39)

We do not know the physical cause of the darkness that came over the land during the final three hours of our Lord's six hours of suffering. Various suggestions have been made, and it is not of course impossible that God used some natural phenomenon to effect this, although this is not certain. What we can say with certainty is that this darkness fittingly symbolized the awful experience of Jesus on the cross. Although personally without sin, he was entering into the darkness that is the portion of those who reject the ways of God. In Paul's profound words, 'Christ redeemed us from the curse of the law by becoming a curse for us' (Gal. 3:13).

It is important for us to approach each Gospel separately and especially to do this as far as the varied records of the passion and death of Jesus are concerned. Often we have a desire to put all four accounts together in order to get a fuller picture, and this is, at one level, quite legitimate and helpful. What such a course of action does, however, is to obscure from view the particular emphases of the individual writers. This is certainly true when it comes to the sayings of Jesus from the cross. We need to remember that God, for his own purposes, gave us the story of Jesus and of his passion in four accounts, not just one, each conveying its distinctive message.

The Gospels record seven utterances from the lips of Jesus as he hung on the cross, all of them brief. Three of these are recorded in the Gospel of John (John 19:26-30) and three different ones in Luke's Gospel (Luke 23:34, 43, 46). That leaves one only, often thought to be the central one of the seven, and this is recorded by two Gospel writers, Matthew and Mark. They then make reference to no other saying from the cross. So these terrible words (v. 34; cf. Matt. 27:46) are allowed to stand in all their awfulness on the page of each of these two Gospels. Not only so, but they stand there uninterpreted. The evangelist makes no comment on them, nothing to help us understand them. Certainly we may think about them in relation to the other sayings, but not until after we have viewed them in their own right, in their own complete isolation on the crucifixion page of Mark and of Matthew.

Why do these words stand in such isolation? Surely it is to challenge us to deep thought and to stab our consciences!

As the Gospel record of our Lord's ministry has proceeded,

the reader is increasingly made aware, not only of the claims that Jesus made for himself and that the Gospel writer himself clearly accepted, but also of the unique character of the Man who made these claims. Here is an unique phenomenon in a sinful world – a Man concerned only to serve God and in so doing to serve others, a Man full not only of great power but also of a deep compassion, and a Man ready to suffer to the utmost in commitment to God's will.

Then, after all that, comes this awful cry! If that does not make us think, then surely nothing will! Jesus himself had already said, 'the Son of Man came ... to give his life as a ransom for many' (10:45). Surely this is the key to the meaning of these dreadful words! Here we get a glimpse into the profound cost of penal substitution, the One dying in place of the many and for the sins of the many. Paul expresses it this way, 'God made him who had no sin to be sin for us, so that in him we might become the righteousness of God' (2 Cor. 5:21).

The words uttered by Jesus are a quotation, taken from the opening of the greatest psalm of the cross, Psalm 22. This deeply-moving psalm, for two thirds of its length, dwells on the sufferings of an innocent man. Some of these sufferings were physical, some were social, some were spiritual. Then in its final third the psalm's whole tone changes and we see that his urgent cry for divine vindication has been answered.

Were there assumptions shared by the writers and the original readers of the New Testament books? We can be sure there were, for they were all Christians. It has been well argued that when the New Testament writers gave a quotation from the Old Testament, they intended their readers to consult the passage concerned and to examine its context, in this way deepening their awareness of the significance of the quotations they used. If the first readers did that here, they might have expected to find God vindicating Jesus even before the Gospel account records the resurrection, for the sufferer in the psalm not only cries out for but also receives such vindication from the Lord (Ps. 22:19-31).

The fact that the words come from a psalm, and that psalms frequently reflect the experience of their authors, makes us ask whether in fact the sufferings of Christ really were unique. In so many psalms, the author cries out for God to come to his aid, especially when he is suffering at the hands of others or is under threat of such sufferings. When the psalmist penned the words of Psalm 22, did they in fact arise out of his own experience? If they did, this must mean that Christ's sufferings do not stand alone.

It is, of course, possible that Psalm 22 is direct prophecy, so that the psalmist wrote of what was to come and not at all of his own experience. In this case, the difficulty simply disappears. Even however if this is not direct prophecy but some kind of typological correspondence, with the psalmist and Christ linked by the sharing of some elements of a common experience, this does not mean that the sufferings of Jesus were not unique. We know from a study of the Old Testament that the same words may reflect quite different outlooks. Both Saul and David, when confronted with their sins, said, 'I have sinned' (1 Sam. 15:24; 2 Sam. 12:13) and yet what they said and did subsequently reveals that their attitudes were very different. For the psalmist, the words which open Psalm 22 need mean simply that he had lost for a while his awareness of the presence of God, not that God had in fact abandoned him. In Christ's case, however, the forsaking had to be completely real as he was bearing sin as our substitute.

In this great cry all the deepest questions human beings have asked, whether they be the most eminent philosophers or quite ordinary men and women, have their meeting-point. Here are deep questions, ultimate questions – the question about the nature of God, the question about the existence of evil, the question about the meaning of suffering, and particularly, of innocent suffering. Such questions have been on the lips and in the writings of a great many and in the hearts of many more. It is most moving to know that Christ has entered so deeply into our profoundest questions as well as being God's answer to our deepest need.

Some in the crowd evidently misheard him (v. 35), for the first two syllables of 'Elijah' practically coincide with those of 'Eloi'. So then Jesus, who had been so often misunderstood, was to suffer misunderstanding to the very end. In his Gospel, Mark occasionally gives some of the words of Jesus in the Aramaic language and explains them for his Roman readers (see also 5:41; 7:11,34), and he does that here. Matthew, who also records the saying, gives it in the Hebrew. Some of the ancient manuscripts of Mark also use the Hebrew form rather than the Aramaic and the NIV follows this particular textual tradition. Most textual scholars, however, regard the Aramaic form as the correct text for Mark's record of the cry.

Perhaps news of the messianic claim Jesus had made before the high priest had been 'leaked' to the crowd, and that this was what lay behind their mishearing at this time, for Elijah's return was associated by the Jews with the advent of the Messiah, as we have already seen in studying Mark 9:1-13. They would take it then that even on the cross Jesus was continuing to maintain his messiahship.

Again there is an offer of a drink. This time, as John tells us (John 19:29,30) Jesus drank it, for this time there is no mention of a narcotic element in it, and so, if this was absent, it would not have the same capacity to dull the senses. The comment of the one who gave him this drink seems to show that he at least was still open to the possibility that the messianic claim of Jesus was true. His words are unlikely to have been cynical when he uttered them in the course of performing an act of kindness.

As we have seen already in the comment on 15:24, the evangelists make no attempt to extract pathos from the story of the Passion. They simply let the facts speak for themselves, and this is deeply impressive, especially with the strong sense of the dramatic which they have, Mark most of all. Yet it is equally remarkable that none of them says simply that Jesus died. They all so word their record as to indicate that his death was his own act. Had he not said of his life, 'No-one takes it from me, but I lay it down of my own accord' (John 10:18)?

The loud cry (v. 37), so extraordinary in its power when coming from somebody who was *in extremis* through terrible suffering, can hardly have been anything other than the triumphant affirmation recorded by John, 'It is finished' (John 19:30). This consists of just one word in the Greek, so that the deepest question ever asked, in verse 34, was followed now by the greatest statement ever to pass through human lips.

The tearing of the great curtain (v. 38), which in the temple separated the Holy Place from the Holy of Holies, was of great significance. This was the God-ordained symbol of the barrier that sin creates between himself in all his holiness and the fallen race of mankind, including even, of course, the Jewish people in whose sanctuary it was located. The tearing of it was clearly a supernatural event, for the curtain was thick and strong, almost more like a carpet for strength than the somewhat flimsy item the word 'veil' (employed in some of our English versions) suggests to us. No human hand could have torn it, certainly not throughout its length. Notice too that Mark tells us that it was torn 'from top to bottom'. This indication of direction is perhaps his way of making sure we realise that this was a supernatural act of God

How did Mark know that this occurred when it did and that the tear first began to appear from the top end, with all its implications of a divine Hand at work? Perhaps there were priests at work there, who were subsequently among those converted to Christ, for the Acts of the Apostles records a remarkable movement of God's grace among them in Acts 6:7, 'a large number of priests became obedient to the faith.' The Writer to the Hebrews, who had a major interest in the implications of the death of Christ for the worship system of Israel, interprets the tearing of this curtain theologically (Heb. 9:1-14; 10:19-22). It is a source of powerful assurance to Christian believers that such a symbol of sin's barrier as this curtain was thus supernaturally torn, for it spells acceptance for us. The way into God's presence is now open for all who will come by faith.

275

What is the climax of the great story told by Mark in his book?

In terms of the life-history of Jesus it is undoubtedly his death. Mark has been leading his readers to this more and more as the story has unfolded. Certainly the resurrection too was of great importance, and so this, which lay beyond the cross, was really a climax beyond the climax. Here was God's vindication of all his Son had done and had been. Here then were two great actions of God, the two greatest since the world began, never to be surpassed. At the level of human reaction to Jesus, however, the utterance of the centurion as he stood at the cross (v. 39) was the greatest moment.

Remember that Mark has been writing primarily for Roman readers. The centurion was a kind of non-commissioned officer and so could represent perhaps an ordinary Roman, with all the strengths and weaknesses of such a person. Without doubt, he would be enamoured by power rather than weakness, by authority rather than submission, by action rather than passive acceptance. Yet here he articulates faith in an apparently helpless Jew who had been crucified by the hands of a military detachment under his own command! This makes his recognition of Jesus truly astounding.

What was it that brought him to faith? In verse 39, Mark seems to be saying that it was the cry and the way Jesus died. He will have known something of the claims of Jesus already, certainly his claim to be King. After all, the actions of the soldiers recorded in verses 16 to 24 were all related to his claim to kingship, and we can be sure that this would have been the subject of many a sarcastic jest among the soldiers at their headquarters. It was of course from there that the centurion had himself led Jesus out to Golgotha. Could he have known that he was called the Son of God? We cannot be sure. It seems it was the manner of his death ('how he died', v. 39) which evoked his faith.

The centurion's faith is one of the great moments in this Gospel because, of course, Mark's desire is to bring his Roman readers to this point, in order to confirm some of them in a faith to which they had already come and perhaps to see others come for the first time. Just as the Prologue to the Gospel of John (John 1:1-18), with its affirmations of deity, is designed to begin a story that led eventually to the great confession of Thomas, 'My Lord and my God!' (John 20:28), so the opening words of Mark's Gospel, 'The beginning of the gospel about Jesus Christ, the Son of God,' are meant to lead the readers to this point and to an affirmation of their own faith in Jesus. If the story of Jesus as told by Mark is a veritable preaching of the good news (1:1), then we would expect something of this nature as the book comes to its climax.

If you compare 8:29 with Matthew 16:16, you will notice that Mark gives Peter's confession of Jesus in a briefer form than does Matthew, omitting the words, 'the Son of the living God'. It is not easy to see why he does this when it is clear from his Gospel that he believed in the divine sonship of Jesus. One possible reason could be that Mark desired to highlight not so much the faith of Peter, a Jewish disciple of Jesus, but the utterance of a Roman Gentile, so that he reserved the full affirmation of divine sonship until its utterance by the Roman soldier.

Did this man understand what he was saying in full Christian terms, or are his words to be understood against the background of a Graeco-Roman world-view in which a number of gods and demi-gods visited this world from time to time? Certainly we should not read too much into what he said, attributing to him as full an understanding of the significance of Christ's Person as the Gospel writers themselves show, but the occurrence of this event in the narrative at this most important point certainly suggests that Mark believed the words were the manifestation of a true if simple faith. He is unlikely to have recorded words which meant markedly less than the phrase 'Son of God' means elsewhere in his Gospel.

2. Dead and Buried (15:40-47)

The women who were to be witnesses of the resurrection were watching at a place which, although somewhat distant, was near enough to enable them to observe what was happening. Without doubt they knew that the death of Jesus was absolutely real. Their presence at that death-scene was a matter of great importance, for they were to be the first witnesses of his resurrection, and, although they were quite unaware of this at the time, they needed to be quite sure that he had suffered a real death.

In 15:47-16:1, Mark mentions three of the women by name. Mary Magdalene came from Magdalan, a fishing-place on the sea of Galilee, which does not figure in the Gospels as much as Capernaum or Bethsaida, but which is so near to them that Jesus is likely to have visited it from time to time. Luke tells us that Jesus had cast out seven demons from her (Luke 8:2). Mary the mother of James the younger and Joses is mentioned in 15:40, 47 and 16:1. Her special mention may well mean that she or members of her family were known to Mark's Roman Christian readers. Salome is the third woman and a comparison with Matthew 27:56 strongly suggests that she was the mother of the disciples James and John. Although these women did not belong to the apostolic band, they were close to Jesus and they were shortly to have a very important part to play in relaying the glad news of his resurrection from the dead.

Mark was writing for Gentiles and so he needed to give some brief explanation of Jewish customs. The Roman readers would have been aware of the Sabbath, for keeping the Sabbath was one of the most obvious features of Jewish life in the Gentile lands of the Dispersion at this time, and of course there were Jewish Christians in the church at Rome, but they might have been less aware of the Preparation Day. Preparation was an important part of the celebration of special days at that time, as it still is in Jewish homes. The Sabbath was the highlight of the Jewish week and, as the afternoon of the previous day moved towards its close, everything was done to make certain that there was no temptation to break its regulations by working after it had begun.

The action of Joseph of Arimathaea deserves more thought than it usually gets. Normally the members of an executed man's family would ask for his body after his death had taken place. It is therefore all the more surprising that Joseph did this. He was a member of the Sanhedrin. Luke tells us that he had refused to agree to the execution of Jesus (Luke 23:51). This in itself says something about his character as a man of integrity with a concern for true justice. It was, however, one thing to vote 'No!' or simply to absent himself from the crucial meeting of the Council, and quite another to stand out boldly as a disciple of the despised Nazarene, which he now did.

What makes his action so extraordinary is that it might well have seemed completely pointless. The Leader of the messianic movement was dead; surely the movement itself could not long survive his demise. Yet this was the moment Joseph chose to come out into the open. Did he have an anticipation of the resurrection which went beyond that of the apostles? On the face of it, that seems improbable. It seems more likely that he simply felt ashamed that he had not declared himself before this. Mark describes this as a bold act and it certainly was. It would hardly have endeared him to most of his fellow-members of the Sanhedrin.

He was 'waiting for the kingdom of God' (v. 43). We might compare this with our Lord's words to the teacher of the Law who asked him a question in the temple, 'You are not far from the kingdom of God' (12:34). We might also compare it with two other descriptions employed in Luke's Gospel. Simeon was 'waiting for the consolation of Israel' (Luke 2:25), and Anna the prophetess spoke of Jesus 'to all who were looking forward to the redemption of Jerusalem' (Luke 2:38). The probability is that all these expressions meant approximately the same thing. In the Old Testament, God had encouraged his people to expect the coming of a new era in his dealings with his people, a time when his great purposes in history would find complete fulfilment. Such promises undoubtedly fostered a deep spiritual longing in the hearts of many people. Joseph was clearly one of these. No wonder his heart went out in faith to Jesus!

This means then that Mark has given us two affirmations of new-found faith at this important point in his Gospel, and he has placed the second almost immediately after the first. Faith is found in the words of the centurion and also in the deeds of Joseph, the one a Roman and the other a Jew. The probability is that both would have faced ridicule from their compatriots as a result of their confession of Jesus. The Gentile and Jewish Christians at Rome will have found these two events and affirmations of great interest and many readers not yet Christians would be challenged by them.

Mark records Pilate's surprise at hearing that Jesus was already dead. This was due, without doubt, to the fact that death did not usually come quickly to those who had been crucified. This again shows that Jesus had dismissed his spirit and so had died at his own time. Again this reveals that God was sovereign over everything, even the moment of the death of his Son. 'He was already dead ... Jesus had already died...' – this reiteration in verse 44 serves to emphasize the reality of his death.

Joseph performed the final act of sealing the tomb with a heavy stone. On Scottish Television's 'Evening Call', a speaker once suggested the kind of conversation Joseph of Arimathaea might have had with a fellow-member of the Sanhedrin, who spoke to him contemptuously of Jesus. 'Fancy you giving your new tomb to that man Jesus!' he said. 'Give!' said Joseph. 'Why yes, I did intend it as a gift. In fact though, he only took it as a loan. You see, as it happened, he only needed it for the weekend.'

What a vindication of Joseph's faith the resurrection of Jesus must have been!

The two closing verses of the chapter convey a sense of finality. The closing of the tomb might have seemed a most decisive act, a fitting conclusion therefore to a book about the life and death of Jesus, as decisive in its own way as the conclusion to the Book of Genesis, where it is said of Joseph, 'after they embalmed him, he was placed in a coffin in Egypt' (Gen. 50:26). But – read on into the last chapter!

Some questions for personal reflection

1. What period am I going to set aside today or in the next few days to think prayerfully about the sufferings of Christ for me and to spend some time in seeking to express my gratitude to him?

2. Identifying with Joseph of Arimathaea, how would I react to the news of the resurrection of Jesus?

Chapter 18

His Resurrection and Ascension (16:1-20)

Florence Barclay's books are not read today as they once were. They are love stories with a high moral tone. Unhappily, our present society has little taste for stories in which the lovers are strongly committed to each other but abstain from physical sex until they are married.

In one of her stories, *The Following of the Star*, she plays a clever trick on her readers. Without in any way incorporating explicit untruth (for even fiction may have untruth in it), she manages to convey the impression that the hero, David Rivers, is dead. The reader feels depressed, for the two main participants in the story are folk of fine character, obviously made for each other, and there is the sense that anticipation has been built up only to be dashed in the end. In fact, however, the reader has read between the lines and has picked up the wrong message. This was, of course, exactly what the author intended in order to effect a surprising, and, the reader feels, a morally appropriate conclusion. In the final chapter of her book, all is revealed. David is alive and he and his beloved are reunited, thankful to have restored to them a love they thought they had forever lost.

The story of Jesus has a 'happy ending', but this is no literary trick. Neither is it contrived by an author more interested in a satisfying story than in fidelity to complete truthfulness. Most of all, it is not a happy ending achieved without pain. It is in fact the very antithesis of this. The pain element is intense, in fact its intensity and even more so its depth are beyond parallel in the annals of human history. It is not then a sense of literary fitness that makes the reader long for a happy ending to this story. It is rather a deep awareness of the fitness of things in a world presided over by a God who is both all-holy and all-powerful. If God is good and sovereign, and if Jesus is the Son of God and throughout his life did his will consistently from the heart, then there has just got to be a happy ending.

You see, what we feel about this true story takes us right to the very root convictions we have, to something that is inwoven into our very beings. We are certain that right must triumph in the end. If it seems to matter even in fiction, it matters desperately in life itself. If right does not triumph ultimately, then there is really no sense to anything. The whole human experience, with its moral choices and its awareness of a judgement to come, cries out for justice to be done.

Not of course that this has always happened, not even in fiction, still less in life. Realism compels us to face this fact. We are however convinced that ultimately justice will be done, the innocent sufferer vindicated and the unpunished wrongdoer brought to the bar of sovereign Holiness. Moreover, it is largely because of God's vindication of Christ that we can be so sure of this.

You see, if it matters in the story of a man like Job, whose innocence can only have been relative anyway (for there has only ever been one perfect life), how much more does it matter in the life of Jesus! As Peter tells us (Acts 10:38), 'he went around doing good and healing all who were under the power of the devil, for God was with him.'

It might perhaps be said that the vindication could wait, that at the end of time God would show that Jesus was truly his Son and that he warmly approved of his life and ministry. It is of course true that this will happen, and there will be a great vindication at the Second Advent of the Lord Jesus. But what is so wonderful about the Christian gospel is the fact that, in a most decisive manner, that vindication has already occurred, that assurance has been given to us, within history itself, of God's vindication of truth and right. For our own commitment, this is exactly what we need.

Make no mistake about it, this is no cleverly contrived fiction. The whole story is filled with pointers to the reality of it all, pointers of such a character that cumulatively they are a very strong basis for faith.

It is Peter, Mark's source of information, who says to the people of Jerusalem, 'You killed the author of life, but God raised him from the dead. We are witnesses of this' (Acts 3:15). This witness, declared so often by Peter and his fellow-apostles in their preaching of the good news, is now put into written form in the Gospel of Mark.

1. The certainty of resurrection (16:1-8)

The triumphant affirmation that death was not the end for Jesus, but that God had brought him out of death into undying life, was so often the message of Peter as he preached the good news of Jesus in the city of Jerusalem. We can imagine him too, sitting perhaps in a Roman tenement (as we suggest on page 16), talking this over with Mark. Mark tells the story briefly but clearly. The other Gospels supply us with more information, but the essentials are all here in this briefest of the accounts of the life, death and rising again of Jesus Christ.

It is important to note that it was the very women who were at the cross, who saw the death and burial of their Lord and who could never be convinced that these events did not happen, who were assured by the angel that he had risen from the dead. It is well worth noting that their names are given three times within nine verses (from 15:40 to 16:1). Why this repetition? After they have been once mentioned by name, why not simply refer to 'the women'? The most likely explanation is that the repetition was deliberately done with an evidential motive.

The same women – precisely the same women, Mark wants to make clear – were witnesses of the three events that are at the heart of the gospel, the same gospel of which Paul writes when he says, 'For what I received I passed on to you as of first importance: that Christ died for our sins according to the Scriptures, that he was buried, that he was raised on the third day according to the Scriptures' (1 Cor. 15:3,4). Dead, buried, and risen again – these are the three main historical facts proclaimed in the evangel of the early church, and all three facts were known to these women. The first two were directly experienced and the third was declared by an angel, although of course they saw that the tomb was empty and eventually saw Jesus for themselves. Nobody was ever going to convince them that Jesus had neither died nor risen again. They would have a rock-hard assurance of these facts.

Why the spices? It was not customary among the Jews to embalm bodies that had been buried. It is in fact such an unusual feature that this in itself testifies to its truth. Those who wish to deceive do not risk embroidering their tales with unusual details when these are quite unnecessary.

A little thought about the facts may yield an answer. The body of Jesus had been in the tomb for about thirty-six hours. Two thirds of this time was during two nights. The hours of the day would have been hot but the inside of a tomb would be cooler than most places. The women may well have reckoned that decomposition might begin during the day in prospect and so, out of their deep respect for Jesus, they had brought sweet-smelling spices in order to reduce the odour. They did not of course realize that the Old Testament had said of him that his flesh should not see decay, in a passage (Ps. 16:10) which was to be quoted by Peter in his Pentecost sermon (Acts 2:27). This would certainly account too for the fact that they were going to the tomb so very early in the morning, before the sun rose high in the sky.

Mark tells us about the rolling away of the stone and also about the young man they saw within the tomb, but he does not say, as Matthew does, that this was an angel, nor that the angel had himself been responsible for rolling away the stone (Matt. 28:1-5). Perhaps he reckoned he had said so much so far about the supernatural power and activity of Jesus that his readers were sure to discern the supernatural nature of the events he recorded here. Not only so, but it may be that he wanted nothing to distract his readers from focusing on the central fact, Jesus had risen from the dead! The reference to the angel as a 'young man', of course, clearly relates to his appearance as far as the women were concerned, for age can hardly have meaning in relation to angelic beings.

The central affirmation of the angel lies in the words, 'He has risen!' This wonderful declaration, just one word in the Greek, is the only one that can be placed, in terms of its importance, alongside the triumphant affirmation of Jesus from his cross (itself also just one Greek word), 'It is finished!' (John 19:30). Together they set forth, with great simplicity, the central truths of the good news of God. A child can understand them and yet the profoundest Christian mind can never plumb their depths.

The two sentences that follow show us that the words were intended to refer to a physical fact, not simply to something like the continued influence of Jesus beyond his death, nor even to the survival of his spirit in some ethereal existence. They were about his body. The resurrection was a physical fact. The body was no longer there.

There is added assurance in the description of Jesus as 'the Nazarene'. This reference to his home-town is a homely touch, for it relates him to the place where he grew up, the place people would most naturally associate with him. It is as if to underline the fact that it was a real Man, a Man who could be named and located, who had conquered death. The invitation, 'See the place where they laid him,' again shows an emphasis on evidence, which is such a marked feature of the story of the resurrection as given in this chapter by Mark.

The women were to be messengers to the disciples. The angel refers to 'his disciples and Peter' (v. 7). Why the mention of his name? Was he no longer to be reckoned among the disciples? This is certainly not the reason for the specific reference to him, for we find him in the Acts of the Apostles as the foremost preacher of the gospel. It is in fact very touching, for it has on it all the marks of forgiveness for one who had so grievously denied his Lord. It is as if they were being told, 'Please do not forget Peter!'

The reference to Galilee so soon after Jesus has been

described as 'the Nazarene' carries its own message. Jesus was going home, to the old familiar territory where they had companied with him for several years. Perhaps this was one more way of telling them that he really was the same Jesus. What could be more natural than a return to his home area?

It is in fact in this combination of the supernatural and the natural, the transcendent and the homely, that the wonder of the resurrection of Jesus consists. The risen One is not some totally supernatural being, but the familiar figure of the great Teacher and Healer and, through his sufferings and death, the great Saviour, so well-known to these disciples. Yet the resurrection makes clear that he is transcendent too. As Paul puts it, 'he was declared to be the Son of God with power ... by his resurrection from the dead' (Rom. 1:4).

The reader discerns a gentle rebuke in the reference to the fact that Jesus had already told them about his resurrection. It seems from the accounts Mark gives of his teaching programme on the way from Galilee to Jerusalem, that Jesus never mentioned his death without speaking also of his resurrection (8:31; 9:9-12,31; 10:33,34). The disciples had perhaps been so preoccupied with the awful disclosure of a destiny of suffering that they could hardly take in the wonderful declaration that death would not be the end, that he would triumph over it. Without doubt, however, they should have absorbed this.

What was the reaction of the women to the empty tomb and to the angel's declaration? Overflowing joy? Thankful praise? No! Mark uses four words to describe it. Let us seek to take in the force of them. They were 'alarmed', 'trembling', 'bewildered', 'afraid'. Not what we might have expected, is it? Or is it? We must give some thought to their significance.

The women must have arrived on the scene in a mood of deep despair. Jesus was dead, and death is the most final fact we know of in this life. Some people are optimists, and are often hopeful in situations where others are in despair. Optimism may give us hope in all kinds of circumstances – from the mere loss of valuable material on a computer disk to the onslaught of terminal cancer – but death is different and utterly beyond the scope of even the most extreme optimism. It belongs to a different order, the order of absolute finality.

Coming to the tomb in that mood, the women were not conditioned for comfort of any order above that of sympathy. The stone rolled back, the body gone, these things were simply aggravations of a despair too deep for description or for utterance. What could anybody have wanted with the body of Jesus? John gives us confirmation of all this in telling us about Mary Magdalene's deep distress (John 20:10-15).

It is possible in fact that they did not really take in the words of this strange young man, although they would mean much to them at a later time. They may not even have realized he was an angel. So they went out with bewilderment and fear added to the deep despondency with which they came. What a combination of negative emotions!

Some have thought that the Gospel of Mark originally ended at this point. This seems hardly likely, but if so, it would mean that Mark leaves the reader to make up his own mind, not compelling faith but leaving room for it.

2. The barrier of unbelief (16:9-14)

There is a textual problem related to verses 9-20, which are absent from some important early manuscripts, while some other manuscripts contain a briefer alternative ending. It is perhaps significant, however, that almost all of those which have this short ending have the longer ending as well. The former rarely stands alone in a manuscript of the Gospel.

This shorter ending is as follows: 'But they reported briefly to Peter and those with him all that they had been told. And after this Jesus sent out by means of them, from east to west, the sacred and imperishable proclamation of eternal salvation.' There is of course nothing in the contents of this briefer ending that presents real difficulties, although some have thought its final phrase rather high-sounding for Mark, whose preference is for plain and often terse writing. It is in fact most unlikely to have been original. The manuscript authority for it is weak.

Are the received words an authentic part of the original Gospel? Were they written later? Is it possible even that they came later from the pen of Mark himself, rather like the epilogue written by John as the last chapter of the Gospel that bears his name (John 21)? If so, what was the reason for this addition? Was the abrupt ending thought to be unsatisfactory, or was the original ending in fact lost? What too are we to make of the existence of the alternative ending? Were two attempts made, probably by two different writers, to complete the Gospel, only one of which found general acceptance?

Without doubt there are real problems to be faced in connection with the received ending. Verse 9 seems a strange and abrupt continuation of the story as told in the earlier verses, especially as Mary Magdalene has already been referred to in verse 1, and there are quite a number of words in verses 9 to 20 which do not occur elsewhere in the Gospel. Objections are also raised to some of the contents, especially to verses 14, 17 and 18, objections we must consider when we look at the verses in question.

What is certain though is that the Longer Ending was known by about the middle of the second century. The evidence for this is quite unambiguous. Also the amount of Christian literature we have which pre-dates the mid-second century is quite limited and so is insufficient to make lack of reference to this passage at all significant.

What then are we to think about this matter? The longer ending has been accepted as genuine by the church for most of its history, and its authenticity was never seriously questioned until the rise of modern textual study. This suggests therefore that Christians never doubted its harmony with all that went before it in Mark and with the other books of the New Testament. The possibility that Mark wrote it certainly cannot be ruled out.

In the providence of God it has been in the possession of the Christian church at least from a very early time. In the absence of evidence unambiguously showing its authorship, however, our wisest approach is probably to view it as a genuine product of the apostolic or immediately post-apostolic ages, whether it is by Mark himself or not, and to treat its material as confirmatory of material from the other Gospels and from the Acts of the Apostles, rather than of undisputed authority in itself. We will in fact see, in our treatment of it, how often its teaching does give such confirmation.

Mark tells us that Mary Magdalene was one of the female witnesses to the death and burial of Jesus and to the resurrection proclamation of the angel (15:47; 16:1-5). It seems quite appropriate then, when we are told that she was the first to see Jesus in his risen form. John gives us a much fuller and deeply moving account of what happened (John 20:11-18). The reference to the expulsion of demons from her is interesting in view of the later reference to exorcism in verse 17, which makes use of the same verb.

The reference to the two disciples is presumably an allusion to the story of the Emmaus Road, recorded in Luke 24, the story which such a sceptic as Ernst Renan surprisingly described as the most beautiful story ever told, perhaps expressing in this a wish that he could believe its truth. What though does 'in a different form' mean? Does it suggest why the two disciples were unable to recognize Jesus (Luke 24:16), that there was in fact something different in his appearance? Alternatively, do the words simply refer to the fact that, because of his resurrection, his body was of such a nature that he could vanish from their sight during the meal in their house? Probably the latter is intended.

The scepticism shown by the disciples at first may have been natural but it was also culpable, for Jesus had told them, clearly, plainly and frequently, that he would rise again. Its very existence, though, shows that the resurrection was based on fact, not wishful thinking. The idea that the disciples created the doctrine of the resurrection of Jesus, because they could not believe his teaching would die with him, does not fit at all well psychologically with this scepticism.

Verse 14 has a counterpart in Luke 24: 36-43 in terms of an appearance to the Eleven while they were eating, but Luke's account makes no reference to the fact that he rebuked them. It does however echo what we have earlier in this Gospel, and especially Christ's rebuke of Peter (8:31-33). Peter had refused to accept the word of Jesus that he would suffer. If the death and resurrection of Christ are the heart of the gospel, as they are, we should not be surprised if we find Jesus rebuking unbelief of the latter as well as of the former.

These verses in fact lay special emphasis on unbelief and faith, and fit well with the beginning of the book, where Mark indicates that what he is producing is a declaration of the gospel. That gospel, as a survey of the various sermons in the Acts of the Apostles shows, always came to its climax in a call for faith. This was what Peter called for in his preaching, as a survey of his sermons recorded in the opening chapters of Acts will show, so that the emphasis on faith here could be reckoned part of a case for the Markan authorship of the longer ending. It is important to note that unbelief's ultimate result is condemnation (16:16), as we are frequently told in the Gospel of John (e.g. John 3:18; 8:24).

3. The responsibility of evangelism (16:15, 16)

At one point during his Galilean ministry Jesus had called the Twelve to him, and had sent them out on a tour, during which they preached and cast out demons and healed many (6:7-13). His original commission given by him to them is now widened. Now they were to take the whole world as their parish.

Can we find any preparation for this earlier in the Gospel? Yes! In his great discourse about the future, Jesus told them that the gospel had to be preached to all nations (13:10). Moreover, shortly after this Mark tells us that the action of Mary of Bethany in anointing Jesus for his burial would be told 'wherever the gospel is preached throughout the world' (14:9). So then this wide commission is not unexpected.

The Great Commission is the name given to the instruction

of Jesus that his disciples were to go into the world and preach the word of the gospel everywhere. This is recorded explicitly no less than five times over, in Matthew 28:18-20, here in Mark 16:15,16, in Luke 24:46, 47, in John 20:21 and finally in Acts 1:8. The wording in each case is different, for not all the passages refer to the same occasion and in any case each evangelist will have made a selection from what were probably a series of statements and commands given by Jesus.

It is surely clear that exceptional emphasis is being laid on this. The importance of the *kerygma* (a technical term for the preached message of the gospel) is widely recognized, and it is seen by many scholars to be the factor that binds all the material in the New Testament together. If this message is needed by all, as it undoubtedly is, then the Great Commission is just what we might have expected. We should recognize the importance of the gospel, but this recognition should go hand in hand with commitment on our part to proclaim it everywhere. Here then is the major task of the church in every age, for the world has not yet been fully evangelized.

Faith sealed in baptism is the response for which the gospel preacher is to call, with a warning of the seriousness of unbelief. We should note both the reference to baptism, showing the importance of this outward expression and witness to inward faith, but also the fact that only unbelief is mentioned in the second part of verse 16. These facts together suggest that faith alone is essential but that the importance of baptism for obedience should not be under-rated.

4. The power of God (16:17-20)

Jesus says that God would give confirmatory evidence of the truth of the gospel and therefore affirm the faith of those who believed its truth by acts of his power.

The word 'sign' is more characteristic of the Gospel of John than of Mark. In the former it is a leading feature of the story of Jesus (e.g. 2:11; 20:30). In fact, some commentators have entitled much of the first half of that Gospel 'the Book of Signs'.

293

There, however, it is related exclusively to the deeds of Jesus himself and never to those of the disciples. It is important to notice, of course, that the performance of these signs is not attributed to the believers themselves, but rather to the activity of God (v. 20). So not only are Jesus and his disciples at one, but they are also to be distinguished, for the works of Jesus as 'signs' are manifestations of his glory (John 2:11), whereas the power at work in those of the disciples is never attributed to them personally.

All but one of the signs to which reference is made here can be documented from the Acts of the Apostles. See, for instance (following the order given here), Acts 5:16; 2:4; 28:3-5 and 28:8. The exception is the reference to drinking deadly poison, but this may be taken as of the same order as picking up snakes, for in both cases it is clearly protection from death through poisoning that is in view.

Note the phrase, 'in my name,' in verse 17. Every verb in verses 17 and 18 has the same grammatical form. This strongly suggests that this phrase is meant to govern the whole series, not just its first clause. This then makes us aware of the fact that these acts could only be accomplished in Jesus' name, which implies not only acting on his authority, but also giving glory to him and seeking his will. Certainly this passage does not mean that such things should accompany the gospel on every occasion of its proclamation, for that is to read into it something that is not there. Nor does it mean that believers should 'put God to the test' by deliberately lifting snakes or drinking poison. Such folly cannot claim the passage here as its warrant. When such things do occur, however, in connection with the authentic gospel of Christ preached in the power of the Holy Spirit, they are witnesses to its truth.

The words of verses 19 and 20 certainly make a most fitting conclusion to the Gospel. The ascension is recorded more fully in Acts 1. In fact, Luke is our chief witness to it as an actual physical fact, for he also refers to it in Luke 24:51. We should remember though that the authority of the ascended Christ is either taught or assumed in many of the New Testament epistles. What could we possibly make of the continued heavenly priesthood of Jesus, so fully expounded in the Letter to the Hebrews, if he had not actually ascended into heaven? If God not only raised him from the dead but seated him at his right hand in the heavenly realms (Eph. 1:20), what sense can we make of this unless it took place by way of ascension?

The Gospel ends with an assurance that the disciples actually obeyed Christ's commission. Perhaps it will make us consider the extent of our own obedience to him.

Some questions for personal reflection

1. In what ways does the story of the resurrection of Jesus give me assurance about the character and purposes of God?

2. In what ways will Christ himself mean more to me now than he did before I began this study of the Gospel of Mark, and in what ways will this mean a change in my life?

What Now?

If you have worked your way through the Gospel of Mark with the help of this book, what will you do to follow this up? There are all sorts of useful possibilities.

You could read more books on the Gospel of Mark in a desire to know it more intimately. If this is your desire, you will find a list of suggested books on page 33.

You could study other books of the New Testament. This could be by reading it right through, or by taking up the detailed study of one of the other Gospels, or you could see how the apostles Christ appointed took the good news of Jesus out to other parts of their land and overseas. The Acts of the Apostles tells some important parts of this story. You could read some of the epistles and see how the great facts about Jesus are interpreted in them, or you could have 'a peep at the end' by reading the Book of the Revelation.

Another possibility is to make a start on some Old Testament book, to see something of the background to the coming of Jesus. Just as Mark gives us the beginning of the good news (1:1), so Genesis tells us about the beginning of everything (Gen. 1:1).

Perhaps, though, God still has some unfinished business with you before you move on. This is because the Gospel of Mark is such a challenging document.

Mark so structured his Gospel as to focus attention on the cross of Jesus, and, after he had recorded that event, he gave his readers a challenge to believe.

Paul's letter to the Romans was written to a church composed both of Gentiles and of Jews, and it is often assumed that 'the weak' and 'the strong' who are in view in chapters 14 and 15 of that letter are two groups composed mostly of Jews and Gentiles respectively.

It is not surprising then to find Mark recording two great

affirmations of faith, one by a Gentile and the other by a Jew, one by word and the other by deed. The significance of the second is not always as fully recognized as is that of the first.

First, there is the story of the centurion's confession of Christ (15:38-39). Here a soldier, who was probably a worshipper of power and who had been responsible for carrying out the act of crucifixion, confesses a despised Jew as Son of God. Mark surely intends his readers to follow this man's example.

Then comes the story of Joseph of Arimathaea (15:42-46). What a great act of faith and of committed discipleship was his visit to Pilate to offer his tomb as a resting- place for the body of Jesus! This faith was wonderfully vindicated in the Saviour's resurrection, and so here too is a challenge to believe.

That challenge still comes to us through Mark's pages.

Perhaps you are already a committed believer in Christ. Has the Gospel a challenge for you?

Yes, it has!

Simon Peter and Andrew, James and John, Levi and others all became disciples of Jesus, and they followed him devotedly. They saw his miracles and they heard his teaching. What caused them real problems though was his teaching about the cross, his insistence that this was absolutely necessary.

We can understand this even though we ourselves have come to accept that he died for us and to put our faith in him as our crucified and risen Lord. If you are a Christian, then without doubt his cross and resurrection will mean a great deal to you.

But let us hear the call of the Saviour to these men. 'If anyone would come after me, he must deny himself and take up his cross and follow me' (8:34)! This call too is an abiding one, as Paul recognized when he wrote Romans chapter 6, with its message that we should reckon ourselves to have been crucified and risen with Christ.

If we love him for what he has done for us, this call comes challengingly to us to surrender personal ambition, and gladly to embrace his will, even if that may mean suffering. If he did so much for me, can I deny him this?

Subject Index

Christian Focus Publications
publishes books for all ages

Our mission statement –

STAYING FAITHFUL

In dependence upon God we seek to help make His infallible word, the Bible, relevant. Our aim is to ensure that the Lord Jesus Christ is presented as the only hope to obtain forgiveness of sin, live a useful life and look forward to heaven with Him.

REACHING OUT

Christ's last command requires us to reach out to our world with His gospel. We seek to help fulfill that by publishing books that point people towards Jesus and help them develop a Christ-like maturity. We aim to equip all levels of readers for life, work, ministry and mission.

Books in our adult range are published in three imprints.

Christian Focus contains popular works including biographies, commentaries, basic doctrine, and Christian living. Our children's books are also published in this imprint.

Mentor focuses on books written at a level suitable for Bible College and seminary students, pastors, and other serious readers. The imprint includes commentaries, doctrinal studies, examination of current issues, and church history.

Christian Heritage contains classic writings from the past.

For a free catalogue of all our titles, please write to

Christian Focus Publications, Ltd
Geanies House, Fearn,
Ross-shire, IV20 1TW, Scotland, United Kingdom
info@christianfocus.com

For details of our titles visit us on our website
www.christianfocus.com